LATIN PROSE COMPOSITION

by the same authors

GREEK PROSE COMPOSITION

also available

ABBOT & MANSFIELD: A PRIMER OF GREEK GRAMMAR

LATIN PROSE COMPOSITION

FOR SCHOOLS

M. A. NORTH, M.A.
LATE ASSISTANT MASTER AT CLIFTON COLLEGE

AND

THE REV. A. E. HILLARD, D.D.
LATE HIGH MASTER OF ST. PAUL'S SCHOOL

DUCKWORTH

This Impression 1978

GERALD DUCKWORTH & CO. LTD.
THE OLD PIANO FACTORY,
43 GLOUCESTER CRESCENT, LONDON NW1.

ISBN 0 7156 13219 (Cased)
ISBN 0 7156 13227 (Paper)

Printed by A. Wheaton & Co. Ltd., Exeter

PREFACE

THE authors wish to explain one or two points with reference to the use of this book.

The arrangement of subjects is meant to adapt it for school use. If a definite section of the book be assigned to each Form, and the division suggested in the Table of Contents be adopted for this purpose, each Form will deal with some new kind of clause in the Compound Sentence, the first with Final and Consecutive Clauses, the second with simple Indirect Statement, and so on. *Pari passu* those subjects are dealt with that concern the structure of the simple sentence (Participles, Case Constructions, etc.). In dealing with the cases the book does not treat each case as a whole, but gives the most necessary constructions (*e.g.* those of Time and Place) to the lowest Forms, and other constructions later on.

The Vocabularies given for the separate exercises (p. 204) are meant to be an important part of the work. They are meant to be learned and kept up by revision. The authors have tried to bring in all words commonly required in Latin Prose Composition below the VIth Form, and any uncommon words required in an exercise have been given in notes, and not included in the Vocabulary to be learnt. These Vocabularies are placed together at the end of the

book, so that they may not be before the eye of a boy
when he does an exercise in school.

The authors have tried to write the exercises so that
no word or construction may be required which has not
previously been given. This applies to the ' connected
pieces ' (which begin from the lowest Form) as well as
to the sentence-exercises. Each piece has been written
expressly for the place in which it stands.

Each exercise is marked either [A] or [B]. This is to
divide the section assigned to a Form into two terms'
work. Either the [A] exercises or the [B] exercises will
make a complete course, and contain sufficient practice in
constructions. But it is recommended that the Vocabularies of both [A] and [B] exercises should be learnt in
any case, and of course the Rules and help given at the
head of exercises are not repeated.

At the end of the book will also be found some further
help in the way of Vocabulary : (1) A list of Military
phrases grouped together (p. 254) ; (2) A list of the most
useful Prepositional phrases (p. 244) ; (3) A list of the
commonest Latin Synonyms (p. 248). These are to be
learnt or referred to as occasion requires.

The rules on the Order of Words in Latin are grouped
at the end of the exercises (p. 196). This seemed better
than scattering them throughout the book, or trying to
bring each in where first required. But the more elementary of them are required in the earliest exercises.

Before beginning this book a boy should be able to
translate simple sentences (including easy questions and
commands) into Latin, and should understand the rules
of agreement, the use of the Passive Voice, the simplest

uses of Pronouns and Prepositions, and the easiest Case constructions. (Ablative of Instrument, Agent, Cause; Dative of Indirect Object and Possessor; Accusative after Factitive Verbs, etc.) But for the occasional revision of this elementary work the 'Preliminary Exercises' (A to K) are prefixed.

The thanks of the authors are due to many colleagues at Clifton for suggestions, and especially to the late Mr. E. N. P. Moor and Mr. W. W. Asquith, and also to Mr. E. H. C. Smith, for kindness in reading through proofs. They wish to acknowledge also the great assistance given them in making the Vocabularies by Mr. R. D. Budworth and Mr. E. G. North. It should be mentioned that the book was used in a privately printed edition at Clifton College during two terms, and that the published edition therefore benefited by the experience thus gained.

PREFACE TO THIRTEENTH EDITION

In this Edition the General Vocabulary has been completely revised by the Rev. J. G. Wilkie and Mr. C. W. F. Lydall of Badingham College, Leatherhead, and the Principal Parts of Irregular Verbs and the Genitive Singular and Gender of Nouns have been added.

CONTENTS[1]

[1] For explanation of the Divisions of this Table of Contents see the beginning of the Preface.

[1] Inserted in these places for convenience of revision before doing the corresponding Indirect construction.

PRELIMINARY EXERCISES

These Exercises from **A** *to* **K** *are meant to supply occasional practice in the more elementary rules not covered by this book. As they are not intended to be included in the course of the book, a separate vocabulary of the harder words is given at the foot of each.*

Exercise A

ACTIVE AND PASSIVE
ABLATIVE OF INSTRUMENT AND AGENT

1. The land was ruled by a good king.
2. The soldier was killed by an arrow.
3. The boy killed the bird with a stone.
4. The Roman general was defeated by Hannibal.
5. The soldier killed the peasant with a sword.
6. We have been conquered by the enemy.
7. The walls were defended by the citizens.
8. Our city was built by Romulus.
9. The Romans fortified their city with a wall.
10. Gaul is separated from Britain by the sea.
11. A high wall defends the camp.
12. We are loved by our friends, and we love them.
13. We shall not be conquered by the enemy.
14. The camp is defended by a long wall.
15. The citizens defended the city.
16. Cities are defended by the citizens.
17. We have taken the camp.
18. The camp has been taken by us.
19. They are teaching the boys.
20. The boys are taught by books.

arrow, săgitta.
stone, lăpis ; *gen.* lapidis.
peasant, agricola, m. 1st decl.
defend, defendĕre.
build, aedificare.

fortify, mūnire.
separate, dīvĭdĕre.
friend, amīcus.
teach, docēı e.

Exercise B

COMMAND; REMOTER OBJECT

1. Give me this book.
2. Do not give him a sword, but give him arrows.
3. Let us go, and let them remain here.
4. Do not go home, but return to us.
5. Let him go away now, but come again.
6. Keep these books.   Do not lose them.
7. Let us fortify the city with walls.
8. Do not let us return to the city.
9. Boys, obey your masters.
10. Let us spend the winter in the city.
11. Do not remain at home.
12. Let them build ships.   Let them not be afraid of the sea.
13. Do not give me the book.
14. This is Caius's book—give it to him.
15. Do not let us remain here.
16. Let him be killed.
17. Do not be afraid of the sea.
18. Citizens, defend the city with your arms.
19. Give me the letter.
20. Let all return to the city.

book, lĭber ; *gen.* libri.
sword, glădius.
remain, mănēre.
(to) home, dŏmum.
at home, domi.
return, redire.
again, rursus.
keep, servare.
lose, perdĕre.

fortify, munire.
obey, pārēre, *dat.*
spend (time), agĕre.
winter, hiems ; *gen.* hiĕmis.
build, aedificare.
be afraid of, fear, tĭmēre.
defend, defendĕre.
letter, epistola.

Exercise C

APPOSITION; COMPOSITE SUBJECT

1. Romulus, son of Mars, was the first king of the Romans.
2. Obey the king, the father of his country.
3. You and your brother will be killed by the enemy.
4. Caius and I are well.
5. The youths were killed by their father, Brutus.
6. You and I and our friends will set out.
7. The king and queen are dear to all of the citizens.
8. By good laws Numa, the second king of Rome, benefited his country.
9. Both men and women were killed by the soldiers.
10. All of us love life, the greatest gift of the gods.
11. The king lost his kingdom and his riches, the things most pleasant to him.
12. Citizens, obey me, your king.
13. Neither the king nor his sons will be killed.
14. The king and his son Caius have been killed.
15. He and I will go away.
16. Give the letter to me, your king.
17. She and her brother have been sent home.
18. His father, the king of Italy, has sent him.
19. I have come to you, my own brother.
20. Both the men and the women are good citizens.

obey, pārēre, *dat.*
country (*fatherland*), patria.
to be well, valēre.
youth, jŭvenis.
friend, amīcus.
set out, prŏfĭcisci.
dear, cārus.
benefit, prodesse, *dat.*

both **men** *and* **women,**
   et vĭri et fēminae.
gift, dōnum.
lose, perdĕre.
kingdom, regnum.
riches, dīvĭtiae.
pleasant, jūcundus.
letter, epistola.

Exercise D

QUESTIONS; USE OF RELATIVE

1. Who saw the man, who killed the king ?
2. Did you, who were present, see him ?
3. Did not Marius, the Roman general, conquer the Teutones ?
4. He was not killed by the enemy, was he ?
5. Has he lost the presents which you gave him ?
6. What general conquered the Teutones ?
7. What did you buy for your brother ?
8. I have lost the book which I bought for my brother.
9. Whose son are you ?
10. Were you not present ?
11. Surely he did not say that ?
12. What name is dearest to you ?
13. This is the book that I lost.
14. What cities has he taken ?
15. By whom was he killed ?
16. Am I not your father ?
17. He did not say that, did he ?
18. She is not the woman, whose son was present.
19. What city do I see ?
20. What man's house have you bought ?

to be present, adesse.
lose, perdĕre.
present, dōnum.
buy, ĕmĕre.

dear, cārus.
woman, mulier.
house, dŏmus.

Exercise E

FACTITIVE VERBS
VERBS GOVERNING TWO ACCUSATIVES

1. The people elected Pompey consul.

2. Marius, who was often elected consul, was a great general.

3. You have often asked me for advice, which I cannot give you.

4. He was thought a good general by all.

5. You wished to conceal the sword from me, but it was given me by the slave.

6. You have been taught many things by your master.

7. Did I not teach you Greek ?

8. The general asked the consul for the soldiers.

9. Marius, who became the enemy of Sulla, killed many Roman citizens.

10. You and I will hide this from our friends.

11. He, having been made king, did not ask his people for advice.

12. We were asked for the sword, which we had concealed from our father.

13. I was asked by Caius for a sword.

14. They were thought to be very wise.

15. I hid from Caius the sword for which you asked me.

16. Were you not taught Greek by your master ?

17. They became consuls, because they were thought to be wise.

18. Why did you hide this from Caius ?

19. You, who did this, were not elected consul by the citizens.

20. The man, whom you asked for advice, has taught me many things.

ask, rŏgare.	*Greek* (language), Graeca lingua
teach, dŏcēre.	*friend*, ămīcus.
hide, *conceal*, cēlare.	*people*, pŏpŭlus.
elect, creare.	*sword*, glădius.
consul, consul, -sŭlis.	*wise*, săpiens.
advice, consĭlium.	*because*, quod.

Exercise F

DATIVE OF POSSESSOR
SIMPLE USES OF *SE*, *SUUS*, *IPSE*, *IS*

1. He killed himself with his own sword.
2. He has a garden which was given him by his friend.
3. He bought the house for himself and his wife.
4. I have never seen him himself, but I have seen his children.
5. His children ask him for bread, which he cannot give them.
6. He has given his children the bread which they asked him for.
7. They have ships and sailors, but they have not many harbours.
8. He wished to conceal his opinion from me, but I asked his friends.
9. You Gauls fear Caesar and his army.
10. He led his army against the Gauls, and took their camp.
11. The citizens themselves wished to make him consul.
12. We have many friends, whom we do not often see.
13. I myself will give you his sword.
14. We ourselves have many ships.
15. He himself gave me his own sword.
16. I killed him, because he wished to make himself king.
17. I had many friends once, but now I have few.
18. I asked you for their bread.
19. They gave us their sailors and ships.
20. We ourselves have been taught many things by him.

garden, hortus, -i.	*harbour*, portus, -ūs.
buy, ĕmĕre.	*opinion*, sententia.
wife, uxor, -ōris.	*fear*, tĭmēre.
children, lībĕri.	*once*, ōlim, quondam.
bread, pānis, -is, *m.*	*few*, pauci.
sailor, nauta, *m.*	

Exercise G

ABLATIVE OF CAUSE
WORDS GOVERNING ABLATIVE

1. A state which has a good king enjoys peace.

2. Relying on the courage of his soldiers, he led them against the enemy.

3. They died of fear.

4. Oxen feed on grass, and lions on flesh.

5. We use riches, and wish to get possession of them.

6. Relying on his wings, Mercury had no need of a ship.

7. A man who performs his duty is worthy of praise.

8. The enemy wish to get possession of our camp.

9. Through his help I can now use my sword.

10. We have need of the soldiers we have asked him for.

11. A man who is contented with little is worthy of a happy life.

12. We shall often use the books which you have given us.

13. You seem to me to be worthy of praise.

14. We have no need of these ships.

15. They attacked the city, relying on the courage of their soldiers.

16. I did this through the advice of Caius.

17. By this courage he took the city.

18. Did you use the riches which were given you ?

19. Many men have died of hunger.

20. You, who perform your duties well, have many friends.

(*For words which govern the Ablative see Voc.* 42.)

state, cīvĭtas.
die, morior.
flesh, căro, carnis.
riches, dīvĭtiae.
wing, āla.
duty, offĭcium.
help, auxĭlium.

little (noun), parvum (neuter of parvus).
happy, beatus.
book, lĭber, -bri.
often, saepe.
hunger, fămes.

Exercise H

EASY PREPOSITIONAL PHRASES

1. Among the captives.
2. At the house of Caius.
3. Over and above the dowry.
4. Before his feet.
5. Without a ransom.
6. From him.
7. With his friends.
8. With you.
9. Because of his age.
10. Owing to his joy.
11. Through fear.
12. Kind towards the poor.
13. To advance towards the city.
14. Through the river.
15. In the presence of the king.
16. Through scouts.
17. By the king.
18. From the fame of his deeds.
19. From that time.
20. Out of the bravest soldiers.
21. He was sent to him with gifts.
22. As hostages.
23. For so great a service.
24. Instead of horses.
25. On the nearest hill.
26. Into his alliance.
27. Under the general himself.
28. At my house.
29. To go under the earth.
30. About terms of peace.
31. Before a year.
32. Round about the city.
33. On this side of the mountains.
34. Besides the messenger.
35. Except the poet.
36. Against Antiochus.
37. About a thousand men.
38. Around the mountain.
39. Within the camp.
40. Outside the gates.
41. Below the city walls.
42. In the power of the enemy.
43. Behind the horsemen.
44. According to the laws.
45. Contrary to the laws.
46. Adjoining the camp.
47. As far as his head.
48. Near the garden.
49. The army was sent under the yoke.
50. It lies under your eyes.

captive, captīvus.
dowry, dos ; *gen.* dōtis.
ransom, prĕtium.
age, aetas.
joy, gaudium.
fear, mĕtus, -ūs.
poor, pauper.

scout, explorator.
gift, dōnum.
hostage, obses ; *gen.* obsĭdis.
service, mĕrĭtum.
nearest, proximus.
alliance, societas.

terms, conditiones.
messenger, nuntius.
poet, poēta, *m.*
horseman, eques.
garden, hortus.
yoke, jŭgum.
lie, jăcĕre.

Exercise K

PREPOSITIONS

1. He came into the city with ten soldiers.
2. After one night he set out against the enemy.
3. In front of the house there is a field.
4. I cannot go across the sea without ships.
5. He was killed by his brother at a feast, amid all his friends.
6. He spoke to me about your house in your presence.
7. He went round about the city, and saw the walls.
8. He came towards me, and called out, ' Who is in the city?'
9. The camp is on this side of the river, the army is beyond the city.
10. On account of the war no one goes outside the gates.
11. Besides these men we have no army in the city.
12. We saw him on the road.
13. He was brought by the soldiers into the presence of the king.
14. They escaped from prison without my knowledge.
15. They sailed past the island in a boat.
16. We sailed as far as Spain (Hispania).
17. They live near the island of Corsica.
18. He did this in sight of all.
19. I did this because of my friendship towards you.
20. Were you not going towards the city ?
21. Men who live underground.
22. He led an army over the mountains against the enemy.
23. After the battle they were killed outside the city walls in the presence of their friends.
24. Before daybreak they came close to (under) the walls of the town.
25. I killed him after these things, not on account of them.

field, ăger ; *gen.* agri.	*boat*, linter ; *gen.* lintris, *f.*
feast, cēna.	*friendship*, amīcitia.
prison, carcer, -is.	*daybreak*, prima lux.
sail, nāvigare.	

EXERCISES

SEQUENCE OF TENSES

Rule 1. The tenses in Latin are divided into two groups :

A. **Primary tenses—**

Ind.	Subj.
Present.	Present.
Future.	Perfect.
Perfect _with_ ' _have._'	

B. **Historic tenses—**

Imperfect.	Imperfect.
Perfect _without_ ' _have_ ' (Aorist).	Pluperfect.
Pluperfect	

Where we have a dependent sentence with its verb in the Subjunctive, the tense of the Subjunctive is determined by the tense of the principal verb. Primary tenses follow Primary, Historic tenses follow Historic.[1]

The English will generally make it quite clear which of the two Primary tenses, or which of the two Historic tenses, is required in each case.

---

[1] The Historic Present may be regarded either as a Primary or as a Historic tense. The Imperative is always followed by a Primary tense.

Exercise 1

In the following sentences Latin requires the dependent verb to be in the Subjunctive. Say (without translating) what *tense* you would put it in.

1. They have come in order that they *may conquer* us.

2. They sent money that we *might buy* our freedom.

3. We had already succeeded so well that we *hoped* to win.

4. We are so tired that we *cannot* work.

5. He ran so quickly that no one *could* catch him.

6. We do not know what he *is doing*.

7. Have you heard what he *has done* ?

8. They did not know what the island *was* like.

9. We shall ask what he *is doing*.

10. We asked whether the war *had been finished*.

11. I do not know how many ships there *were*.

12. We were wondering why you *feared* us.

13. Tell me why you *are* afraid.

14. We shall work in order that we *may become* rich.

FINAL CLAUSES

Rule 2. **Final Clauses** (*i.e.* clauses expressing a *purpose*) **have their verbs in the Subjunctive, introduced by** *ut* **when positive, by** *ne* **when negative.**

EXAMPLES

Laborant pauperes **ut** divites **fiant.**
Poor men work to become rich.

Se receperunt **ne** consilia ab hostibus **cognoscerentur.**
They retreated in order that their plans might not be discovered by the enemy.

Exercise 2 [*A*]

1. I am going to the city to buy bread.
2. He went to the city lest he should see his father.
3. We have gone home [1] to see our friends.
4. We shall go to Caesar to ask for peace.
5. Do not send me to ask for peace.
6. We were running fast that we might not be caught.
7. I have bought a horse that I may not be tired.
8. Give him a sword that he may not be killed.
9. You had gone to Italy to see the king's son.
10. We were sent to ask for peace.

---

[1] domum.

Exercise 3 [*A*]

1. The enemy retreated in order to avoid a battle.

2. We shall send 200 men in order that we may hinder the enemy's march.

3. They marched quickly so that the enemy might not learn their plans.

4. We advanced to the top of the hill[1] to see the enemy's camp.

5. He is marching with Caesar so that he may not be accused by us.

6. We work in order to become rich.

7. They have come to ask for arms from us.

8. In order that we may not think you a coward, fight bravely.

9. He did this in order that a poor man might not be consul.

10. We ought not to do this to be praised.

---

[1] summus collis.　So with some other words :

　　　　the middle of the *stream*=medium flumen.
　　　　all of *us*=omnes nos.
　　　　the rest of the *army*=reliquus exercitus.
　　　　the whole of the *city*=tota urbs.
　　　　the end of the *year*=extremus annus.

In all these Latin uses *adjectives* where English uses the words ' rest,' ' all,' ' middle,' etc., as *nouns*.

Exercise 4 [B]

1. I was sent to ask for peace.

2. I shall do this in order to help my friends.

3. They have gone away lest they should be seen.

4. They had gone away that they might not be seen.

5. We will leave the sick that we may not be hindered.

6. To help our friends we are willing to suffer pain.

7. To help us they had marched very quickly.

8. He did this in order to become consul.

9. They retreated that they might not be killed.

10. Let us go to the top of the hill to see the plain.

Exercise 5 [B]

1. In order not to be accused myself,[1] I accused my friend.

2. We ought to praise good men to make others good.

3. To avoid the enemy march very quickly.

4. We left the sick so that we might not be hindered.

5. I have not come to avoid my enemies.

6. To be safe stay in the city.

7. All of us will come with you,[2] so that you may be safe.

8. Do not come in order to save me.

9. In order that the enemy might not take the city the whole of the army set out.

10. That they may not be caught by the enemy do not send many men.

---

[1] 'ipse,' in agreement with subject expressed or understood.

[2] 'tecum.' ' Cum ' follows its case in the same way in mecum, secum, nobiscum, vobiscum, quibuscum.

CONSECUTIVE CLAUSES

Rule 3. Consecutive Clauses (_i.e._ clauses expressing a _consequence_) have their verbs in the Subjunctive introduced by _ut_. When the consequence is negative we have _ut non_, _ut nemo, ut nullus, ut nunquam_, etc., according to the sense.[1]

EXAMPLES

Tantum est periculum **ut** omnes **terreantur.**
So great is the danger that all are frightened.

Tam celeriter se receperunt **ut** hostes eos capere **non possent.**
They retreated so speedily that the enemy could not catch them.

---

[1] The sequence of tenses is the same as for Final clauses, with one exception ; _viz._ the Perfect Subj. is often used after a historic tense. But only use it thus when (_a_) the result is ' momentary,' not continuous, and (_b_) the result actually did follow.

   _e.g._ Tantus erat ardor militum ut nemo motum terrae **senserit.**
    The soldiers were so engrossed that no one felt the earthquake.

Exercise 6 [A]

1. The soldiers are so brave that they always conquer the enemy.

2. He has done this in such a way that we do not praise him.

3. The enemy were so many that all our men were afraid.

4. He escaped so quickly that no one [1] could catch him.

5. The battle was fought [2] so fiercely that all the soldiers were killed.

6. The danger is so great that no ships can be saved.

7. So deep is the river that no one can cross it.

8. They have conquered the enemy so often that now they despise them.

9. Their fear was so great that they did not dare to cross the river.

10. So great a storm had arisen that all the sailors were terrified.

---

[1] Nemo is a noun, '*nobody*,' '*no one*.' Nullus is an adj., '*no*,' '*none*.'

[2] pugnatum est=*the battle was fought.*

Exercise 7 [*A*]

1. We were so tired that we remained in the plain.

2. Are you strong enough to defeat the enemy ?

3. The snow was so deep that we did not set out, but remained in the camp.

4. He has said this so often that now I am weary.

5. So numerous [1] were the enemy that they easily took the city.

6. The tree was so high that it fell, and lay on the ground.[2]

7. We were not brave enough to return to the battle.

8. Such was his courage that all men praised him, and wished to follow him.

9. He has done this so easily that he is not tired.

10. These trees were of such a kind that we could not climb them.

---

[1] *so numerous* = tot.

[2] *on the ground* = humi.

Exercise 8 [B]

1. Let us work in such a way that all men may praise us.

2. So many soldiers had arrived that the camp was full.

3. We have crossed the sea so often that we do not fear storms.

4. He asked me so often that I gave him the book.

5. The forces of the enemy are so great that we cannot espise them.

6. We were so greatly terrified that we all fled.

7. So many men were killed that we did not fight again.

8. They are such cowards (so cowardly) as not to dare to urn into battle.

9. We are strong enough to save you.

10. We were not strong enough to fight against them.

11. They are so strong that they are always willing to work, and [1] do not [1] become weary.

---

[1] *and . . . not*=neque. Never put ' et ' before a negative ; *e.g.* do not say ' et nunquam,' but ' neque unquam ' ; do not say ' et nulla navis,' but ' neque ulla navis.'

Exercise 9 [B]

1. The tree was so high that it fell.

2. The sea is so great that we cannot cross it.

3. Will the snow be so deep that we cannot set out ?

4. The sailors were so terrified that they left the ship.

5. He was so brave that he crossed the sea, and returned home.

6. The hill is so high that we cannot climb it.

7. The boys were so idle that I did not praise them.

8. He is so brave that he ought to be praised.

9. Such was his courage that all men praised him.

10. The island is of such a kind that I do not wish to see it.

11. They worked so well that they became rich, and were praised by all.

Exercise 10 [*A*]

In the following exercises Final and Consecutive clauses are mixed. When the sentence is negative remember that a negative final clause *always* begins with **ne,** a consecutive clause *never* does. Therefore for

'that no one' use **ne quis** in a final, **ut nemo** in a consecutive clause.
'that no . . .' use **ne ullus**   ,,   **ut nullus**   ,,   ,,
'that never' use **ne unquam** ,,   **ut nunquam**   ,,   ,,

1. We have come to defend the walls.

2. There is no one here so brave as to climb the walls alone.

3. The wall was made so high that no one might ever climb it.

4. The wall was made so high that no one could ever climb it.

5. I am so tired that I cannot work.

6. The messengers, who were sent to ask for peace, have returned.

7. The laws which the Romans made were so good that no one wished to break [1] them.

8. Speak about [2] me so that he may never accuse me again.

9. The rich helped the poor so that they might not die of [3] hunger.

10. He was so hurt that he died.

---

[1] violare.   [2] When *about* or *of* means *concerning* use de.

[3] *Of* here means *by*, denoting cause or instrument. Therefore use simple abl.

Exercise 11 [A]

1. He was sent to ask for peace, that the citizens might not die of hunger.

2. The messengers arrived so quickly that no one died.

3. Go away quickly that no one may see you.

4. We defended the walls so well that the enemy retreated, and did not take the city.

5. The snow was so deep that many men died of cold.

6. Set out quickly that no one may see you.

7. Are you brave enough to set out alone ?

8. Do not do this, lest you should seem to be a coward.

9. We have made the ditch deep that no one may cross it.

10. The ditch was made so deep that no soldiers could cross it.

Exercise 12 [B]

1. So many weapons were thrown that no place was safe.

2. His shield was large enough to defend him.

3. That no one may be idle, this work has been given to all.

4. They were so cowardly that they retreated, and did not defend the city.

5. Our forces are great enough to repel the enemy.

6. We put him to death that he might not hurt us.

7. He is so brave that he does not fear the enemy, but loves battles.

8. He did the work in such a way that all men praised it.

9. Be brave that we may praise you and call you a friend.

10. He went away so quickly that we never saw him again.

Exercise 13 [B]

1. He sent so few men that we could not defend the walls.

2. We shall return so quickly that you ought not to fear danger.

3. The man who [1] dares to despise his enemies is brave enough to conquer them.

4. No man is so brave that he is never afraid.

5. We have come to help you so that nothing may hinder the work.

6. He bore a shield so that no weapon might hurt him.

7. He bore so big a shield that no weapon could hurt him.

8. They all were put to death so that no messenger might ever return home.

9. I am accused by so many men that I dare not defend myself. [2]

10. In order never to be conquered never be afraid.

---

[1] Is qui. Wherever 'the man' or 'men' is equal to 'he' or 'those' translate by 'is.'

[2] me ipsum.

Exercise 14 [A]

A poor soldier was one day leading a mule laden with gold which had been sent to Alexander [1] the Great. The mule was so tired that it could no longer bear the burden, and the soldier was compelled to carry the gold himself. But by chance Alexander himself was following the man, and he admired his kindness so much that he said, ' My friend, try to carry the gold home, for I give it all to you.'

Exercise 15 [A]

The enemy advanced quickly to capture the city. There were so few soldiers in the city that they were hardly able to defend the walls. But reinforcements were advancing, and they resolved to resist bravely, that these might arrive and defeat the enemy. The attack was so fierce that the walls were almost taken, but at length the fresh forces arrived, and the enemy retreated. So great was the joy of the citizens that they went to the temples, and gave many gifts to the gods.

---

[1] Alexander, -dri.

Exercise 16 [A]

The soldiers, who had been marching all day,[1] were so tired
that they could scarcely climb the hill. Some, in order to
march quickly, threw away their arms; others were so
exhausted that their friends carried them. But their courage
was so great that at last they came to the top of the hill, and
saw the enemy's camp. Here they hid themselves that they
might not be seen by the enemy.

Exercise 17 [B]

They had been so often defeated by Caesar that they sent
messengers to him and asked for peace. In order that they
might not wish to fight again, Caesar asked them for hostages,
which they gave him. But the army of the Gauls was so great
that Caesar was not willing to remain near them, and he went
away. Lest the enemy should follow he led his soldiers very
quickly, and before night they came into their camp.

---

[1] Acc.

Exercise 18 [B]

A Persian,[1] who had been banished from Persia, came to the city of Athens to see Cimon. He brought much gold and silver, in order by presents to make Cimon his friend. ' Do you bring this money to buy my friendship ? ' asked Cimon. ' I wish to make you my friend,' replied the Persian. ' Take away the money,' Cimon said, ' lest I should think you an enemy. Friendship is not bought and sold.'

Exercise 19 [B]

Pyrrhus, the Greek, gave money to Fabricius, the Roman general, that he might betray the Roman army. But no present was great enough to tempt Fabricius. A Greek came to the Roman camp that he might receive a reward, and then kill the king. But so upright was Fabricius that he sent the man back to the king to be punished by him.

---

[1] *Persian*=Persa, 1 decl., m. Cimon, *gen.* Cimonis.
Athens=Athenae, -arum, f. pl. ' *The city of Athens* '=' the city Athens ' in Latin, the two nouns being in apposition.

INFINITIVES

Rule 4. **The simple use of the Infinitive is as the subject or complement of a finite verb.** It thus corresponds to the English verbal noun in -_ing_.

> _e.g._ laborare est orare = _working is praying._

Here 'laborare' is the subject of 'est,' and 'orare' is the complement, just as, in the sentence 'laborare est difficile,' 'difficile' is the complement. This last sentence we usually translate '_It_ is difficult to work,' but the Latin is 'To work is difficult,' and 'laborare' is a true subject.

All verbs whose meaning is incomplete in itself require a complement, and this is usually in the Infinitive. We call it the **Prolate Infinitive.**

> _e.g._ volo abire   = _I wish to go away._
> conor laborare = _I try to work._
> possum vincere = _I can conquer._
> te sino proficisci = _I permit you to depart._

Exercise 20 [*A*]

1. Hoping is easier than believing.

2. Those who wish to command ought to learn to obey.

3. He was thought to be a good general.

4. It is the duty of [1] all soldiers to be willing to die for their country.

5. Cease to be idle, and learn to work.

6. We have determined to go to the help of our friends.

7. These men are not accustomed to fight.

8. Did they seem to you to be true friends ?

9. The general decided to pitch his camp on a hill.

10. They did not dare to lie.

11. Were you not compelled to leave your home ?

12. They do not allow us to remain in the city.

---

[1] Lat. '*it is of all soldiers*' (Genitive). So with such phrases as '*it is* (*the part*) *of* . . .' '*it is* (*the nature*) *of* . . .'

Exercise 21 [A]

1. It is (the part) of good citizens to try to help the poor.

2. Learning is easier than teaching.

3. If soldiers are unwilling to march they are punished.

4. He desires to benefit himself alone.

5. The barbarians are said to be very brave.

6. They determined to follow the enemy into the city.

7. It is pleasant to help those who can help themselves.

8. All men ought to think it disgraceful to lie.

9. Some men are accustomed to rule, others to obey.

10. Those who are accustomed to command others ought to learn to obey.

11. They think it foolish to die for their country.

12. All men ought to praise those who seem to be wise.

Exercise 22 [B]

1. I used to learn more quickly than I can learn now.

2. To complain is useless.

3. He never ceases to complain of his friends.

4. We have decided to remain in the plain.

5. He seemed to me to be very brave.

6. Ruling is more difficult than being ruled.

7. If we try to help others, they are willing to help us.

8. I prefer to remain, you to depart.

9. They determined to work that they might not be punished.

10. They were accustomed to go home with their friends.

11. They were compelled to retreat.

Exercise 23 [B]

1. You ought not to desire to be a man.

2. The general determined to set out against the enemy.

3. Speaking is easier than persuading.

4. You ought never to cease to learn.

5. If we desire to learn we can always have masters.

6. Not helping our friends is the same as [1] hurting them.

7. Punish him if he is unwilling to learn.

8. We decided to defend the city.

9. We have been compelled to buy many things which do not seem to be useful.

10. You force me to speak against my will.

---

[1] *the same as*=idem ac.

PARTICIPLES

Rule 5. English sentences which require to be translated by participles in Latin are not usually in the Latin form at first. The English has to be *turned*; *e.g.* 'The Greeks, *having captured Troy*, burnt it,' cannot go straight into Latin, because Latin has no Perfect Participle *Active*.

(*a*) **Wherever possible, make the participle agree with the subject or object.**

e.g. The Greeks, having captured Troy, burnt it.
> = Trojam captam Graeci incenderunt.[1]

The chiefs were taken and massacred.
> = Capti duces trucidantur.

(*b*) Wherever this is not possible, use the construction called **Ablative Absolute**; *i.e.* a Participle agreeing with a Noun in the Ablative, the whole phrase being an Abl. of Manner or 'Attendant Circumstances'; *e.g.* in the sentence '*Having taken the city, he marched on*,' the participle cannot agree with the subject because there is no Perfect Participle Active in Latin, nor can '*the city*' be made the object of the verb. We therefore turn it: '*The city having been captured, he marched on*' = Capta urbe progressus est.

---

[1] Never write such a sentence as 'Capta urbe, Graeci eam incenderunt.' The Abl. Abs. is only to be used where the participle *cannot* agree with subject or object.

Exercise 24 [A]

1. The army having been defeated the general fled.

2. Regulus having been given up to the enemy was put to death.

3. Having conquered the enemy the general returned home.

4. Having summoned the citizens he spoke as follows.[1]

5. The soldiers having been captured gave up their arms.

6. Having collected his forces he led them against the enemy.

7. The Gauls [2] having thrown away their arms were taken by the Romans.

8. Having taken the messenger they put him to death.

9. Having killed his brother he fled into the woods.

10. The enemy having captured the messengers put them to death.

Exercise 25 [B]

1. Having been made king he tried to benefit the state.

2. Kings having been driven out consuls were elected.

3. The soldiers, throwing away their arms, fled from the battle.

4. Caesar having conquered the Gauls demanded hostages.

5. Our men having taken the chiefs brought them to Caesar.

6. Seizing his sword he tried to kill his enemy.

7. Having taken the camp we set it on fire.

8. Having conquered the enemy the soldiers wished to return home.

9. Having set the prisoners free he sent them home.

10. The Gauls having been defeated asked for peace.

---

[1] haec dixit.   [2] Galli.

Exercise 26 [A]

1. **Do not invent a Passive Participle of Intransitive Verbs.** Saying ' Caesare pervento ' is as absurd as saying ' perventus est ' for *he arrived.* Latin having no Perfect Part. Active, the only way to render ' Caesar having arrived ' is ' Caesar cum pervenisset.' [1]

2. On the other hand, remember that **Deponents have Perfect Participles with an Active sense,** though their form is Passive ; *e.g.* locutus=having said, aggressus=having attacked, ratus= thinking, etc.

1. My horse having stumbled I was caught.
2. Having said these things the messenger departed.
3. Having come to the gate of the city they halted.
4. Having advanced ten miles our men reached the river.
5. Having seen the enemy's forces our men retreated.
6. Our men being afraid, the general retreated.
7. Having halted we pitched a camp.
8. Being about to die he called his sons.
9. The enemy having set out we retreated.
10. The Gauls having attacked the walls the city was taken by storm.

Exercise 27 [B]

1. Having reached the gates our men tried to open them.

2. Having opened the gates our men marched in.

3. Having attacked the walls the Gauls took the city by storm.

4. My house having fallen down I went to Caius' house.

5. Having entered the house I called to Caius.

6. Night approaching we pitched a camp.

7. Winter beginning we retreated across the river.

8. His father being about to die he returned home.

9. Having slept in the house he went away early.

10. The messenger having returned brought this answer.

---

[1] See the first part of Rule 26, p. 144.

Exercise 28 [*A*]

1. '*Saying this,* he fled' is a loose way of expressing '*Having said this,* he fled'; and in Latin must be 'Haec **locutus** fugit.' **The Present Participle denotes an action going on at the same time as the action of the principal verb, whatever the tense of that verb may be;** *e.g.* Hoc jam moriens dixit=he said this while dying.

2. We must often use participles in Latin where they are not used in English—

(1) **Where English uses two simple verbs joined by ' and ' or ' but ' ;** *e.g. Numa died and Tullus became king*=Mortuo Numa Tullus rex factus est ; *He took him and slew him*—Captum eum interfecit.

(2) **Where English uses phrases with prepositions or conjunctions ;** *e.g. He was killed while hunting*=interfectus est venans ; *on the death of Numa*=mortuo Numa ; *after advancing a mile*=mille passus progressus.

(3) **Where English uses clauses denoting time, cause, etc. ;** *e.g. When Tullus was king*=regnante Tullo ; *As the soldiers would not follow, he remained*=nolentibus sequi militibus, mansit.

1. On leaving the wood we saw the camp of the enemy.

2. We departed after saying these words.

3. Saying these words he left the camp.

4. The Greeks returned home after the capture of Troy.

5. When Romulus was ruling Rome was a small city.

6. The youth was killed while fighting for his country.

7. The enemy took the messenger and put him to death.

8. They pitched their camp, and fortified it with a rampart.

9. They collected an army and marched against the enemy.

10. Not being able to resist us the Gauls threw away their arms and fled.

Exercise 29 [A]

1. Having made silence he spoke as follows.
2. He died while sleeping.
3. On the death of Remus Romulus became king alone.
4. Seeing the great walls of the city we did not attack it.
5. Having received reinforcements we were able to resist the enemy.
6. During the consulship of Crassus there was peace.
7. He exhorted his soldiers and led them out.
8. After burning the town we departed.
9. After killing his brother he fled into the woods.
10. Being followed by the enemy we did not halt.

Exercise 30 [B]

1. On their return home they were received gladly by their friends.
2. Having gone out of the city the soldiers returned to the camp.
3. He was killed while trying to save his friend.
4. On the approach of night we left the camp and advanced against the enemy.
5. On hearing this the general resolved to retreat.
6. Saying this he threw himself at the king's feet.
7. This is the tenth year from the foundation of Rome.
8. Having killed the Gaul he buried him in a wood.
9. Having set out at the approach of spring they marched against the enemy.
10. He took these presents and gave them to his son.

Exercise 31 [B]

1. They were attacked by the enemy while fortifying a camp.

2. Some having already gone out of the camp it was attacked by the enemy.

3. The enemy attacked some of them when they had gone out of the camp.

4. Caesar having arrived in the camp the soldiers resisted the attacks of the enemy more bravely.

5. With these exhortations he left his men.

6. Having betrayed the town they went away.

7. Leading back the army into the city he demanded hostages.

8. After the banishment of the kings the Romans had consuls.

9. They left the sick in the camp and pursued the foe.

10. He was killed while pursuing the foe.

Exercise 32 [A]

The enemy being now defeated, the general led his men back to the camp, which had been fortified by a rampart. The lieutenant [1] having been left in the camp, had not heard about the battle. When he saw the army at a distance, he went to the top of the rampart to await them. As they approached, he went out and asked them about the fight. But they were so tired that they would tell him nothing, but threw away their arms and went to their tents.[2]

---

[1] legatus.   [2] tabernacula, n. pl.

Exercise 33 [*A*]

The bread being now all eaten, we were dying of [1] hunger. But the general, calling us together, gave us the bread which he had kept hidden in his house; then, opening the gates, he and the soldiers escaped through the enemy's camp. The wounded only being left [behind] in the city, we gave ourselves up to the enemy. They soon left us, taking away much gold and silver from the city.

Exercise 34 [*B*]

Seeing the enemy the Gauls crossed the river, and breaking down the bridge waited for Caesar's arrival. Caesar did not wish to fight immediately as his men [2] were wearied. Marching therefore into the hills he pitched a camp, then came down against the enemy when they had gone out of the camp and were seeking corn. Having conquered them he sold those whom he had captured, and after repairing the bridge returned to the city.

---

[1] See note 3, p. 13.   [2] *his men* = sui.

Exercise 35 [B]

Returning to the top of the hill the scout saw the enemy slowly advancing across the plain. Coming to the camp he told these things to the general. Immediately our camp was moved, and we set out to the other side of the river. Having broken down the bridge, so that the enemy might not follow us, we marched the whole day through the woods, and as night approached reached the city of Spoletium. Here we determined to collect provisions and defend ourselves. The walls and gates of the city having been made by the Romans were very strong.

TIME, PLACE, SPACE

<u>Rule 5A.</u>

TIME

To be expressed **without a preposition.**

Time during which. Accusative. *e.g.* Triginta annos vixit.
He lived 30 years.

Time when. Ablative. *e.g.* Tricesimo anno mortuus est.
He died in the 30th year.

Time within which. Ablative. *e.g.* Multis annis Romam non venit.
For many years he did not go to Rome.

N.B.—Undeviginti annos natus.
Nineteen years old.
Tribus ante (post) diebus.
Three days before (after).
Abhinc tres dies.
Three days ago.

PLACE

To be expressed **with a preposition,** except in the case of towns, small islands, domus, rus.

Place whither. Accusative. *e.g.* In urbem, *into the city.*
Athenas, *to Athens.*

Place whence. Ablative. *e.g.* Ex Italia, *out of Italy.*
Romā, *from Rome.*
Domo, *from home.*

Place where. Ablative. *e.g.* In urbe, *in the city.*

But to express *place where* use the *Locative* of towns, small islands, domus, rus, humus; *e.g.* Romae, Athenis, Corinthi, Rhodi, ruri, humi.

EXTENT OF SPACE

To be expressed by the **Accusative without a preposition.**

e.g. Tria milia passuum progressus.
Having advanced three miles.
Tredecim pedes altus (latus, longus).
Thirteen feet high (broad, long).
Castra ab urbe aberant milia passuum ducenta.
The camp was distant from the city 200 miles.

Exercise 36 [A]

1. In the country. At home. From Asia. From Athens. In summer. In the night. All night.

2. He sent the forces to Labienus in the camp.[1]

3. Augustus died at Nola (when) seventy years old.

4. Cicero was consul a few years before.

5. I will go into the country next summer.

6. Ten years I stayed at your house.

7. In three days you will reach Athens.

8. I went to Syracuse in winter. The snow was two feet deep.

9. I saw my friend at Carthage three months ago.

10. The snow was deeper in the country than in the city.

Exercise 37 [A]

1. The new ship is fifty feet long.

2. At Messana. At Carthage. At Saguntum. In Sicily. From Florentia. To Pisae.

3. We shall remain at Athens or Corinth for three years.

4. On that day on which the battle was fought.

5. Nine years afterwards in the night I came home.

6. I shall come back to Carthage in nine days.

7. Do you not wish to go and see your friends in Italy ?

8. Setting out from Sicily he went to Brundisium, and afterwards to Greece.

9. Will you be at home ?

10. Ten days ago I came back to the city from the country.

---

[1] In Latin, 'into the camp,' in close connection with the verb of motion. So in **Exercise 37**, sentence 7, ' to go into Italy to see your friends.'

Exercise 38 [B]

1. The Romans were severely defeated at Cannae.

2. For five days the army advanced.

3. Within fourteen days help will come to the city.

4. While marching to Athens he delayed at Corinth.

5. Sailing from Asia to Brundisium he perished in a storm.

6. I am going to the country to see my farm.

7. Hannibal waged war in Italy for fourteen years.

8. Three days afterwards he was killed by his brother.

9. On the fifth day a storm arose and compelled us to go to the harbour of Tarentum.

10. Will you come to see my house at Florence ? [1]

11. I am now nineteen years old, and have never gone to Athens.

12. The enemy having attacked us at dawn we were fighting the whole day.

Exercise 39 [B]

1. Out of Spain. To Rome. At Florentia. From Alba. Into France. To Zama.

2. The city was so beautiful that I remained in it for many years.

3. I have not seen my friends for many years.

4. They stayed in the country all the summer, and on the approach of winter returned to the city.

5. My friends came from Athens to see me at Corinth.[1]

6. He left the camp at sunset and went to the nearest town with one companion.

---

[1] See note 1 to **Exercise 36.**

7. On the following day he pitched his camp about seven miles from the enemy.

8. In the evening they reached the river Allia, which is about eleven miles distant from Rome.

9. This river is thirty feet broad and ten feet deep.

10. On that day he returned to his country, from which he had set out (when) fifteen years old.

Exercise 40 [A]

Three days after we crossed a river forty-five feet broad. From this river we marched along a good road [1] for four days, and came to Carthage. For a short time we stayed in the city, but for fear of the citizens soon left it and made a camp upon the seashore. Food was brought to the camp from the country every day. At the beginning of spring we marched to Utica, a town which [2] had been captured by the Romans five years before.

Exercise 41 [B]

For many days we remained within our camp awaiting the enemy's attack. All night we heard their shouts and songs, but by day we did not see them, nor did we dare to go out to explore. Their camp seemed to be pitched about six hundred yards from us, and there was a river between about twenty feet broad. At last we resolved to escape by this river. Accordingly on a dark night we left the camp, and a large boat having been got ready we began to advance up the river without the knowledge of the enemy.

---

[1] The *way by which* one goes is expressed by the ablative without preposition.

[2] In Latin, ' which town.'

Exercise 42 [A]

ABLATIVES OF COMPARISON, QUALITY, MEASURE
OF DIFFERENCE; WORDS GOVERNING THE
ABLATIVE

(1) Quid mollius undā ? [1]   *What is softer than water ?*
(2) Stătūrā fuit humili.   *He was of low stature.*
(3) Multo
    Multis partibus } major est.   *It is much greater.*

1. Having gained possession of the enemies' camp, he gave the booty to the soldiers.

2. More citizens were dying of hunger than of disease.

3. My brother was a man of weak body.

4. The wise man is contented with his lot, and performs his duties well.

5. I never saw a house more beautiful than this.

6. Being a man of great courage he remained.

7. Hercules undertook twelve labours of great difficulty.

8. The army, which he has equipped, is much larger than ours.

9. Relying on his wings Mercurius had no need of a ship.

10. He was killed by the arrow which had been shot by the soldier.

11. War was waged much oftener by sea than by land.

12. My brother is two feet taller than I am.

---

[1] The Abl. of Comparison is only to be used where two things are directly compared with one another by means of a Comparative Adjective. Otherwise use *quam*. The case of the noun following quam will be the same as that of the noun corresponding to it in the first part of the sentence.

e.g. Facilius est mihi quam tibi.   *It is easier for me than for you.*
    Balbi domus quam Cai altior   *Balbus' house is higher than*
    est.   *Caius'.*

Compare with these—
    Facilior est somnus labore.   *Sleep is easier than toil.*
    Domus muro altior est.   *The house is higher than the wall.*

In these sentences we have direct comparison between the two things denoted by the nouns, and can therefore use the Ablative of Comparison.

Exercise 43 [B]

1. Let us feed on the same food as [1] the soldiers.

2. He is much more like you than Caesar (is).

3. Solon, a man of great wisdom, gave laws to Athens.

4. The walls, which have been built by Balbus, are of great height.

5. We shall be saved more by courage than by our walls.

6. On the march we saw more friends than enemies.

7. No walls are higher than those of [2] Babylon.

8. I admire this house much more than that.

9. The enemy's forces are a little smaller than ours.

10. We were attacked by the enemy with a shower of darts.

11. He was beaten by the bows which the soldiers used.

12. We crossed a river many feet deeper than the Rhone.

13. Our city is many times larger than yours.

---

[1] Use the Relative (eodem . . . quo).

[2] Omit *those*. So with the words ' that of ' in comparisons, *e.g. my house is higher than that of Caius*=mea domus quam Cai altior est.

INDIRECT STATEMENT

In the sentence 'He said *many things*' the verb governs a noun as
direct object.   In the sentence 'He said *that I was unwise*' a
clause has taken the place of a direct object.   When in this way
a sentence becomes the object of a verb of 'saying' or 'thinking' we call it an 'indirect statement.'

When the verb of 'saying' or 'thinking' is in the Passive the 'indirect statement' becomes the subject, *e.g.* nuntiatur hostem
adesse='*that the enemy are near*' *is announced.* So with
'impersonals' like constat (*it is agreed*).

Rule 6. **When a statement is made dependent on a
verb of 'saying' or 'thinking' the subject of the dependent clause is put in the Accusative, and the Verb in
the Infinitive.**

Verbs of 'saying' and 'thinking' include all such verbs
as *learn, perceive, know, hear, pretend, inform, hope, promise,
threaten* — of which **hope, promise, threaten** are always
followed by the **Future** Infinitive.   The subject of the
Infinitive must always be expressed.

'I deny' and 'I say that . . . not' are both translated in
Latin by **nego**.   Never use *dico . . . non*.

EXAMPLES

DIRECT STATEMENT	INDIRECT STATEMENT
Ille vir bonus est.	Putamus **illum virum esse bonum.**
He is a good man.	*We think he is a good man.*
Legiones sequentur.	Dixerunt **legiones secuturas** esse.
The legions will follow.	*They said the legions would follow.*
Copiae advenerunt.	Senserunt **copias advenisse.**
Forces have arrived.	*They perceived that forces had arrived.*

Urbs non capietur.
The city will not be taken.

Negant urbem captum iri.[1]
They say the city will not be taken.

Regrediar.
I shall return.

Spero me regressurum esse.
I hope to return.

Exercise 44 [A]

1. We know that forces will arrive.
2. They say the king is dead.
3. We have heard that peace has been made.
4. It was reported that the enemy had struck their camp.
5. Messengers say that the city has been taken.
6. We perceived that the king would be killed.
7. It is agreed that the citizens are cowardly.
8. Tell your friend that I am ready.
9. We promised to give Caesar arms.
10. Do you not know that the arms will be taken ?

Exercise 45 [B]

1. We promised to give hostages.
2. It was announced that the city had been taken.
3. They say that fresh forces are at hand.
4. We hope that our men will not yield.
5. It is well known that the Gauls are good soldiers.
6. It is announced that a great disaster has been sustained by our men.
7. It was announced that Caesar had defeated the Gauls.
8. We hope Caesar will be defeated by Ariovistus.
9. They perceived that the camp had been taken by Ariovistus.
10. Did you not think that your friends would come ?

[1] For the explanation of this construction see p. 82, note 1.

SE, IPSE

Latin has no separate Reflexive Pronoun of the 1st and 2nd Persons, the oblique cases of the Personal Pronoun being used reflexively. Where special emphasis is required ipse may be used in agreement with subject or object; *e.g.* ipse tibi obstas=you get in your own way; te ipsum laudas=you praise yourself.

In the 3rd Person se is the Reflexive Pronoun, both Masc. and Fem., Sing. and Plu. It has no Nom., and for 'he himself,' 'they themselves' we must use ipse, ipsi in agreement with the subject.

Rule 7. In simple sentences 'se' refers to the subject of its own clause. In Indirect Statement (Acc. with Inf.) use 'se' with reference to the subject of the principal verb; *i.e.* the verb of 'saying.' 'Eum,' 'eos' must not be used for the speaker.

The adj. suus follows the same rule, and *ejus* must not be used for it.

EXAMPLES

Ad eum discedite (vos) ipsi.
Go to him yourselves.

Se sua pecunia liberavit.
He freed himself with his own money.

Ariovistus respondet non sese iis sed eos sibi bellum intulisse.
Ariovistus replied that he had not waged war on them (the Gauls), but they on him.

Exercise 46

In the following sentences translate only the pronouns in italics :

1. Cato slew *himself* with *his own* hand.

2. Lentulus *himself* was put to death.

3. He *himself* knows best.

4. Come with me *yourselves*.

5. I sent for *them themselves*.

6. They gave the greatest share to *themselves*.

7. He said *he* did not know *them*.

8. *I myself* told them that *they* would be punished.

9. The king said *he* should set *them* free.

10. The judges replied that *they* did not fix the penalty, but the laws *themselves*.

11. Cato told *his* men that *they* would escape.

12. Who said *he* would give me the money ?

TENSES OF THE INFINITIVE IN INDIRECT STATEMENT

Rule 8. **If the time referred to by the Infinitive is the same as the time of the verb of saying or thinking, the Present must be used. Otherwise use the Perfect or Future according to the tense of English.**

The tense of the Infinitive is always the tense that was used by the speaker in Direct Statement; _e.g._ ' He said he was ill.' The actual words were, ' I _am_ ill.' Therefore use the _Present_ Infinitive.

EXAMPLES

Caesar per exploratores cognovit et montem a suis **teneri** et Helvetios castra **movisse.**

Caesar ascertained through scouts that the mountain was being held by his own men, and that the Helvetii had moved their camp.

Exercise 47 [_A_]

1. Few men knew that the walls had been taken.

2. Have you heard that the king's army is advancing?

3. He does not believe we shall ever finish the journey.

4. He says we shall not finish the journey.

5. Promise that you will not follow me.

6. I hope to give it you within a few days.

7. The soldiers cried out that they had never been conquered, and would not now yield.

8. I pretend to be his friend.

9. I did not know that he had deceived you.

10. They said they had not heard about the king's arrival.

11. We threatened to attack them as they were returning home.

12. Men say that the citizens are very rich.

Exercise 48 [*A*]

1. They informed the general that hostages would be given by all the states.

2. Our men [1] were told [2] that the enemy had fortified their camp, and were expecting an attack.

3. It was reported that the Gauls were close at hand.

4. The soldiers all declared that they would never leave their leader.

5. You have promised to come to me in the camp.

6. They declared that reinforcements had been seen, and would soon arrive.

7. I know that they promised to come before sunset.

8. They were so terrified that they did not see that the enemy were charging.

9. Ambassadors had told the king that war was finished.

10. They pretended to have told the king about the disaster.

11. Do not pretend to be wiser than your father.

---

[1] Nostri alone.

[2] certiores facti sunt. *To inform*=aliquem certiorem facere (literally ' to make more sure '). *I informed him*=eum certiorem feci. In the Passive ' *to be informed*,' ' *to be told*,' ' *to hear* '=certior fieri. *They will be informed*=certiores fient. Remember that dicor =*I am said*, never *I am told*.

Exercise 49 [*B*]

1. It is said [1] that the enemy are at hand.

2. News was brought that the enemy were at hand.

3. He was told that the legions would follow as soon as possible.[2]

4. It is agreed that the traitors were rightly killed.

5. Having been told that the city was taken, we retreated.

6. He promised to give the booty to the soldiers.

7. He said they had never asked him for money.

8. You know that they will not return.

9. The prisoners themselves declared that they were Gauls.

10. They said they were sure that the camp would be taken.

---

[1] Do not use *dicitur*.   Latin prefers the personal construction, *e.g.* hostes dicuntur. . . . Similarly do not use *videtur* for *it seems* where the sentence can be made personal ; *e.g. It seems that the ambassadors have returned*=Legati videntur redisse.

[2] quam primum.   Quam with a superlative (adj. or adv.) always has this sense ; *e.g.* Quam plurimos milites collegit (*he collected as many soldiers as possible*).   Quam celerrime progressi sunt (*they advanced as quickly as possible*).

Exercise 50 [B]

1. The general perceived that the enemy were about to attack.

2. It was announced by scouts that reinforcements were coming up.

3. They said he had not given them the promised reward.

4. I hope to see you at Rome next year.

5. Having ascertained that the enemy would soon attack them, they began to retreat.

6. Having been told of this disaster they declared that they would retreat.

7. We ourselves noticed that our men wished to yield.

8. Do you not perceive that we are surrounded by the enemy ?

9. The messengers tell us that the enemy left their camp two days ago.

10. The ambassadors informed the king that they would give him reinforcements.

Exercise 51 [A]

An old man used to complain to his wife in these words. He used to say that he went to the fields every day, and returned home in the evening tired with work ; but that she sat at home idle. The wife replied that she did not wish to be idle, and promised that she would go to the fields the next day. The husband accordingly stayed at home to prepare the supper, but not being skilled in [1] such things he prepared nothing which they could [2] eat in the evening ; and in the morning he said he would rather work and eat than sleep and be hungry. So he went to the fields himself.

---

[1] peritus with Gen.   [2] Subj.

C

Exercise 52 [A]

It was told Philip that the Romans were at hand. Crying out that he had been betrayed he ran out into the forum, and sent some men to throw his treasures [1] into the sea and others to burn the ships. Men who saw him say he was like a madman.[2] He declared that the passes had been purposely abandoned by his generals, and that he would punish the guilty. At the same time he promised to give a large sum of [3] money for every Roman killed in his kingdom.

Exercise 53 [A]

On hearing that [4] the Roman general had sent 3000 soldiers to besiege the town, the citizens, whose food was already beginning to fail, were greatly alarmed. So they resolved to send ambassadors to the camp to ask for peace. The Romans answered that this would be given when hostages had been surrendered (*abl. abs.*). The Roman general demanded these before night; but the citizens refused [5] to obey the order: they said that they would rather die than accept such a peace. And accordingly the city was blockaded for four months. Then the Romans withdrew to defend their own territories against the Suevi.

Exercise 54 [B]

At daybreak Leonidas perceived that he had been surrounded by the enemy. Nevertheless, being endowed with great bravery, he resolved to engage in battle and die for his country. Having praised the allies, he sent them all to their homes. Many of the Spartans also he wished to dismiss, but they all

---

[1] thesaurus. [2] madman=furens (participle).
[3] a large sum of=multus.
[4] Translate by '*having been informed that.*'
[5] Use nego (said they would not . . .).

said they would never leave their king. At length Leonidas perceived that the enemy were approaching, and drew up his men in line of battle to withstand their attack. They all knew that the enemy's forces were so great that there was no hope of escape ; but they fought bravely for many hours, and all to a man were killed.

Exercise 55 [B]

When Romulus had returned to the Campus Martius to review the army, a great storm having arisen suddenly, he was hidden by so thick a cloud that the citizens could not see him. Nor was he afterwards seen by any mortal. But on the following day a young man, by name Proculus Julius, came to Rome, and said that Romulus had appeared to him, and had told him that the gods wished Rome to be the capital of the world. Therefore the Romans perceived that they ought to practise the art of war, and become good soldiers, that all men might know that Romulus had spoken the truth.

Exercise 56 [B]

I have many friends, but of them all I think Caius is the cleverest. Once the brother of Caius was accused on account of some offence, and Caius was compelled to give evidence.[1] The accusers wished to make him angry, so that he might deny what he had already said. But he knew that they desired this, and gave his evidence without anger. At length one of the accusers said, ' Go away, my friend : you are a very clever man.' Caius replied that he wished that he could say the same of them, but that he had sworn to tell the truth.

---

[1] testimonium dicere.

Exercise 57 [A]

PRICE AND VALUE

The 'Genitive of Value' (tanti, quanti, minoris, minimi, magni, pluris, flocci, etc.) is to be used of indefinite value with verbs of *estimating* or *valuing*.

If the price is stated (with verbs like *buy, sell*) the Ablative of Price (which is really an Abl. of Instrument) must be used.

e.g. **Multis talentis** emptam domum **nihili** aestimat.
  A house bought for many talents he values at nothing.

1. How much do you think this horse is worth ?

2. I bought this book for four denarii.

3. Do you value liberty highly ?

4. I bought this house at a low price,

because Caius thought it of no value.

5. This house cost me 5000 sesterces.

6. He will sell the horse for 1500 sesterces.

7. I am selling my farm for a great sum of money.

8. I do not care a straw for wisdom.

9. A slave can buy his freedom for a talent.

10. I think this worth less than that (is worth).

Exercise 58 [*B*]

1. Buy a horse for 1250 sesterces.

2. I value this so greatly that I do not wish to sell it.

3. This house cost them a very great sum of money.

4. They set a very high value on virtue.

5. The victory cost Hannibal many men.

6. For how many talents will you sell this slave ?

7. How much do you think the slave is worth ?

8. Value money less and virtue more.

9. He bought the farm for 9000 sesterces, but **now** cares nothing for it.

10. For how much money was he liberated ?

Exercise 59 [*A*]

PARTITIVE GENITIVE

Britannorum fortissimi = *Bravest* { *of* / *among* } *the Britons.*

Nimis
Parum
Satis
Aliquid
} virtutis = {
Too much
Too little
Enough
Some
} *courage.*

1. I know that they waste too much time.

2. He had too little confidence in himself.

3. You both have sufficient boldness.

4. They do this that the State may not suffer any [1] loss.

5. Three thousand of our best soldiers have perished.

6. Some of the citizens wished to surrender, others to resist.

7. Our country, which was once the greatest in the world, still keeps some of its old strength.

8. Most of you [2] have shown more courage than wisdom.

9. I think there is some good in all men.

10. Where in the world do you live ?

---

[1] quid.

[2] Nos has two genitives—nostrum and nostri ; vos has vestrum and vestri. Use the forms in -um for Partitive Genitive, the forms in -i for the Objective Genitive.

Exercise 60 [*B*]

1. Most of our old friends are dead, and some have ceased to be friends.

2. Caesar has always been considered the greatest of the Romans.

3. The Gauls have too much eloquence and too little wisdom.

4. They said that the Helvetii were the greatest nation in the whole of Gaul.

5. So great a storm arose, that the greater part of the ships were lost.

6. Some of us have lost all hope.

7. You, who have some love for your country, ought not to do this.

8. He was the first to march [1] into this part of the country.

9. I do not consider Crassus the greatest man in our country.

10. Send to our help the best of your ships.

---

[1] *He, the first* (adj.), *marched.*   So ' *he left last* ' is ultimus abiit.

Exercise 61 [A]

DATIVE VERBS

1. He promised me wealth, but he has no money himself.

2. He satisfied me, and I think I can trust him again.

3. The enemy spared those who survived the battle.

4. Labienus was put in command of the army by Caesar.

5. A man who is angry with his friends without a cause does himself more harm than them.

6. This does not seem to me to be a place fit for a camp.

7. It is difficult to heal such a disease.

8. My friend Atticus came out of the city to meet me.

9. Having been put in command of a legion, he took part in many battles in Gaul.

10. The cavalry pressed the Gauls hard in their flight.[1]

11. A thousand Gauls threw themselves in our way, and we scarcely held our ground against them.

12. Caesar waged war against the Gauls, but his victories did not please his enemies at Rome.

13. They threatened me with death, but I had not injured them.

---

[1] =*flying.* Use Participle.

Exercise 62 [B]

1. Let us declare war immediately against the French.

2. You, who were put in command of the legion, ought to lead us against the enemy.

3. Did your friend marry Claudia ?

4. It is the king's pleasure to entrust the command to you.

5. They made war on their countrymen.

6. The judges threatened the prisoners with tortures.

7. Caesar exacted many hostages from the Aedui.

8. The general has sent these troops to our aid.

9. Who does not prefer freedom to slavery ?

10. I am unwilling to entrust Caius with this money.

11. Labienus, who was at the head of the sixth legion, resisted the onset of the Gauls.

12. They are much more devoted to agriculture than to war.

Exercise 63 [A]

[Exercises 63-70 are intended for revision.]

The Greeks valued their liberty so highly that they determined to resist the Persians and never [1] yield to them. Themistocles was put in command of the Greek forces. By his advice the Greeks trusted to their ships, and fought the Persians [2] by sea. The Greek fleet was near the island of Salamis,[3] and most of the leaders wished to withdraw from this place, and leave Athens in the hands of the Persians ; for they valued their own safety more than the city of Athens. Then Themistocles declared that he and the Athenians [4] would sail to Athens with the fleet of two hundred ships. But he was not able to persuade the others.

Exercise 64 [A]

Thereupon [5] Themistocles formed the following [6] plan to save both Athens and the other States of Greece. He sent a messenger secretly to the king of the Persians to tell him that the Greeks were about to depart. He pointed out that the Persians with their large fleet would easily surround the small forces of the Greeks. There are some who [7] say that by this advice he wished to please the king, and that he put his own safety before the freedom of his country. But the advice was of great service to Greece ; for the ships of the Persians hindered one another,[8] and the Greeks routed the enemy.

---

[1] See note on p. 11.   [2] *against* the Persians.
[3] Salamis, f. ; *Gen.*, Salaminis ; *Acc.*, Salamina.
[4] Athenae, -arum, f. ; Athenian=Atheniensis.
[5] quo facto.   [6] *this.*   [7] sunt qui, with Subj.
[8] *one another* here translate by se.

Exercise 65 [A]

In the battle which Caesar fought in that place with the Gauls he lost many of his men. For when he had arrived at the top of a hill, and had begun to fortify a camp, suddenly the enemy made an attack. The Romans, who were not standing in line of battle, at first were unable to resist, and took to flight; but afterwards Caesar sent the tenth legion, which he had with him,[1] to their aid, and at last the Gauls were driven down to the river. Here, however, they again made a stand, and Caesar himself says that they fought very bravely.

Exercise 66 [A]

When the king was told of this, he sent an officer [2] with 150 soldiers to take the robbers and bring them to him. On arriving at the place where the robbers were, they found that a very strong camp had been made in a wood, and that all the approaches had been blocked by cutting down trees.[3] At length, however, the place was stormed, and the robbers being taken were put to death : but the king pardoned the leader's son, a boy twelve years old.

---

[1] secum.

[2] Here ' centurio.' The centurion corresponds to the English *captain* ' and also to ' *sergeant*.' If a superior officer (*e.g.* colonel) is meant use tribunus militum. If the commander of a separate division is meant (a lieutenant-general) use legatus.

[3] Abl. Abs.

Exercise 67 [B]

When the crops began to ripen the general marched through the wood, making use of [1] a guide whom his horsemen had taken prisoner. On his march he sent out scouts to discover the enemy's camp. They having returned informed him that the enemy, with their wives and children and a large number of cattle, had made a camp in the middle of the marsh, and were awaiting his arrival. When he learnt this he advanced so quickly that he reached their camp at midnight; and such was the bravery of the Romans that few of the Germans escaped in safety.

Exercise 68 [B]

Calenus received a letter from Caesar, who told him that all the harbours and the shore were held by the enemy. On hearing this he recalled all his ships; but one of them, which did not obey his orders, was captured by Bibulus. All the sailors were put to death by the cruel general; he spared neither man nor boy, and hoped by his cruelty to finish the war more quickly. But Calenus pursued his fleet with forty ships, and defeated him at Oricum three days after the massacre.

---

[1] usus (utor).

Exercise 69 [B]

The kings of England and Germany declared war against Philip,[1] king of France. They felt sure that they would conquer him, on account of the number [2] of their troops, and because they held the French forces in small esteem. Nevertheless he defeated them in a great battle at Bovinium. It was a desperate battle,[3] and all showed the greatest bravery. It was observed that a certain priest had killed great numbers [2] of the enemy. The weapon which he used was an iron club. He had chosen this because he declared that a priest ought not to shed human blood,[4] and by this means his enemies died from the violence of the blow.

Exercise 70 [B]

The French king himself was the bravest knight in his army. He himself was wounded, and his horse was killed under him ; but he rose immediately, and led his men again against the enemy. They charged a squadron of Germans, amongst whom was the emperor himself. The Germans, thinking [5] that their emperor would be taken prisoner, came up to his help, and opened for him a way of escape. Thereupon Philip remarked to his men that they would only see the emperor's back on that day. After the flight of the emperor the French pursued his army, and defeated them with great slaughter.

---

[1] *Philip*=Philippus.

[2] ' number,' ' numbers,' meaning ' *great* numbers,' is always multitudo.

[3] atrociter pugnatum est.

[4] blood of men.

[5] Deponent—reor.

PASSIVE OF INTRANSITIVE VERBS

<u>*Rule* 9.</u> **Intransitive Verbs cannot be used personally in the Passive, but they can be used impersonally:** *e.g.* Pugnatum est diu = *the battle lasted long.*   Concurritur undique = *men run together from all sides.*   We can often express the same English by an intrans. or by a trans. verb : *e.g.*

The Romans are helped = succurritur Romanis, or juvantur Romani.

I was commanded = imperatum est mihi, or jussus sum.
I was advised = suasum est mihi, or monitus sum.

N.B.—Remember that all 'Dative Verbs' (*i.e.* all verbs that govern the Dative *only*) are Intransitive.

Exercise 71 [A]

1. The rich are envied by the poor.
2. A fierce battle was fought at Cannae.
3. You will not be believed again.
4. You have been advised by many of us.
5. The enemy were resisted for almost three hours.
6. At Rome many criminals are pardoned.
7. You shall be satisfied.
8. I was persuaded by the majority.
9. Many men more ill than you have been healed.
10. Shall such men be favoured among us ?

Exercise 72 [B]

1. Is a man believed who has once lied ?
2. The work is only hindered by such people.[1]
3. Do not be persuaded by him.
4. Help was brought to the Romans when hard pressed.
5. No man is hurt by advice.
6. They will not be pleased.
7. Orders are given to an army by the general only.
8. What rich man is envied by the wise ?
9. Be advised by us.
10. You will be accused and not spared.

---

[1] Here ' such people ' may be expressed by ' tales ' only. Very frequently *people* may be thus omitted or translated by ' ii ' : *e.g. people who lie* = ii qui mentiuntur. ' Populus ' is a people in the political sense, a nation, or ' the public,' *e.g.* ' populus vult decipi.'

DIRECT COMMAND OR PETITION[1]

<u>*Rule* 10.</u>

Second Person.　　If positive = Imperative.

　　　　　　　　　　If negative = (*a*) Ne with Perfect Subj.

　　　　　　　　　　　　　　　　(*b*) Imperat. of nolo with Inf.

First and Third Persons.　　Present Subj., with ne if negative.

EXAMPLES

Do not buy this horse = $\begin{cases} \text{Hunc equum } \textbf{ne emeris.} \\ \text{Hunc equum } \textbf{noli emere.} \end{cases}$

Let us (*not*) *buy this horse* = Hunc equum (**ne**) **emamus.**

When a command is double, and the second part negative, use **neu** or **neve** instead of *neque*, before the second part.

　　e.g. Maneamus in urbe **neve** discedamus.

　　　　Let us remain in the city and not depart.

　　　　Ne iratus sis **neve** me reliqueris.

　　　　Do not be angry or leave me.

---

[1] This is inserted here for convenience of revision before doing Indirect Command.

Exercise 73 [A]

1. Let us escape to the woods.

2. Follow me into the city.

3. Do not try to escape.

4. Let us go to Rome, and let us not remain here.

5. Let them not return to the city.

6. Do not remain at home, nor fear the storm.

7. Do this that you may be praised.

8. Do not give him a sword, but give him a bow and arrows.

9. Do not let us ask our friends for help.

10. Hold your ground, and do not retreat.

Exercise 74 [B]

1. Take away this shield.

2. Do not bring cavalry, but bring infantry and archers.

3. Let us try to bring help to our friends.

4. Give me the books which I asked you for.

5. Come to me, and do not be afraid.

6. Do not let us help our enemies or [1] injure our friends.

7. Let them remain where they are.

8. Do not despise the poor.

9. Let us die for our country.

10. Do not let slip this opportunity.

---

[1] In Latin 'nor.' The second half of the sentence is really negative.

INDIRECT COMMAND AND PETITION

In the sentences ' He commands *the building* of a bridge,' ' He demands *the payment* of the money,' the verbs ' commands ' and ' demands ' govern direct objects. But usually the place of this direct object is taken by a clause ; *e.g.* ' He commands *that the bridge be built,*' ' He demands *that the money be paid.*' These clauses are ' noun sentences,' and are as truly the objects of the principal verbs as the nouns ' building ' and ' payment ' in the first sentences. These object-sentences after verbs of asking and commanding are what we mean by ' Indirect Commands.'

Rule 11. **Indirect Commands are expressed in Latin by ut (when positive), ne (when negative), with the Subjunctive.**

The construction is exactly the same as that of Final Sentences.

Exceptions.—**Jubeo, veto,** take Present Infinitive. Avoid *jubeo . . . non,* for which *impero ne* or *veto* must be used.

Neu (neve) is used for *neque* in Indirect as in Direct Commands and Final Sentences.

EXAMPLES

(*a*) Persuadet Rauracis **ut** una cum Helvetiis **proficiscantur.**
He persuades the Rauraci to set out with the Helvetii.

(*b*) Pontem, qui erat ad Genavam, jubet **rescindi.**
He orders the bridge at Geneva to be broken down.

(*c*) Se gladio transfixit **ne** fame periret **neve** ab hostibus caperetur.
He fell on his sword that he might not die of hunger or be taken by the enemy.

Exercise 75 [A]

1. I asked him to follow me into the streets.
2. I beg of you not to let him escape.
3. He ordered Minucius not to attempt a battle.
4. I will persuade them not to leave me here alone.
5. Caesar had encouraged his men to hold their ground.
6. I forbade your asking him for money.
7. I warn you against despising the friendship of such a man.
8. Caesar demanded that the Germans should not cross the Rhine, nor leave their own territories.
9. The Gauls begged Caesar to spare their town.
10. The journey was so long that he told his men to leave the baggage in the town.
11. I have persuaded him to devote himself to his books.
12. Order the vanguard to halt.

Exercise 76 [B]

1. They have persuaded me to stay at home.
2. Tell your men to follow you.
3. We were asked to bring help to the citizens.
4. I told you not to leave us here alone.
5. They were advised not to leave their lands.
6. I will urge my friends to come to me at Rome.
7. I told the boy not to buy himself a horse.
8. Tell your brother not to cross the river or come into the town.
9. I have ordered the vanguard to halt and wait for reinforcements.
10. He had received such a serious wound that he asked his slave to kill him.
11. They urged their fellow-countrymen not to surrender nor send hostages to the Romans.
12. The people of the town begged Caesar to spare them.

WORDS THAT MAY INTRODUCE STATEMENTS AND COMMANDS

Rule 12. **The verbs moneo, persuadeo, suadeo, may intro-**
duce either an Indirect Statement or an Indirect Command.
In the former case, of course, they take Acc. with Inf. *E.g.*
in the sentence 'I will persuade him that this journey is
dangerous,' the word 'persuade' introduces a statement;
but in 'I will persuade him to abandon this journey' it
introduces a command.

EXAMPLE

Civitati persuasit ut de finibus suis **exirent** : perfacile esse
totius Galliae imperio potiri.

He persuaded the State to migrate from their territories (Ind.
command) ; *saying that it was easy to become supreme in
Gaul* (Ind. statement).

There is a similar ambiguity in the use of the English 'tell,' which
may introduce either statement or command; *e.g.* '*I told him
the journey was dangerous,*' and '*I told him to abandon the
journey.*'

Exercise 77 [A]

1. He ordered his men [1] to break down the bridge which had been made over [2] the Rhone.

2. He persuaded his men not to retreat, and warned them that the whole country was in the hands [3] of the enemy.

3. Caesar told his men that he was persuaded that the Germans had crossed the Rhine.

4. Cicero set out with the cavalry after telling [4] the infantry to follow him in three days.

5. Our men were advised to advance with great caution, that the enemy might not attack them off their guard.

6. The prisoners begged Caesar to spare their lives, and send them back to their friends.

7. You will never persuade me that the Romans will be conquered by barbarians.

8. So great was the determination of the prisoners that no one could compel them to speak.

9. Were you told that our men had been ordered to lay down their arms ?

10. Thereupon he dismissed the council, and ordered them not to assemble again.

11. They knew that Caesar had forbidden them to attack the enemy, but in his absence [5] they began to prepare for battle.

---

[1] sui.   [2] *in*, with Abl.   [3] in potestate.

[4] Abl. Abs. Remember that in this construction *impero* cannot be used. See Rule 9.   [5] Abl. Abs.

Exercise 78 [B]

1. I have been asked to stand for the consulship.

2. I shall forbid their crossing to this side of the river.

3. I warn you that you will be punished.

4. Caesar exhorted the legion with many prayers not to betray him to the enemy, or throw away their last hope of safety.

5. We have been forbidden to plunder the houses.

6. Orders have been sent us to try again to storm the town.

7. I was advised by Caesar not to trust you, or take you with me.

8. Our men were incited to search for the treasure by the promised reward.

9. Catiline is believed to have ordered Rome to be set on fire.

10. Persuade him that it is dangerous to cross the mountain.

11. Divitiacus tried to persuade the Gauls to remain faithful to Caesar, and not to revolt from him.

Exercise 79 [A]

Cincinnatus lived on the other side of the Tiber on a little farm, which he cultivated with his own hands. The messengers, who had been sent by the senate, found him sitting in the fields. They told him that they had come to inform him that he had been appointed dictator, and asked him to set out with them as soon as possible. Thereupon he bade his wife Racilia bring him his toga, in order that he might not displease the messengers of the senate. When it had been brought, he said he was willing to obey their commands, and would go with them at once.

Exercise 80 [A]

A certain [1] king found one of his slaves sleeping and holding a letter in his hand. He read the letter, in which the boy's mother thanked him because he had sent [2] her money, and begged him to obey his master faithfully. The king put the letter back with gold into the boy's hand, and then told another slave to wake him. At first the boy was frightened, when he saw the gold; but the king told him that good fortune often came to men when sleeping, and bade him give the gold to his mother, and say that the king greatly praised the mother of so good a son.

Exercise 81 [A]

In the evening a spy was caught by the guards at the gate of the town. Being brought to the commander of the garrison he fell down, and besought him with tears to spare him. He said he could persuade many of the besieging army to desert, and promised to assassinate their general. But the commander said he did not wage war in that way; and he ordered the guards to conduct the man to the enemy's camp. At the same time he sent a letter to the general, in which he advised him not to make use of traitors again—for (said he) they are always willing [3] to betray their masters to save their own lives.

Exercise 82 [B]

After this battle the Spartan commander sent a messenger to Sparta to tell the citizens that their good fortune had been lost, Mindarus slain, and that the soldiers were dying of starvation. Soon, however, Darius sent his younger son

---

[1] quidam, following its noun.

[2] Verb in Plup. Subj.

[3] This sentence is an Indirect Statement; but the word for 'said he' will be omitted in Latin, being understood from 'advised.'

Cyrus to the coast to supply pay to the Spartan sailors. These then attacked the Athenians so suddenly that they easily beat them, and took the whole fleet. At length the Athenians, being compelled by famine, surrendered their city, and became allies of the Spartans.

Exercise 83 [B]

On the next day the English advanced by forced marches with the intention of [1] attacking the French off their guard. But the latter had already learnt by means of [2] spies that the English were advancing, and had taken up their position on the top of a mound. When the English came within range, the archers began to shoot their arrows at the enemy. But the French general told his men not to fire back, but to allow the English to approach the bottom of the mound. When they were a few paces distant, he ordered his men not to wait any longer, but to get ready their arms. Then when the signal was given the French charged with such force that the English were routed and took to flight.

Exercise 84

The general vainly tried to persuade his men to follow him through the wood. He told them that the enemy had retreated, and that no one would attack them on the march. But they replied that night was approaching, and that many enemies could conceal themselves behind the trees ; and they begged him to allow them to pass the night in the camp. But the general would not allow this, but said that he himself would advance at once even with a few men. The rest he advised to return to the city, and tell their friends that they had been unwilling to march against the enemy.

---

[1] eo consilio ut.   [2] per.

Exercise 85 [*A*]

DATIVE OF PURPOSE, OR PREDICATIVE DATIVE

Exitio est avidum mare nautis.
The greedy sea is a destruction to sailors.
Hosti ludibrio esse.
To be a laughing-stock to the enemy.
Auxilio Caesari mittitur.
He is sent to the help of Caesar.

These Datives are never qualified by an epithet, except the simplest of quantity ; *e.g. magno* dedecori esse=*to be a great disgrace.* They are almost always accompanied by a *Dativus Commodi*, as *nautis, hosti, Caesari* in the above examples.

1. I shall only be a burden to you.
2. To sound a retreat will serve as a signal for flight.
3. This negligence has brought disgrace upon him.
4. It was to the advantage of the Romans to banish the kings.
5. His punishment was the cause of his death.
6. Let your father's constancy be an example to you always.
7. He sent money to help me while ill.
8. It was to my credit that (quod) you got home safely.
9. This will be a great disgrace to you.
10. He ought not to be hated by you.
11. They persuaded him that such a plan would mean destruction to the whole army.

Exercise 86 [*B*]

1. Avarice is a great evil to men.
2. This is a great proof of his courage.
3. He left three legions for the protection of the camp.
4. He ordered me to sound the signal for retreat.
5. I think this defeat was a great disgrace to the Romans.
6. Let us try to set a good example to others.
7. I believe this plan will prove the destruction of our army.
8. He was an object of hatred to all good men.
9. It is to your credit to have spared the prisoners.
10. This victory was the salvation of the state.
11. The position itself was a great help to the Gauls.

Exercise 87 [A]

ABLATIVES OF ORIGIN, SEPARATION, ASSOCIATION [1]

(1) Jove natus   =*Son of Jupiter.*
(2) Libera nos metu=*Free us from fear.*
(3) Divitiis abundat=*He has plenty of money.*

1. Having been banished from his country, he said he was freed from her laws.

2. He was descended from kings, but he did not enjoy kingly power himself.

3. The exiles were compelled to depart from their land.

4. The king was persuaded to set free the captives from prison.

5. Not only was he free from fault, but he also deserved praise.

6. Being the son of such a father, all the people obeyed him willingly.

7. He lived so far from the city, that even his friends did not see him often.

8. The slaves could not be persuaded to speak even by tortures.

9. When kings were banished from Rome, the people were full of joy.

10. Men are often injured even by praise.

11. Not only does the island abound in fruits and flowers, but it is inhabited by a race descended from the gods.

---

[1] Earlier exercises on the Ablative are given on pages 36, 37.

Exercise 88 [B]

1. This victory has freed us from all fear.

2. The camp was pitched on a hill not far from the town.

3. Even good men are not always free from blame.

4. Being descended from a noble race, he tried to set an example to the rest of the citizens.

5. Not only the men, but also the women and children were banished from their country.

6. The soldiers were ordered to desist from the siege.

7. Even safety will not induce me to live far from the city.

8. This land abounds in all kinds of [1] riches.

9. We were compelled not only to depart from the city, but also to give up all our goods.

10. They were begged by all of us to set free the captives from prison.

11. These people were rich both in cattle and money.

12. He left the city in a passion.

---

[1] all.

Exercise 89 [A]

ABLATIVES OF RESPECT AND MANNER

(1) Numero superiores   =*Greater in number.*
(2) Summa diligentia naves armare=*To fit ships with great care.*

The Ablative of Manner must have an epithet, except in a few words : *e.g.* jure (rightly), injuria (wrongly), fraude (treacherously), silentio (in silence), etc. If there is no epithet use cum : *e.g.* cum diligentia naves armare.

1. The troops were few in number, but they fought with great bravery.

2. He replied in a loud voice that he would never yield.

3. They were told that the enemy were advancing in great disorder.

4. Having armed as many men as possible,[1] they charged the enemy with the utmost fury.

5. I have been wrongfully accused of treachery [2] by my private enemies.

6. They said they had been accustomed to live in the fashion of their ancestors.

7. These traitors were rightly put to death with all speed.

8. He is younger than his brother, but excels him in wisdom and talents.

9. You, who are an Englishman by birth, ought to resist bad laws with all your power.

10. I had not even heard that they were inferior to us in numbers.

11. By your leave I shall ask him to come home with me as often as possible.[1]

12. Not even you, he said, will persuade me that Caesar was rightly killed.

---

[1] See note to Ex. 49.   [2] Gen. of *crime.*

Exercise 90 [B]

1. The Athenians joined battle with the utmost fury.

2. What he has learnt with care he values most highly.

3. They are superior in skill, not in courage.

4. He spoke this with sorrow.

5. In everything else they employ Greek characters.

6. I believe that we ought to act according to the customs of our ancestors.

7. With your leave I will tell the slaves to withdraw.

8. He seems to have been rightly punished.

9. To live in the fashion of rich men seems pleasant to you who are poor.

10. He replied in great anger that his enemy had lied.

11. The consul with a smile said, ' Go home and do not come here again.'

12. We are inferior to the enemy in numbers, but our men excel others in courage.

Exercise 91 [A]

[Exercises 91-98 are intended for revision.]

Numa being dead, Tullus Hostilius was made king. While he was king war arose between the Romans and Albans. In order that the war might be finished without great loss, the kings ordered that three Romans should fight for their fatherland against three Albans, and decide the contest. The fight lasted a long time, but at last two of the Romans were killed, and all three Albans were wounded. The third Roman, whose name was Horatius, pretended to flee, and induced the Albans to pursue him. In following him they were separated, and Horatius, turning round, killed them in turn.

Exercise 92 [*A*]

Eurystheus then set [1] Hercules the eleventh labour, which
was harder than those which we have mentioned above.　For
he ordered him to take away the golden apples from the gardens
of the Hesperides.[2]　These were nymphs of remarkable beauty,
who lived in a distant land, and some golden apples had been
entrusted [3] to them by Juno.　Many men had before this tried
to take away these apples ; but it was a difficult thing to do,[4]
for the garden in which the apples were was surrounded by a
high wall on all sides.　Moreover a dragon,[5] which had a
hundred heads, guarded the gate of the garden carefully by
day and night.

Exercise 93 [*A*]

Hearing that the Belgae were conspiring against the Romans,
Caesar determined to go himself without delay to central Gaul
with two legions, ordering the rest to follow in a few days.
On his arrival the Remi, who live on the borders of Gaul, sent
ambassadors to say that they were willing to give hostages,
and help the Romans with corn.　They said that the rest of
the Belgae were under arms, and that the Germans had joined
them.　On hearing this, Caesar promised to come with all
possible speed to the help of the Remi, that having joined
their forces they might repel the invasion of the Germans.

---

[1] proponere.　　　　　　　　[2] Hesperides, -um.

[3] committere.　　　　　　　[4] factu (supine).

[5] draco -onis, *m.*

Exercise 94 [A]

The Romans, having set out about the third watch, advanced
with great caution, for they had been informed that the enemy
were close at hand. They advanced until late in the night,
and then were told to pitch their camp. In the middle of
the night shouts were heard on all sides, and they saw that
great forces of the enemy were making an attack. So they
took up their arms as quickly as possible to repel the onset.
But when the enemy perceived that they had not been able
to attack our men off their guard, the signal for retreat was
given, and they withdrew.

Exercise 95 [B]

Louis [1] could not at this time besiege Tunis,[1] because he had
not received reinforcements from his brother Charles,[1] King of
Sicily; and meanwhile his army was attacked by a disease
which carried off the greater part of his soldiers in a few days.
The king himself was seized with the disease, and felt that he
would die of it. But, to sustain the courage of his soldiers, he
performed all the duties of a king, and attended in every
way to the safety of the camp. But at last he was compelled
to remain within his tent, and before long [2] died, after telling
his men never to abandon the siege.

---

[1] *Louis* = Ludovicus. For *Tunis* use Carthago. *Charles* = Carolus.
[2] before long = mox.

Exercise 96 [B]

Nothing had been heard of the army for many months, and the citizens began to think that it had been defeated and all their fellow-countrymen killed. The women used to go every day to the temples, and pray the gods to send them back safely their husbands and sons. At last, when winter was approaching, and all had begun to give up hope, a messenger was seen at a distance who was approaching the city with great speed. The citizens all rushed out to meet him, and implored him to tell them without delay about the army. So tired was the messenger by his journey that at first he could not speak; but at length he said that the army had both won many victories and taken many towns of the enemy, and that the soldiers hoped in a short time to return home with a great quantity of booty and many prisoners.

Exercise 97 [B]

As the people of Veii [1] often made incursions [2] for the sake of plunder, the Romans were scarcely able to defend their own territories. Their soldiers went home to their fields in the spring to sow, and in the autumn to gather the harvest, at which times the Veientines did a great deal of harm to [3] their lands. At last the Fabii promised the Senate that they would be under arms the whole year, and undertake the whole war themselves. The Senate thanked them, and going out from Rome they made a camp near the river Cremera. For a little time they checked the Veientines, but at length they were surrounded, and slaughtered to a man.

Exercise 98 [B]

We set out from Moscow [4] about the third watch, so that no disturbance might be excited by our friends. I never expected to see my brothers again. For thirty-three days we marched along a road covered by snow a foot deep. Sometimes one of us fell down, and was unable to move further. Our guards did not try to urge him on, for they knew well that the wolves would have him for [5] their prey before the next day. I now often envy those who were thus left on the road, and prefer death to the evils which daily press upon me. I am compelled to work, but that is the least of my ills; I am compelled to see the sufferings of the women who with us dared everything for the sake of liberty.

---

[1] Veientes.   [2] Abl. Abs.   [3] *harmed much.*
[4] Moscova.   [5] pro, or simple acc. in apposition.

D

GERUNDS AND GERUNDIVES

Distinguish the Gerund and Gerundive.

(1) The Gerund is a Verbal Noun of the Active Voice, corresponding to the English verbal nouns in *-ing ;* not to be confused with the Present Participle in *-ing*, which is really an Adjective.

(2) The Gerundive is a Verbal Adjective of the Passive Voice.

Rule 13.—**A. The oblique cases of the Gerund are used simply as the cases of a Noun. But the Accusative can only be used governed by a Preposition.**

e.g. Acc.   natus ad regendum   =*born to rule.*
    Gen.   cupidus discendi   =*desirous of learning.*
    Dat.   studuit discendo   =*he was devoted to learning.*
    Abl. (in) discendo sapientior fio=*by learning I become wiser.*

When the Gerund is in the Genitive case or the Ablative without a Preposition it may take a direct object.

e.g. Gen.   pacem petendi causa   =*for the sake of seeking peace.*
    Abl.   scribendo fabulas   =*in writing stories.*

B. But when the Verbal Noun governs a direct object[1] instead of the Gerund we generally use the Gerundive. This attracts the object into its own case, but agrees with the object in number and gender. This construction is known as 'Gerundive Attraction.'

e.g. Acc.   ad pacem petendam   =*in order to ask for peace.*
    Gen.   pacis petendae causa   =*for the sake of asking for peace.*
    Dat.   legibus mutandis studuit=*he was eager for changing the laws.*
    Abl.   in scribendis fabulis   =*in writing stories.*

---

[1] The Gerundive being *Passive*, none but transitive verbs (governing a direct object in the Acc.) can have a Gerundive.

Exercise 99

The art of writing.	The signal for striking the camp.
The art of writing letters.	
By obeying the laws.	The desire of having riches.
By changing the laws.	By dying.
For the sake of pleasing our friends.	For the purpose of preserving the state.
For the sake of saving our friends.	For the purpose of helping the state.
In order to injure the Gauls.	
In order to defeat the Gauls.	For saving the king.
The signal for advance.[1]	For serving the king.

Exercise 100 [A]

1. We have done this for the sake of helping our friends.

2. By teaching others we learn ourselves.

3. By learning letters we are able to enjoy reading.

4. They hastened to Rome for the purpose of defending the city.

5. Are you not desirous of saving your friends ?

6. The Romans became great through their desire to obey the laws.

7. The art of ruling others is not easily learnt.

8. For the sake of winning honour we suffer much pain.

9. An opportunity has been offered for fighting.

10. This seems a good opportunity for defeating the enemy.

---

[1] When the Gerund or Gerundive depends on a substantive, put it in the Genitive Case.

Exercise 101 [A]

1. Caesar sent cavalry to bring help to the allies.

2. The officers sent their men to forage in all directions.

3. By obeying the laws we show that we are desirous of preserving our state.

4. He gave his men the signal to advance.

5. The signal was given to advance the standards.

6. The Athenians sent men to Delphi to consult the god.

7. For the sake of pleasing their friends the Senate did many disgraceful things.

8. He sent messengers to the Aedui to demand hostages from them.

9. No opportunity was left them for retreating.

10. They are anxious to devote themselves to letters.

Exercise 102 [B]

1. They were led on by the hope of taking the city.

2. I was induced to do this for the sake of pleasing the soldiers.

3. We were sent to ask for help.

4. They were sent to bring help to the allies.

5. Time is often wasted in writing books.

6. By obeying wise laws the Roman state became great.

7. The people of this city seem anxious to change their laws.

8. Let us not let slip this opportunity of winning a victory.

9. I am anxious to consult your interests.

10. Caesar was anxious to exact hostages from the Gauls.

Exercise 103 [B]

1. Let us not talk of flying, for only by holding our ground shall we conquer.

2. To save his country a man ought always to face death.

3. How many of us are fit for commanding an army ?

4. He gave the signal for crossing the river.

5. In our zeal for pursuing the cavalry we advanced too far.[1]

6. For learning one needs [2] talent and a great desire of knowledge.

7. We were sent for to defend the king from harm.

8. A great cause of crime is the desire of having wealth.

9. Officers were ordered to enter the citadel to receive the arms which the enemy had promised to give up.

10. For the sake of filling the ships and sailing at once they bought merchandise at a great price.

11. They are here to ask for pardon.

---

[1] Comparative.   [2] *one needs* = opus est.

SUPINES

Besides the Gerund there is another Verbal Noun in Latin called the Supine. It only has two cases—an Acc. in **-um**, and an Abl. in **-u**.

Rule 14. **The Supine in -um can only be used to express purpose after Verbs of Motion. It may govern an object.**[1]

The Supine in -u can only be used after Adjectives,[2] **and corresponds to an Infinitive following an Adjective in English,** _e.g._ ' a question _hard to answer._'

EXAMPLES

Abii **dormitum**   = _I went away to sleep._

Venerunt **pacem petitum** = _They came to ask for peace._

Mirabile **dictu**   = _Wonderful to relate._

---

[1] The Future Infinitive Passive is made up of the Supine with iri, so that in the sentence ' Dixerunt nos interfectum iri,' _interfectum_ really governs _nos_, being a supine of purpose after _iri_.

[2] Also certain indeclinable nouns used as adjectives, _e.g._ **fas** (right), nefas (wrong).

Exercise 104 [A]

1. It is easy to say, but difficult to do.

2. They say that the city will not easily be captured.

3. Go out to play.

4. Do not always eat what is pleasant to eat.

5. The story is a strange one to tell.

6. Send him to pay the money at once.

7. The general told the officers to send some men to forage.

8. Fire is dangerous to touch.

9. They left Rome to found a new colony.

10. All agree that the city will never be surrendered.

Exercise 105 [B]

1. Aeneas had gone away from the camp to ask for help.

2. I do not believe that the money will be paid.

3. It is not lawful to do this.

4. The mother and wife of Coriolanus were sent to him to ask pardon on behalf of the city.

5. I shall go to bed soon.

6. They often do things disgraceful to relate.

7. I hope the soldiers will be sent home again.

8. The story is easy to tell.

9. Send men to give an answer.

10. He spoke with a voice difficult to hear.

Exercise 106 [*A*]

Our men saw that they were surrounded on all sides ; and
no opportunity being left for retreating, they resolved to
charge with all their might in the hope of striking terror
into the enemy. They knew that they had been brought into
these dangers by delaying too long [1] before, and they hoped
that by fighting bravely now they would force the enemy
to give ground. Therefore, when the signal for advance was
given, they ran forward with a loud shout against that part
of the line which seemed weakest.[2] The enemy were thrown
into such confusion [3] by this unexpected attack that their line
was broken at once, and no one resisted our charge.[4]

Exercise 107 [*A*]

A messenger had been sent to France to ask for help, and
to invite French troops to Ireland. Arms and money were
promised for the purpose of assisting an Irish army. These
were conveyed [5] by a French ship, and a hundred men
assembled on the shore to receive the arms which it was going
to land.[6] But in a storm two of their boats had been broken,
and in repairing them time was wasted.[7] Meanwhile, to
scatter the rebels, a troop of horse had been sent out from
Cork, at the sight of whom [8] the rebels fled in all directions ;
and to effect their own escape the French sailors threw the
arms overboard [9] ; they lie sunk [10] in the harbour to this day.

---

[1] Comparative of *diu.*
[2] tenuis.
[3] *were so disturbed* (perturbare).
[4] *them charging.*
[5] *convey by sea*=transportare.
[6] expositura erat.
[7] Use Historic Present.
[8] Abl. Abs.
[9] e navi projicere.
[10] submersus.

Exercise 108 [*B*]

The French general was unwilling to attack us at close quarters, because his troops were inexperienced in battle, and he thought they would fight best (when) sheltered[1] by ramparts. Moreover, three years before his troops had been unable to resist the English hand to hand, but having been withdrawn into the town, had defended the walls obstinately. The recollection of that time and the desire to prolong the war induced him to remain where he was. However, in order to give the Belgians[2] an opportunity of deserting us, he sent out troops of cavalry as far as our outposts. But for fear of this we employed no Belgians as sentinels. For throughout the whole year we were expecting every day they would desert us.

Exercise 109 [*B*]

The Athenians hoped that a Spartan army would march into Boeotia, and had taken no measures[3] to save their families and property. Therefore they saw with the utmost fear and dismay that the Barbarians were advancing with all their forces for the sake of attacking their city. It was evident that in six days Xerxes would be at Athens, and this seemed a very short time for removing the population of a whole city. But they knew that it was of the greatest importance[4] to them to accomplish this, and before his arrival they had safely removed all who were willing to leave their homes. Some were taken to Aegina, others to Troezen ;[5] but many could not be induced to proceed farther than Salamis.[6]

---

[1] tectus = *covered*, in the sense of *sheltered* ; opertus = *covered*, in the sense of *hidden*.

[2] Belgae.   [3] ' *had done nothing.*'

[4] maximi interesse = to be of the greatest importance.

[5] Troezen, *Gen.* Troezenis f.

[6] Salamis, *Gen.* Salaminis, *Acc.* Salamina f.

DIRECT QUESTIONS [1]

Rule 15. **Direct Questions** may be asked without any special Interrogative word, but they are frequently introduced

(*a*) by Interrogative Pronouns or Adverbs, such as **quis,** *who ?* **quando,** [2] *when ?* **ubi,** *where ?*

(*b*) by Interrogative Particles. These Particles are in Single Questions **-ne** (enclitic), **nonne** (expecting answer 'yes'), **num** (expecting answer 'no') ; in Double Questions **utrum . . . an, -ne . . . an, utrum . . . annon.**

EXAMPLES

(*a*) **Caesarne** ad castra advenit ?
Has Caesar reached the camp ?

(*b*) **Nonne** Caesar ad castra advenit ?
Has not Caesar reached the camp ? Surely Caesar has reached the camp ?

(*c*) **Num** Caesar ad castra advenit ?
Caesar has not reached the camp, has he ? [3]

(*d*) **Utrum** Caesar (or **Caesarne**) ad castra advenit **annon ?**
Has Caesar reached the camp or not ?

[N.B.—Do not append the **-ne** to an unemphatic word.]

---

[1] This rule is inserted here for convenience of revision before doing Indirect Questions.

[2] *When* in questions is never *cum* but *quando*. Notice also that *where* is often used in English for *whither*, and in this sense must be translated by *quo*.

[3] Notice the form of the English. ' Has he ? ' ' is he ? ' ' isn't he ? ' etc., is only our way of showing what answer we expect, and is fully represented in Latin by the *nonne* or *num* at the beginning of the sentence.

Exercise 110 [A]

1. Did you say that you would come ?
2. Were you or your brother the first to arrive ?
3. What sort of country do you live in ?
4. Surely you do not hope to see him again ?
5. Where have you come from ?   Where are you going to ?
Where have you decided to live ?
6. Do you not believe that this loss will increase the panic ?
7. How many books have you ?
8. How often have you seen him, and when do you expect
him to return ?
9. Have you determined to accept these terms or not ?
10. How great is the army of the enemy, and who commands it ?
11. What plan have you formed now ?

Exercise 111 [B]

1. Is it easier to command or to obey ?
2. Have you seen the horse which I gave your brother ?
3. How many times have you been to France ?
4. Surely you do not think me worthy of blame ?
5. They did not ask you to go to Rome, did they ?
6. How large is the house in which you live ?
7. Which of these two books do you prefer ?
8. Why do you prefer England to France ?
9. What plan have you formed now ?
10. How great is the army of the enemy, and who
commands it ?
11. Where did you buy this horse ?   Where did you send
the letter ?   Where did these ships come from ?

INDIRECT QUESTIONS

In the sentence 'He asked *what I was doing*' the clause 'what I was doing' is really the object of the verb 'asked.' In the sentence '*What he is doing* is uncertain' the clause 'what he is doing' is really the subject of 'is.'

When a direct question becomes thus the subject or object of a verb we call it an *Indirect Question.*

Rule 16. **A clause expressing an Indirect Question in Latin always has its verb in the Subjunctive.**

The principal verb may be any such word as *ask, know, doubt, consider, tell,* etc.

Primary Tenses

$$
\left\{ \begin{array}{l} \text{Rogat}\ ^1 \\ \text{Rogabit} \\ \text{Rogavit} \end{array} \right\} \text{quid} \left\{ \begin{array}{l} \text{agam} \\ \text{acturus sim} \\ \text{egerim}\ ^2 \end{array} \right\}
$$

$$
\left\{ \begin{array}{l} \text{He asks} \\ \text{He will ask} \\ \text{He has asked} \end{array} \right\} \text{what} \left\{ \begin{array}{l} \text{I am doing} \\ \text{I am going to do} \\ \text{I did} \end{array} \right\}
$$

Historic Tenses

$$
\left\{ \begin{array}{l} \text{Rogabat} \\ \text{Rogavit} \\ \text{Rogaverat} \end{array} \right\} \text{quid} \left\{ \begin{array}{l} \text{agerem} \\ \text{acturus essem} \\ \text{egissem} \end{array} \right\}
$$

$$
\left\{ \begin{array}{l} \text{He was asking} \\ \text{He asked} \\ \text{He had asked} \end{array} \right\} \text{what} \left\{ \begin{array}{l} \text{I was doing} \\ \text{I was going to do} \\ \text{I had done} \end{array} \right\}
$$

In the above examples it will be noticed that we supply a **Future Subjunctive** by what is called the **periphrastic conjugation,** *i.e.* the Fut. Participle with *sim* in Primary, *essem* in Historic sequence.

> *e.g.* Nescio quando **venturi sint.**
>
>   *I do not know when they will come.*
>
> Nesciebam quando **venturi essent.**
>
>   *I did not know when they would come.*

The interrogative particles are the same as in direct

---

[1] The Imperative is a Primary tense—

$$
\text{Roga quid} \left\{ \begin{array}{l} \text{agat} \\ \text{acturus sit} \\ \text{egerit} \end{array} \right\} = \text{Ask what} \left\{ \begin{array}{l} \text{he is doing} \\ \text{he is going to do} \\ \text{he did} \end{array} \right\}
$$

[2] The Perfect represents a **completed** action. Therefore use the Perf. Subj. when the governing verb is primary and the dependent verb relates to an action completed in past time, *e.g.* —

Nescio quomodo mortuus sit = *I do not know how he died.*

questions (whether single or double). But in indirect questions *num* does not necessarily expect the answer 'no,' and **necne** must be used for *annon*. ' If ' meaning ' whether ' introducing a question must never be translated *si*, but in single questions by **num**, in double questions by $\left.\begin{array}{l}\text{utrum}\\ \text{-ne}\end{array}\right\}$. . . **an.** ' When ' in questions is **quando**, never *cum*.

Exercise 112 [*A*]

1. Tell me why you did that.

2. We have not been told when reinforcements will arrive.

3. It was doubtful if they would arrive before night.

4. We did not know where our friends had gone, nor where we should find them.

5. It is uncertain whether we shall see him again.

6. I was not told whether I ought to remain or go away.

7. Tell me where you have come from.

8. I do not know how I ought to do this.

9. Have you heard what plan the general has formed ?

10. I was told how bravely our men had fought.

Exercise 113 [*A*]

1. I have not heard when he arrived.

2. It is doubtful whether we ought to do this or not.

3. I do not know if he told the truth.

4. It is hard to say whether this was done on purpose or not.

5. I was not told how I ought to answer.

6. I cannot say how often I have been asked to come.

7. Nobody seems to know how great the enemies' forces were.

8. It was doubtful how many soldiers would arrive.

9. We had not been told what sort of man he was.

10. Can you tell me if he was rightly punished ?

Exercise 114 [B]

1. Nobody knows whether he said that or not.
2. Have you heard which of the two was elected consul ?
3. The soldiers did not know what plan the general had formed.
4. He said he did not know if Crassus had been put in command of the army.
5. It is uncertain how many men he is in command of, and where he has taken up his position.
6. We asked them who they were, where they lived, where they came from, and where they were now going.
7. I cannot tell you when they have promised to come.
8. It is doubtful how he is able to do such things.
9. We, who are old, understand how happy are the young.
10. I do not know whether you deserve praise or blame.

Exercise 115 [B]

1. He wants to know what I am going to do to-morrow.
2. It matters a great deal [1] whether they intend to send out cavalry or infantry.
3. We did not know whether the enemy were going to attack in the evening or late in the night.
4. It was doubtful what news the messenger would bring.
5. Let us ask if one regiment will be enough.
6. When the enemy would cross the river was quite uncertain.
7. Tell me if your father is dead.
8. It makes a great difference whether he bought the horse at a low price or not.
9. Have you heard if he has been persuaded to return ?
10. It is uncertain whether he will hinder us more than he will help us.

---

[1] maximi interest.

Exercise 116 [*A*]

N.B.—Abstract nouns should generally be translated by concrete expressions; *e.g.*—

What is the *character* (*nature*) of the island ?=Qualis est insula ?
What is the *size* of the island ?=Quanta est insula ?
What are the *numbers* of the enemy ?=Quot sunt hostes ?
Their *decision* is=constituerunt.

What is your { *reason* for doing this ? / *intention* (*object*) in doing this ? } =Quo consilio id agis ?

1. The general tried to discover the numbers and intentions of the enemy.

2. Have you been able to discover his reason for doing this ?

3. Nobody seemed to understand their object in asking for such terms.

4. I almost think we ought to retreat.

5. They had not heard the decision of the king.

6. It was doubtful where our friends were, and when they would come to meet us.

7. I rather think he has been advised to depart.

8. He sent me to discover the nature of the island.

9. It is uncertain where they started from, and when they will reach the city.

Exercise 117 [B]

1. I could not discover his reason for saying that.

2. We cannot find out the size of the enemy's camp.

3. I did not tell him by what road we should march.

4. The generals did not inform the soldiers of their decision.

5. Spies were sent forward to learn what was going on in the enemy's camp.

6. Can you tell me how many miles the town of Veii is distant from Rome ?

7. We could not easily discover the numbers of the enemy.

8. Do you know the destination of these travellers ?

9. I almost think they have been compelled to retreat.

10. We could not discover their reason for returning home.

Exercise 118 [A]

It is said that a certain prophetess brought nine books to Tarquin,[1] king of Rome, and asked him if he wished to buy them. The king asked for what price she was willing to sell them ; to which she replied that she would sell them for three hundred pieces of gold. The woman went away, but afterwards she returned with six books. Tarquin asked where she had left the others, and she replied that she had burnt them, but that she would sell him these for the same price. Tarquin would not buy them, and she again left him. But once more she returned with only three books, and asked whether he was willing to buy these at the same price or not.

Exercise 119 [A]

The king, who wondered why she had returned so often, now asked his senate whether he ought to keep them. They first asked him what sort of books they were, and if the prophetess had shown them to him. The king replied that she had said nothing, but that she had burnt six books out of [2] nine, and now offered three at the same price. It seemed doubtful to the senators what they ought to do, but at last they advised the king to buy the books. Then the woman, having received the money, advised the Romans to keep the books very carefully, and went away.

---

[1] Tarquinius.   [2] de.

Exercise 120 [A]

The story is told of King Tarquin that he once determined to add new companies [1] to the Roman knights. Attius the augur said it could not be done. Moved by anger the king demanded that he should show by a sign what the gods wished. Attius replied that he would tell the king what he had in his mind. But Tarquin said, ' Tell me rather whether that which I have in my mind can be done.' ' It can be done,' said Attius. Then the king bade him cut a whetstone [2] in two, for he said he was thinking of that. Without any delay (so they relate [3]) Attius cleft it with a razor.[4]

Exercise 121 [B]

In the following year Cleon was sent to Macedonia to recover the cities which had been taken by the Spartans. He first marched to Amphipolis, and encamped on rising ground near the city. In the meanwhile Brasidas, the Spartan general, who knew what sort of man Cleon was, resolved to deceive him by a trick. He ordered his men not to show themselves on the wall, but to conceal themselves behind the ramparts. Meanwhile he sent out spies to discover how large the forces of Cleon were, and if reinforcements were coming. These men brought back word that the army of the enemy was small, and was not drawn up carefully. Then Brasidas ordered his men to throw open the gates and attack the enemy at once. The Athenians, who did not trust their general, took to flight, and most of them were killed.

---

[1] centuriae.   [2] cos, cotis f.   [3] ut ferunt.   [4] novacula.

Exercise 122 [*B*]

The prisoner was brought before the king, who asked him where he had concealed his money. To this the man replied that he had indeed been rich once, but that now all his money had been taken away from him by the soldiers, and that nothing was left. The king asked the soldiers if this was true, but they all declared that they had not taken the gold, and did not know where the prisoner kept it. Then the king said that he would discover by means of tortures who was telling the truth ; but the prisoner, being overcome by fear, asked if the king would pardon him when the money was given up.[1] The king promised to do this, whereupon the prisoner said he would show them at once where he had carried the money.

Exercise 123 [*B*]

I once went to the house of a celebrated man, who had formerly been a friend of mine, to ask if he would help me in a matter which I had in hand.[2] The servant (slave) said he was not at home, but as I had caught sight of my friend, I knew the fellow [3] lied. Some days after the great man [4] came to my house, and I, having no servant,[5] opened the door to him myself. On seeing him I exclaimed, with unmoved countenance, ' He is not at home.' In astonishment my friend asked whether I was mad. To which I replied, ' I believed your servant when he told lies about you. Are you not willing to believe me when I speak about myself ? '

---

[1] Abl. Abs.
[2] *undertaken* (suscipere).
[3] homo—often contemptuous.
[4] ille.
[5] ' *to whom there was no servant.*'

SUBORDINATE CLAUSES IN INDIRECT STATEMENT, ETC.

Rule 17. **All clauses which are subordinate to an Indirect statement or command or question have their verbs in the subjunctive.**

EXAMPLE

Ariovistus respondit se non in eas partes Galliae venire audere **quas Caesar possideret.**

Ariovistus replied that he did not dare to come into those parts of Gaul which Caesar held.

Exercise 124 [A]

It was the custom of the Falisci to send their children to a schoolmaster to live with him. When the Romans were waging war with the Falisci, this schoolmaster thought that he would please the Romans if he gave them these children as hostages. He therefore purposely led them, without the knowledge of the citizens, to the Roman camp, and offered them to the general. The latter, however, asked him how he had dared to betray children who had been committed to his care, and threatened him with severe punishment. Then he told the children to take such rods as their master was himself accustomed to use, and with these to drive him to the city.

Exercise 125 [*A*]

The news reached [1] Rome that their army had been defeated, and that of the two consuls who were in command one had been killed and the other was a fugitive. At first the whole city was full of panic and grief. But soon the Senate assembled to take measures [2] for the safety of the State. They decreed that those who were able to fight should go with the women and children to the capitol ; but they declared that they themselves, who were old men, and unable to bear arms, would remain in the city. The Gauls found these old men sitting in silence, and clothed in their state robes. [3] At first they wondered greatly, but finally they approached the Senators, and a soldier stroked the long beard of one of them with his hand. The Senator, being enraged, struck the man, whereupon the rest of the Gauls slew all the Senators.

---

[1] *to bring news* = afferre nuntium.   [2] = *consult*.   [3] toga laticlavia.

Exercise 126 [B]

Solon, the wisest of the Athenians, went once to visit
Croesus at Sardis.[1] You have all heard how these two
men became friends, and discussed many things together.[2]
But the story is worthy of [3] being told again. Croesus
considered that that man was most fortunate who had great
power and riches, and who could do whatever he wished ; and
he thought that he himself was such a man. He therefore
showed Solon all his gold and silver, and told him how many
nations he ruled. He then asked him whom he considered the
happiest of mortals. He was sure that Solon would answer
that he who ruled the city of Sardis and such a great kingdom
was the happiest. But Solon replied that two young men,
Cleobis and Biton, were the most happy.

---

[1] Sardes pl., *gen.* Sardium. Solon, Solonis.

[2] ' inter se,' which often translates words like ' *together.* ' ' *mutually,*'
' *one another,*' etc.

[3] digna quae, with Subjunctive.

Exercise 127 [B]

Croesus said he had never heard of these men, and asked Solon who they were. The latter replied that they were two youths of great piety, whose mother was a priestess. [He said that] when she wished to go to the temple the oxen which used to draw her cart had died, and that her two sons had drawn her there instead of the oxen; that therefore she had prayed to the gods to give them their best gift, and in the night they had both died. By this story Solon wishes to prove that those who are alive must not be accounted [1] happy, since all are liable to misfortune; but that those who have met [2] an honourable death are indeed the happiest.

---

[1] *to be reckoned, thought*=duci or haberi.   [2] obire.

Exercise 128

IMPERSONAL VERBS

1. In using oportet there is the same difficulty as in using debeo. In English we say, ' *I ought to have come*,' expressing the Perfect tense in the Infinitive. In Latin the tense must be expressed in the modal verb, not in the following Infinitive ; *e.g.* **Debui** venire *or* **oportuit** me venire. There is the same difference in the use of possum ; *e.g.* **Potui** hoc facere=*I might have done this*.

2. Remember that *se* refers to the subject of the sentence. An impersonal verb has no subject, and therefore cannot be followed directly by *se* ; *e.g. He was ashamed*=**eum** puduit. If, however, the impersonal is used in an indirect statement *se* must be used for the third person, because it refers to the subject of the verb of saying ; *e.g.* Dixit se pudere=*He said he was ashamed.* See Rule 7, p. 40.

I repented of my crime.	We are resolved to banish the kings.
Do you pity the prisoner ?	It happened that the king was killed.
They are weary of life.	
He was ashamed of his deed.	
It becomes us to do this.	It is the lot of all men to die.
You ought to speak.	You ought not to be ashamed of your friend.
You ought to have spoken.	
It is lawful for us to use arms.	You might have pleased the gods.
Do not repent of your deed.	
You may go away.	It is our duty to fight.
You might have gone away.	I happened to be present.

Exercise 129 [*A*]

1. I am sorry for your grief.

2. I am ashamed of my country.

3. It seemed good to the judge to put the prisoners to death.

4. He said he pitied me.

5. I believe you repent of your crime.

6. He replied that he was tired of living in the city.

7. Every man has not the good luck to go to Corinth.

8. You ought to know what you are doing.

9. You ought to have done this of your own accord.

10. It is becoming to children to obey their parents.

11. Do not be ashamed of such a deed.

Exercise 130 [*B*]

1. Do not get tired of living in the country.

2. He said we ought to leave our home.

3. A man who runs away in battle soon repents of his cowardice.

4. We happened to be present at that time.

5. I was sorry for his sufferings.

6. He said he was ashamed of his deed.

7. I do not think you ought to have done that.

8. Do not repent of your kindness to us.

9. It happened that the general was present with his staff.

10. You might have escaped before the battle.

11. Why do you repent of saving the state ?

Exercise 131 [A]

GENITIVE CASE [1]

1. Through fear of death the bravest men forget their courage.

2. He is ignorant of many things which he ought to be skilled in.

3. Looking after [2] other people's affairs is difficult.

4. I pitied them all as they came back from the battle.

5. Skill in addressing his soldiers was necessary for a Roman general.

6. The remembrance of his past life brings one man joy, another pain.

7. Your care for me reminds me of my father.

8. I am anxious to thank you for your kindness, which I shall never forget.

9. He is skilled in every labour which you demand of him.

10. I am sure he will be mindful of us in our absence.

11. Under the emperors Romans were made consuls for the sake of honour, not for the sake of administering public affairs.

12. My knowledge of Caesar made me eager for his friendship.

---

[1] An earlier exercise on the Genitive will be found on page 50.

[2] Use the noun *cura*.

Exercise 132 [B]

1. No one will repent of a life well spent.

2. You have a chief mindful of others, forgetful of self.

3. Pity a man suffering undeservedly.[1]

4. He was charged with treachery.

5. His love for his country is more powerful than his fear of death.

6. The best men are fonder of doing than of speaking.

7. Out of pity for the woman he gave up his design.

8. He is unaccustomed to swimming.

9. They were unaccustomed to toil, but despised danger.

10. I hope you will not forget your country through your eagerness to see new things.

11. Caesar's friendship for me I value very highly.

12. These barbarians seem skilled in making bridges.

---

[1] *unworthy things.*

Exercise 133 [*A*]

[Exercises 131-140 are for revision.]

Now when they had sailed for several days, it chanced that they caught sight of a ship of war approaching them. Some were afraid, and wished to turn back, but the captain [1] said that he was ashamed to turn back, ' For,' said he, ' brave men ought to meet an enemy boldly, and I do not believe that by flight we shall escape from so large a vessel.' As the ship came near they saw that there were on board [2] many soldiers, one of whom, by his proud looks and splendid dress, seemed to be the king. This man called out to them to come on board his ship. And when they had done this he asked them where they came from, and why they had left their homes.

Exercise 134 [*A*]

On hearing their answer he asked them to sail with him, and promised to give them lands in his country, because they seemed to be good soldiers, and because he pitied them for their misfortunes. But they declared that they wished to discover what fortune the gods would give them in distant regions. Then the king replied that he was sorry for this resolve, [3] but that he would no longer try to persuade them to follow him. He asked them if they needed gold or provisions ; and when they said that they had no need of such things, he dismissed them kindly, and held on his course.

---

[1] dux.   [2] *to be on board*=in nave vehi.   [3] consilium.

Exercise 135 [*A*]

I have lately with much care found out and written in a book the strange stories which the inhabitants [1] of this district believe. Among other things they believe that a man who throws a garment into the stream which flows near our town will be free from disease for a year. I have asked why they believe this, and they say that a god dwells in the stream ; but why the god of a river wants such gifts they do not understand. They also believe that a certain spring which rises outside the town is able to make rich the man who visits it on a certain night in the summer ; but on which of all the nights of summer one ought to visit the spring no man can tell, and I have never found a man made rich in this way.

Exercise 136 [*A*]

The gallant Brutus,[2] who had been blockaded for a long time, wished to know when the reinforcements would arrive. Accordingly he sent away two ships, under the command of his lieutenant, with the intention of informing the Roman commander [3] in what great danger he was. But these ships being wrecked, the enemy surrounded them, and asked the lieutenant who they were and where they came from. On learning that they were Romans, they promised to spare their lives, and be their guides. But when they had led them two miles they surrounded and slew them. The Roman commander, on hearing of this through his scouts, decided not to delay any longer, but to send forward two legions as soon as possible.

---

[1] incolae.   [2] Lat. ' Brutus a very gallant man.'

[3] *Commander-in-chief*=' imperator ' ; in a general sense, *commander*=' dux.' The ' legatus ' is the second in command, properly the general to whom the command of a separate division was assigned.

Exercise 137 [B]

When the king of France was besieging Amsterdam [1] the
citizens were greatly terrified, and summoned a council to
consider what they ought to do. Most of them said that there
was no hope of holding out any longer against the enemy, and
advised that the keys of the city should be given up to the
king. But they observed that one of the elders was asleep,
and had not given his opinion. So they woke him up, and
asked him what he advised about giving up the keys. He
inquired if the king had demanded them; and when they
said that he had not done so, he replied, ' Then let us wait at
least till [2] he be pleased to ask for them.' It is said that [3]
these words saved the city.

---

[1] Amstelodamum.   [2] Use dum with Subj.

[3] See Note 1, page 44.

Exercise 138 [B]

The soldier, thus recognised, was soon surrounded by a mob
of citizens asking who he was, where he came from, where he
was going, for what purpose he was in the town, and why he
had not come through the gates, but had climbed over the wall
in the night time. In nowise terrified, he replied that neither
could he answer so many things at once, nor was it the
business of private citizens to know what was his name or
what he came for. On which he was dragged with much
violence to the magistrates, who questioned him again as to his
purposes.[1] As he would not speak, they were deliberating
whether they ought to detain him or set him free ; but there
came up a soldier who pretended to recognise the prisoner, and
asked whether he had not been seen in the rebels' camp.

---

[1] See head of Exercise 116.

Exercise 139 [B]

A boy and his sister were once found by the inhabitants
of a village, near the entrance of a cavern. They were
in form like other men, but they were different in the
colour of their skin, which was tinged with a green colour.
No one could understand what they said. When they were
brought to the house of a certain knight they wept bitterly.[1]
Food being set before them they refused to touch it, though
it was clear that they were tormented by great hunger. At
length, when some beans [2] were brought into the house, they
asked by signs that these should be given them. They
fed on these with great delight, and for a long time would
eat no other food. The boy, however, was always languid [3]
and sad, and died in a short time.

---

shed (fundo) many tears.   [2] fabae.   [3] languĭdus.

Exercise 140 [B]

The girl, however, becoming accustomed [1] to various kinds of food,[2] at length lost that green colour. For many years she remained with the knight to whom she and her brother had first been brought. Being frequently asked about her country, she declared that the inhabitants were of a green colour, and that they saw no sun, but enjoyed such a light as we see after sunset. Being asked how she came into this country, she replied that as they were following their flocks they came to a certain cavern, where they heard a delightful [3] sound of bells.[4] Led on by this they wandered for a long time through the cavern, and at last reached its mouth. When they came out of it they said they were stupefied by the excessive heat of the sun, and were thus caught by the inhabitants of the village.

---

[1] assuefactus ad.   [2] omne genus cibi.

[3] jucundus.   [4] tintinnabulum.

E

RELATIVE WITH THE SUBJUNCTIVE

Rule 18. **A relative with the subjunctive may express many adverbial meanings, especially a Purpose or a Consequence.**

This is the regular way of expressing a _Purpose_—
  (1) When the subject of the subordinate sentence is the same as the subject or object of the Principal Verb.
  (2) When the subordinate clause contains a comparative, in which case **quo** (the abl. of the relative) is regularly used for _ut_.[1]

A _Consequence_ is most often expressed in this way with the phrases _is qui, dignus qui,_ and _sunt qui._

EXAMPLES

Final

Duas legiones reliquit quae auxilio duci possent.
He left two legions to be brought up as reinforcements.

Nervii murum aedificaverunt quo facilius equitatum impedirent.
The Nervii built a wall the more easily to hinder the cavalry.

Consecutive

Non is sum qui mortis periculo terrear.
I am not the man to be frightened by the fear of death.

Dignus erat qui rex fieret.
He deserved to be made king.

Sunt qui non habeant.
There are some who have not (or _some men have not_).

---

[1] We thus have four ways of expressing purpose in Latin, viz. as in the following sentences :
  (1) Legatos miserunt _ut pacem peterent_ (Rule 2).
  (2) Legatos miserunt _qui pacem peterent._
  (3) Legatos miserunt _ad pacem petendam._
      Legatos miserunt _pacis petendae causa_ (Rule 13).
  (4) Legatos miserunt _pacem petitum_ (Rule 14).
Occasionally also purpose is expressed by the Future Participle ; _e.g._ Legatos miserunt _pacem petituros._

Exercise 141 [A]

1. Caesar has sent out scouts to discover where his reinforcements are.

2. These men are here to give an answer.

3. Hannibal left part of his army to blockade Tarentum.

4. They carried food with them, so that they might march the quicker.

5. I have few men to send.

6. Send cavalry, so that we may the more easily check the enemy.

7. To become wiser, read many books.

8. He promises to send books for me to read.

Exercise 142 [B]

1. In order that the flight might be shorter he drew up his line near the camp.

2. I have no one to trust.

3. On the next day men were sent to kill Cicero.

4. There are guards in the streets to restrain the multitude.

5. He went into the country to live more quietly.

6. To make your son better you ought to live better yourself.

7. Caesar set chosen men in the woods to fall on the enemy when fighting.

8. He left Labienus to command the camp.

Exercise 143 [A]

1. He is not a man to rejoice even at his enemy's death.

2. He deserves to be put to death.

3. The consul is doing things that do not benefit the state.

4. Shall I find a soldier brave enough to go with me ?

5. There were some who were willing to give Caesar large sums of money.

6. There is no one who could endure such insolence.

7. Does he deserve to receive so great a reward ?

8. Is he a man to be trusted with money ?

Exercise 144 [B]

1. I am not the man to refuse money to my own brother.

2. Send such troops as can help me.

3. There are men who accuse him of theft.

4. We did not deserve to be put in prison.

5. Men are not easily found who can endure pain patiently.

6. Is he a man to be admitted into my house ?

7. There were some who could run faster.

8. The ships are not fit to be launched.

Exercise 145 [A]

1. No one was found to face death for him.

2. I am not the man to shirk danger.

3. They sent five priests to consult the god at Delphi.

4. I will say such things as may persuade him.

5. Five men have to-night entered the camp to announce that the city will be surrendered.

6. Caesar left his baggage at Ravenna in order to reach Rome more quickly.

7. He is worthy of being made a Roman.

8. There are some men who do not desire riches.

9. He led out the tenth legion to attack the enemy in the rear.

10. He drew up his line in this way in order that his forces might appear greater.

Exercise 146 [B]

1. Men were sent by the general to choose a suitable place for a camp.

2. The more easily to cross the river he gave orders for making a bridge.

3. He was not the man to bring his soldiers rashly into danger.

4. Towards evening fresh men arrived to take the place of those who were disabled by wounds.

5. There are some who think that we ought to strike the camp and advance to higher ground.

6. Men who free their country from slavery deserve to be praised by all.

7. A mound was made, and ladders brought up that we might the more easily scale the walls.

8. I am not the sort of man, he said, to wish to avoid danger.

9. Spies were sent to see if the enemy's troops were advancing.

10. There were some who advised the general not to summon a council.

11. These barbarians are not men whom we ought to despise.

12. He placed elephants in front of his line of battle to strike more terror into the enemy.

Exercise 147 [*A*]

Hannibal first crossed the Pyrenees [1] with an army of fifty thousand foot soldiers and nine thousand horse, without any difficulty. No Roman army appeared to hinder his march. He reached the Rhone safely, and found no Romans to oppose him. The Gauls, however, were prepared to bar his way, and Scipio, the Roman general, had arrived at Massilia ; so Hannibal determined to cross the river without delay. He ordered such boats as were ready to be brought to him, and trees to be cut down from which to build others. In two days the boats were ready, but the Gauls were drawn up on the opposite bank to prevent the landing. Accordingly Hannibal sent a large number of his men some miles up the river, ordering them to cross and attack the Gauls in the rear upon a given signal.

---

[1] Pyrenaei.

Exercise 148 [B]

The Carthaginians had now reached the highest point of the mountains; they encamped on a large plateau[1] where they could rest for some days. But it was a cold and desolate place, and not one where they could remain long, especially as winter was approaching. Many had been left behind on the march, overcome with want and hardships; and the cold was terrible to men who came from Spain and Africa. But Hannibal encouraged them, and pointed out that from this place the road led downwards, and that it would soon lead them to a country where they would find friends. 'There lies Italy,' cried he; 'yonder[2] is the way to[3] Rome.'

---

[1] planities, f. 5.   [2] ille.   [3] Use *dūcĕre*.

GERUND AND GERUNDIVE EXPRESSING OBLIGATION

(Translation of 'ought,' 'must.')

Rule 19. **The Nominative of both Gerundive and Gerund is used to express obligation. The Gerundive is used with Transitive Verbs, the Gerund with Intransitive Verbs.**

e.g. Gerundive—leges mutandae sunt = *the laws must be changed.*

Gerund—succurrendum est amicis = *we must help our friends.*

When these statements become *indirect* the Acc. is used in the same sense of obligation.

e.g. Gerundive—dixit leges mutandas esse.

Gerund—dixit succurrendum esse amicis.

Rule 20. **In this construction the person on whom the obligation lies is expressed by the Dative.** This is often called **Dative of the Agent.** But for the sake of clearness, where there is another Dative, the Agent is expressed by **ab** with the Abl.

e.g. **Leges** nobis mutandae sunt   = *we must change the laws.*

Legibus a nobis parendum est = *we must obey the laws.*

N.B.—(1) The English words 'ought,' 'must,' etc., are often to be translated into Latin by this construction. Remember that the Gerundive is a *Passive* Adjective, and before translating we must turn the English in thought into a Passive form.

> e.g. *We must change the laws =*
> *The laws are to-be-changed by us =*
> Leges nobis mutandae sunt.

(2) Observe also that the Gerundive can be used with any tense of *sum* according to the sense, and the English translations will be very various, because our words 'must' and 'ought' have only one tense.

> *e.g.* Leges nobis mutandae **erunt** =
> *We* shall have to *change the laws.*
>
> (Literally, the laws will be to-be-changed by us.)

> Leges nobis mutandae **erant** =
> *We* ought to have changed *the laws.*

The Gerund in like manner can be used with any tense.

> *e.g.* Legibus a nobis parendum **fuit** =
> *We* had to *obey the laws.*

Exercise 149 [A]

1. We must set out at once, and you must guard the camp.

2. Caesar had to do everything at the same time.

3. It is agreed by all that the laws must be obeyed.

4. All good citizens must obey the laws.

5. Crassus was ordered to see to the repairing of the fleet.

6. We have undertaken the construction of a bridge over [1] the Rhine.

7. This should not have been done.

8. We must not injure those who are desirous of helping us.

9. Caesar caused a camp to be fortified.

10. They must not be accused of treachery by us.

---

[1] 'in' with Abl.

Exercise 150 [A]

1. We must not remain here any longer.
2. Let them see to building another bridge.
3. I think we must choose a place for a camp.
4. They will have to return in fifteen days.
5. We must start at once and march until evening.
6. Caesar pointed out that hostages must be surrendered by all the states.
7. We must take measures for the good of the state.
8. Do you think Crassus ought to have done this ?
9. He promised to undertake the repairing of the fleet.
10. We have to wait here for reinforcements.

Exercise 151 [B]

1. We must help the poor.
2. The general decided that he must not delay any longer.
3. We shall have to send forward two legions.
4. Caesar entrusted to Labienus the repairing of the ships.
5. They had to remain a long time where they were.
6. They had to leave their winter quarters in spring.
7. He should not have said that.
8. They promised to see to holding a levy.
9. They did not know where they were to pitch the camp.
10. We must come to the help of our allies.

Exercise 152 [B]

1. We have to cross the sea.
2. We must not delay too long.
3. The soldiers were told to see to fortifying the camp.
4. Crassus ought not to have gone to Asia.
5. All of us must obey the laws.

6. We shall have to leave our country.

7. We were entrusted with holding a levy.

8. They ought to have helped their allies.

9. Hannibal caused his camp to be pitched on the top of a mountain.

10. We should not accuse them of treachery.

Exercise 153 [A]

While the Romans were waging war against the Samnites[1] their general Postumius tried to lead an army into Samnium through a narrow pass. There is in the midst of this pass a broad and open plain, but in order to reach it an army must enter a narrow defile, and afterwards either it must go back by the same way or must get out by a still narrower defile into Samnium. The Romans reached the open plain, but attempting to proceed they could not escape, for meanwhile the Samnites had blocked both the defiles. To escape they had to climb the mountains, and having tried to do this many times in vain they had to fortify a camp where they were.

Exercise 154 [B]

Accordingly Postumius sent ambassadors to ask for fair terms. Pontius the Samnite replied that they must give hostages and surrender their arms, and must themselves be sent under the yoke. At length these disgraceful conditions were accepted, and the Romans were allowed to depart. To reach home they had to pass through the country of their Campanian allies, and even ask them for food and clothes. The Roman Senate refused to accept the treaty, and sent back the consul to surrender himself to the Samnites.

---

[1] Samnite=Samnis, *Gen.* Samnitis.

VERBS OF FEARING

Rule 21. **Verbs of Fearing** have three constructions—
  (_a_) **Prolative Infinitive.**   (_b_) **ne with Subjunctive.**
  (_c_) **ne non with Subjunctive.**

EXAMPLES

  (_a_) Timeo **redire.**
     I am afraid to return.

  (_b_) Timeo **ne redeat.**
     I am afraid that he will [1] _return_ (_of his returning_).

  (_c_) Timebam **ne non rediret.** [2]
     I was afraid he would not return.

     Timeo **ne non redierit.**
     I am afraid he has not returned.

     Timebam **ne non rediisset.**
     I was afraid he had not returned.

N.B.—(_b_) and (_c_) are _Final_ Sentences, Latin preferring to express the _object_ or _desire_ of the person fearing, while Eng. gives the exact opposite ; viz. the thing you wish to _avoid_. Of course (_a_) is only possible when the subject of the two verbs is the same.

---

[1] In clauses after Verbs of Fearing there is no need to express the English Future (as in Indirect questions) by the Periphrastic Conjugation (Rule 16).   The Present (in Primary sequence) and Imperfect (in Historic sequence) are used for it without causing any ambiguity.

[2] _Ut_ may sometimes take the place of _ne non_ (especially after vereor).

Exercise 155

1. I am afraid to do this.
2. I am afraid he will do this.
3. I was afraid you would not do this.
4. I am afraid he is dead.
5. I was afraid he had not seen me.
6. Do not fear to return.
7. Are you afraid of speaking ?
8. We were afraid of being seen.
9. I am afraid lest they should see us.
10. I am afraid they will not see us.
11. They were afraid not to tell the truth.
12. I fear that he has lied.

Exercise 156 [A]

1. As they were afraid to follow me, I went away alone.

2. The soldiers were afraid that the enemy would surround them.

3. As the camp was not yet fortified, they were afraid of being attacked by the barbarians.

4. Though [1] he was not afraid to die, he wished to live a long as possible.

5. Fearing that the ships would not be able to keep ol their course, they returned to the harbour.

6. He was afraid that his plans had been discovered by the enemy.

7. Fearing to advance farther, they took up their position ten miles from the town.

---

[1] 'cum' with Imp. Subj.

8. Though the city had walls one hundred feet high, the inhabitants feared they could not resist an assault.

9. They were afraid that they would not be able to conceal their departure from their enemies.

10. He was afraid of being betrayed by his own men, and therefore resolved to kill himself.

11. They loved their country so much that for its sake they were not afraid of dying.

12. I am afraid the prisoners have escaped.

Exercise 157 [B]

1. You ought not to be afraid to tell the truth.

2. I am afraid that you have not told the truth.

3. Our men were afraid of being surrounded by the enemy.

4. Most men are afraid of dying.

5. I am afraid they will not be able to follow the standards.

6. The general was afraid to give the signal for advance.

7. Were you not afraid that the soldiers would seize and kill your son ?

8. Fearing that they would be taken prisoners, they fled for refuge into the woods.

9. The general told his men not to be afraid of crossing the river.

10. We were afraid that the city had been taken.

11. I was afraid that we should not reach the camp before sunset.

12. They set out at daybreak, fearing that the enemy might overtake them.

Exercise 158 [A]

News having been brought of Caesar's approach, the Arverni, fearing that he would invade their territory, resolved to break down all the bridges over the river. Caesar was very anxious to cross as soon as possible, for he was afraid of being hindered all the summer by this river. He accomplished this by the following trick. He sent forward the greater part of his forces, and the enemy followed these, thinking that the whole army had set out. Thereupon Caesar, who had remained with a few men, ordered them to repair one of the bridges with all speed, fearing that they might not be able to finish the work before the return of the enemy.

Exercise 159 [B]

A peasant on the point of death [1] summoned his sons, and told them that the end of his life was near. ' My sons,' he said, ' I am not afraid that you will disobey my commands, or forget me when I am dead.[2] I therefore bid you work diligently in my vineyard, for by doing this you will discover great riches.' When the old man died, his sons remembered his words, and began to dig up the soil with all their might, hoping to find great riches concealed there. Soon however they were afraid that they had been deceived, for they could find neither gold nor silver ; and at first they regretted their labour. But at last they discovered what their father had intended, for by carefully digging up the ground, they made it so fertile that it produced excellent vines.

---

[1] Future Participle. [2] *when I am dead*—use Past Participle.

CAUSAL CLAUSES

A Causal Clause is one which gives a reason for the statement of the principal clause.

<u>Rule 22</u>. Causal Clauses have their verb

(a) in the **Indicative** when the **actual cause** of a fact is given.

(b) in the **Subjunctive** when only a **suggested reason** is given. But cum (since) always takes Subj.

N.B.—Of course the Indicative of a Causal Clause becomes Subjunctive if it forms part of an Indirect Statement. See Rule 17.

EXAMPLES

(a) Tacent quia periculum **metuunt.**
    They are silent because they fear danger.

(b) Socrates accusatus est quod juventutem **corrumperet.**
    Socrates was accused on the ground that he corrupted the youth.

(It is not asserted by the writer that Socrates did corrupt the youth.)

Exercise 160 [*A*]

1. As you have heard this, you ought to announce it to all.

2. Under these circumstances I shall leave the city.

3. This being the case, no one would remain.

4. I am rejoiced that you have decided to come.

5. They declared that they had done this, because it seemed to be for the good of the state.

6. We were told that they had been condemned to death, because they had displeased the king.

7. He must be considered a coward, since he is unwilling to become a soldier.

8. Since night is at hand, let all depart to their tents.

9. In this condition of affairs it was to our interest to withdraw from the meeting.

10. I rejoice that you and the army are safe.

11. They pretended to be glad that we were safe.

12. I pity you greatly, because no one seems to love you.

Exercise 161 [B]

1. The slave was blamed for coming too late.

2. You deserve praise, because you have served your country well.

3. Under these circumstances the general decided to sound the retreat.

4. They were condemned to death for setting fire to the city.

5. I am rejoiced that such men have been condemned to death.

6. He said they ought to be punished, because they had fled from the battle.

7. They were charged with treason, on the ground that they had threatened the king with death.

8. This being the case, we must advance at once.

9. As they have shown themselves brave soldiers, let them receive the promised reward.

10. Our friends declared that they rejoiced that we had returned in safety.

11. Since this is so, you must remain in exile.

12. They were brought to trial on the charge of conspiring against the state.

Exercise 162 [A]

The triumph of Camillus, after the fall of Veii, was disliked by the Romans, because he showed too much pride. Amongst other things he was accused of making himself equal to the gods, because he had entered the city in a chariot drawn by four white horses, which were sacred to Jupiter and the Sun. He also made the soldiers still more angry, because he ordered them to return part of the spoils taken at Veii, that he might offer them to the god Apollo. Finally he was accused of having hidden some treasures which he ought to have given up to the people, and was obliged to go into exile.

Exercise 163 [B]

Some Irishmen [1] had been brought to trial on the charge of stirring up a revolution [2] in their country. They asserted that they had done nothing contrary to the law of nations, since the English were oppressing their land, and they themselves were only trying to free her from an unjust dominion.[3] Under these circumstances they declared that they by no means repented of their deed, especially because they had shown that it was not easy to govern Irishmen against their will. These words displeased many who were present ; but since the prisoners were young, and had never before been accused of any crime, they were spared.

---

[1] Hiberni.
[2] seditionem facere *or* novis rebus studere.
[3] dominatus.

Exercise 164 [A]

(Exercises 164-167 are for Revision.)

Now when the Delphians [1] knew what great danger they were in, great fear fell upon them. In their terror they consulted the oracle concerning the holy treasures, and inquired if they should bury them in the ground, or carry them away to another country. The god replied that they must leave the treasures untouched. ' He was able,' he said, ' without help to protect his own.' So the Delphians, when they received this answer, began to deliberate how to save themselves. First of all they sent their women and children across the gulf into Achaia. After which the greater number of them climbed to the top of Parnassus, and placed their goods in a cave. In this way all the Delphians quitted the city, except sixty men and the prophet.

Exercise 165 [A]

A great plague had broken out [2] in the city, and many of the people,[3] both rich and poor, had perished. A great number of those who survived, who had neither wives nor children, resolved to leave the city and sail away to discover new lands. They pitied those whom they were leaving behind, but they knew that they could not help them. Accordingly they set

---

[1] Delphi.   [2] =*arisen.*

[3] *People* (=*persons*) should be omitted (as here) or sometimes be translated by *ii.* In the political sense (=*a nation*) it is *populus.* In the sense *race* or *tribe* use *gens, natio.*

sail by night, and meeting with a favourable wind, were many
miles away from the city before dawn. They did not know to
what lands they would come, but they had resolved to sail
towards the west.

Exercise 166 [B]

The two armies had been gazing at each other a long time.[1]
At last an old man came forward, and asked that a warrior
from each army should be chosen to fight for his countrymen.
Accordingly Sohrab [2] came forward from the one army and
Rustum,[2] his father, from the other ; but neither [3] of them
knew who the other [4] was. For it happened that when Sohrab
was born and carried off by the Scythians,[5] his father was
absent. At first Sohrab prevailed ; for Rustum hurled his
spear with such violence that he slipped and fell on the
ground. But quickly rising, he dealt [6] his son a deadly wound ;
for Sohrab had heard Rustum, as he rushed forward, shout out
his name, and knowing [7] him to be his father, he did not even
move a hand to defend himself.

---

[1] jamdudum (Imperf. Indic.).

[2] It is best not to try to turn these names into a Latin shape. In
turning a piece into Latin it is often possible to omit the proper names.
Where it is not, try to recall some parallel incident in Roman history,
and adopt the names from that. Where (as here) this is difficult, it is
better to adopt *any* classical names than to talk of ' Sohrabus ' and
' Rustumius.'   [3] neuter.   [4] alter.

[5] Scythae.   [6] infligere.   [7] cum with Imp. Subj.

Exercise 167 [B]

King James's [1] army was far [2] superior to Monmouth's in numbers, but with such great carelessness did they take up their position on that night that they were almost surprised and destroyed by the rebels. By chance the guides whom Monmouth trusted had not told him that there was a ditch twenty-five feet wide which defended the king's camp in front. Therefore when the rebels were just going to rush forward to attack the ramparts, they were stopped [3] by this trench.   The officers ordered their men to throw the waggons into it, but the guards of the other army were now aroused, and their artillery [4] began to play upon [5] the rebels. It is said that Monmouth, having exhorted his men to fight bravely and hold their ground, himself rode out [6] of the fight, hoping to find [7] some place where he might be safe.

---

[1] James has a Latinised form *Jacobus*. But here call him Octavianus and call Monmouth L. Antonius, who caused an insurrection against Octavianus soon after the battle of Philippi.

[2] longe, multo.   [3] impedire.

[4] *artillery*=tormenta or ballistae.   [5] saxa ingerere in.   [6] avehi.

[7] *hoping to,* si forte (with Subjunctive).

QUIN

Rule 23. **Quin with Subjunctive is used**

(1) (a) after verbs of **doubting and denying**[1] ⎫ **when these**
                                              ⎪ **verbs are pre-**
    (b) ,,   ,,   **hindering** and   pre- ⎬ **ceded by a**
                    venting[2]   ⎭ **negative.**

In these uses quin = quî-ne, _by which not_, quî being an old Ablative of the Relative.

EXAMPLES

    (a) **Non** {**dubitare**} debemus **quin** fuerint ante Homerum
               {**negare**[1]}   poetæ.

        We ought not to {_doubt_} _that there were poets before_
                           {_deny_}   _Homer._

    (b) **Nihil** me **deterrebit quin** proficiscar.
        Nothing will prevent my setting out.

        Haud multum **afuit quin** Ismenias interficeretur.
        Ismenias was very near being killed. (_There was **not**_
            much to prevent Ismenias being killed.)

Under (1) (b) come the important phrases—

non possum facere quin . . .   = _I cannot help_ . . .
non potest fieri quin . . .   = _It is impossible that_ . . .
                                      not . . .
haud multum afuit quin (ego) . . . = _I was very near_ . . .
                            or _I was not far from_ . . .

(2) In certain phrases where quin = qui-ne, _who not_, qui being Nominative.

    _e.g._ **Nemo est quin** . . . **nulla navis est quin** . . . etc.

        Nullum est aedificium **quin** collapsum sit.
        There is no building that has not fallen.

    N.B.   In all its uses quin is preceded by a negative, or virtual negative (_e.g._ vix, aegre, or a question expecting the answer ʻno,ʼ like ʻCan any one prevent . . . ?ʼ).

---

[1] The use of this construction with **negare** is not earlier than Livy.
[2] **Prohibeo, veto,** prefer Infinitive.

Exercise 168 [A]

1. There can be no doubt that he did this on purpose.
2. I could not deny that I was guilty.
3. There is no man who does not often do wrong.
4. Do not prevent their setting out.
5. I cannot help writing to you.
6. We had no doubt that he was on our side.
7. It is impossible that the guilty man should escape.
8. I was very near dying of hunger.
9. We must not doubt that he will keep his word.
10. There was no man in the city who had not a son or a brother in the army.

Exercise 169 [B]

1. They do not deny that they desire peace on fair terms.
2. There was no man of noble birth who did not scorn Catiline.[1]
3. They were not far from taking the city by force of arms.
4. I have no doubt that he is already consul.
5. Do not hinder his leaving Rome.
6. He said he had no doubt the news was true.
7. It is impossible for us not to believe him.
8. We cannot doubt that this pleases the multitude.
9. There is no ship that has not been hurt by the storm.
10. I could not help consulting you.

---

[1] Catilina.

QUOMINUS

Rule 24. **Quominus with Subjunctive** is used after verbs of **hindering and preventing,** whether they are positive or negative.[1]

Exception.—Prohibeo, veto, prefer an Infinitive.

EXAMPLES

Nihil deterret sapientem **quominus** reipublicae **consulat.**
Nothing prevents a philosopher from serving the state.

Per Africanum stetit **quominus dimicaretur.**
It was due to Africanus that there was no battle.

Exercise 170 [*A*]

1. It was owing to you that the army was not destroyed.

2. Who hindered you from coming to our help?

3. They were prevented by the snow from crossing the Alps.

4. You ought to have prevented the fleet from weighing anchor.

5. We could not deter the soldiers from charging the enemy.

6. It was due to us that the house was not burnt.

7. We ought to prevent them from attacking us.

8. The soldiers could not be prevented from rushing into the river.

9. I believe it was through me that we were not defeated.

10. I could hardly restrain them from burning the ships.

11. They refused to leave the city.

---

[1] Quominus = quo minus, and is really a special case of the Relative with the Subj. making a Final sentence.

Exercise 171 [B]

1. It was owing to Horatius that Rome was not taken.

2. The soldiers must be prevented from plundering the town.

3. The general could hardly prevent his men from burning the houses.

4. Let not fear deter you from speaking the truth.

5. You ought to forbid the fleet to set sail.

6. Was it not due to our king that we did not perish ?

7. The tribunes were able to prevent laws from being passed.

8. The ambassadors were the cause of peace not being made.

9. By surrendering the city to the enemy, we prevented the inhabitants from dying of hunger.

10. You prevented them by your threats from speaking the truth.

11. Did you not refuse to supply the army with provisions ?

Exercise 172 [A]

QUOMINUS AND QUIN

1. Every one knows that this ought to be done.

2. We must prevent the enemy from crossing the river.

3. There is no doubt that they ought to have remained.

4. They hesitated to speak, but I had no doubt that they were angry.

5. The city was within a very little of being destroyed.

6. There is no one present who does not know that you are lying.

7. It was due to Themistocles that the Athenians did not leave Salamis.

8. All the world knows that I fought for my country.

9. Do not try to prevent these men from escaping.

10. There is no doubt that they have betrayed us.

11. I cannot help hoping that we shall be saved.

Exercise 173 [B]

1. It is impossible that you have not heard this.

2. There is no doubt that there lived brave men before Agamemnon.[1]

3. Who is there so base as not to love his country ?

4. It is owing to the gods that we did not die of starvation.

5. Do not refuse to help those who have benefited the state.

6. I had no doubt that they wished to deceive me.

7. Our men could hardly be restrained from making the assault at once.

8. I easily prevented the slaves from reporting this to Caius.

9. There is no doubt that this news will cause great panic to the citizens.

10. It is impossible for us to save the state.

Exercise 174 [A]

All the world has heard how gallantly Horatius Cocles defended the bridge by which the enemies of Rome hoped to enter the city. First with two companions and afterwards alone he resisted all the attacks made upon him, and prevented the enemy from crossing ; and there is no doubt that he was the salvation of the Roman state. Again and again the enemy charged, but were always repulsed with great loss. At last, when the bridge was all but broken by the Romans, his countrymen called to him to come back, and, offering a prayer to the river god, he threw himself into the water. His friends feared that he would be drowned ; but contrary to the expectations, both of friends and enemies, he reached the other bank in safety.

---

[1] *Acc.* Agamemnona.

Exercise 175 [B]

In this year the Gauls, under the leadership of Brennus, crossed the Alps, and threatened Rome with war. It is said that they were provoked by certain Roman ambassadors, who violated international law by taking part in a battle fought between the Gauls and Etruscans. As the Senate refused to punish the ambassadors, the Gauls vowed with the help of the gods to avenge this wrong, and set out for Rome. At the river Allia they won a great victory over the Romans, nor were they afterwards opposed. They were greatly amazed at [1] no one trying to prevent their entering Rome, and stopped some time outside the walls.

Exercise 176 [A]

[*Exercises* 176–181 *are for revision.*]

At the time when Russia [2] had as many enemies as neighbours, the king of Sweden laid siege to Novgorod, and the Swedes soon got possession of the city. There is no doubt that this happened through the carelessness of the inhabitants, and there are some who say it was the result of treachery. But there were some who determined to hold out to the last, and among these was a certain priest. He shut himself up in a house with a few friends, who, animated [3] by his courage, refused to surrender, and fired [4] on the enemy. Messengers were sent again and again to command them to surrender, and at last the enemy set fire to the house. But these brave men chose to be burnt in the house rather than to yield, for they had determined not to survive the independence of their country.

---

[1] quod.

[2] Russians=Scythae. Swedes=Suevi. Novgorod=Forum Novum.

[3] confirmatus.

[4] tela immittere. Of course the idea of *fire-arms* can never be reproduced in Latin. *Cannon* must be tormenta; *rifles, guns, shot*, etc., must be turned by some phrase with tela or pila.

Exercise 177 [A]

Antiochus greeted the Roman ambassadors on their arrival,
and was stretching out his hand to Popilius; but the latter[1]
gave him the despatches, and bade him read these first. After
reading them through the king said he would consult his
friends as to what ought to be done. But Popilius drew a
circle round the king with a rod which he was carrying in his
hand, and said, ' Before you leave this circle[2] give me an
answer to take to the Roman Senate.' The king at first was
on the point of refusing to obey the ambassador; but he knew
that it would be to his advantage to keep the friendship of
the Roman people, and at last replied that he would do what
the Senate wished. Then at last Popilius stretched out his
hand to the king as[3] to a friend and ally.

Exercise 178 [A]

When ambassadors came to Hannibal in Italy to recall him
to Carthage, he received them with great anger, and could
hardly refrain from shedding tears. ' There is no doubt,' he
cried, ' that it is not the Romans who have conquered me,
but my own people through their hatred and jealousy. Take
me where you will; it matters little to me where I go, since
I have to leave Italy.' The ambassadors were now afraid
that he would refuse to serve the state any longer, and
tried to persuade him that the most important thing was
to defend Carthage. But he replied that a city which
feared to trust its generals did not deserve to be defended
by them.

---

[1] qui tamen.　　[2] priusquam hoc circulo excedas.　　[3] velut.

Exercise 179 [B]

Elated by the rapid departure of the Roman fleet from Africa, the Carthaginians still more rejoiced on hearing of its destruction. They could now boast that they were 'friends of the sea, and enemies of all who sailed on it.' This being the case the Romans could not prevent them from transferring the war to Sicily, with all the land forces, with 140 elephants, and with a fleet to help the army. They made straight for that island, and, taking the field,[1] prepared to ravage the open country.[2] But the Romans, with unconquerable resolution, undertook[3] the construction of a new fleet, and within three months 220 new vessels had been built, and were ready for action.

---

[1] copias educere.

[2] campestres loci.

[3] suscipere, followed by Gerundive.

Exercise 180 [B]

The command was entrusted to Xanthippus, who seemed
to all to be the man whom they could best trust. A cry
was raised for instant battle,[1] for none doubted that they
would conquer under the command of Xanthippus. Being
thus appointed general, he led his army into the plain, and
prepared to give battle to the Romans. He first ordered the
elephants to charge the Roman centre, and the cavalry to fall
upon the wings on both sides. The Roman horse, who were
greatly inferior in numbers, fled without striking a blow,[2]
and the elephants, rushing [3] into the foremost ranks of the
Roman infantry, laid the enemy low [4] in every direction.
Attacked in front by the infantry, on the flanks by the
cavalry, and on the rear by the elephants, the majority of the
Roman soldiers of the line stood their ground bravely, and
died where they were standing.

---

[1] that a battle should be fought at once.

[2] re integra.

[3] invecti.

[4] prosternere hostem.

Exercise 181 [B]

Ten years after, Caius, the younger brother of Tiberius, thinking he ought to avenge his brother's death, brought forward laws to upset the whole constitution.[1] The people had not forgotten the death of Tiberius, and all the power of the senators could not prevent their electing Caius tribune of the plebs. But Tiberius had proposed his laws because he pitied the common people; Caius proposed his in order that he might the more easily satisfy his desire for revenge.[2] He was accused also of aiming at kingship. For two years he delivered many speeches before the people, and continued to propose [3] all such laws as might lessen the senate's power, but the most iniquitous of them was that which caused [4] bread to be given to the common people at a very low rate.[5]

---

[1] evertere rempublicam.
[2] ulciscendi libido.
[3] Imperfect.
[4] efficere ut.
[5] vili (Abl. of Price).

TEMPORAL CLAUSES

<u>Rule 25.</u> Conjunctions used in a purely temporal sense are followed by the Indicative. But the verb is put in the Subjunctive (a) when it is in Oratio Obliqua, (b) when some other idea than that of time (*e.g.* purpose) is introduced.

N.B.—*Cum* is an exception. Also *dum* in the sense of *while*. For these see *Rules* 26, 27.

EXAMPLES

(a) **Postquam**[1] omnes Belgarum copias ad se venire **vidit**, ad exercitum properavit.

After he saw that all the forces of the Belgians were coming to him he hastened to join the army.

(b) Caesar **priusquam** se hostes ex terrore **reciperent** in fines Suessionum exercitum duxit.

Before the enemy could recover[2] from their panic, Caesar led his army into the territories of the Suessiones.

When the temporal clause refers to Future time the verb will be in the Future (or Fut. Perf.) in Latin, though in English the Present is preferred.

(c) Nos **ante** abibimus **quam** tu **redieris** (Fut. Perf.).

We shall go away before you return.

---

[1] *The English Pluperfect should be rendered by Latin Perfect after* postquam, *and* simulac. *But with* postquam *the Plup. may be used if the exact interval of time is mentioned.* Tertio post anno quam veneram=*three years after I had come.*

[2] Implying that Caesar wished to prevent their recovering.

Exercise 182 [A]

1. As soon as they saw us they went away.

2. I knew they would go away as soon as they saw us.

3. After you have heard what has taken place, you will know what you ought to do.

4. He refused to leave before he had seen the general.

5. From the time when we heard of the destruction of the army we gave up all hope of safety.

6. No sooner was the signal given than all the soldiers ran forward together.

7. As often as messengers arrive we all run to the gates.

8. They would not depart until they received their pay.

9. Caesar had embarked all his troops before Pompey could reach Brundisium.

10. Before Pompey reached Brundisium Caesar had embarked all his troops.

Exercise 183 [A]

1. We were defeated almost before battle was joined.

2. The Gauls attacked the camp before our men could man the walls.

3. After landing the soldiers burnt their fleet.

4. We were informed that the general had dismissed his men after giving them their pay.

5. A crowd assembled before I could reach the temple.

6. No sooner had the king appeared, than all the citizens raised a shout.

7. When you return you will hear what has taken place.

8. Advance the standards, my men, before the enemy catch sight of us.

9. They waited in the road until the king had passed.

10. We must remain here until our friends arrive.

F

Exercise 184 [B]

1. I will come to you when I have finished this work.

2. As soon as I had finished the work I left the city.

3. The camp was attacked by the enemy before we could take up arms.

4. Caesar addressed his men before leaving winter quarters.

5. It was announced that the cavalry had been sent forward before the scouts had returned.

6. Wait at Rome until you receive another letter.

7. They decided not to leave Rome till they had received our letters.

8. No sooner was war proclaimed, than the general took the field.

9. The prisoners escaped into the woods before the soldiers could overtake them.

10. Our men advanced in close order until they saw that the enemy were retreating.

Exercise 185 [B]

1. Horatius stood firm until the bridge was broken down.

2. I will leave the army as soon as the new consul arrives.

3. Cicero refused to go to a province after he resigned his consulship.

4. I will be here as soon as you call me.

5. He refused to leave the army till the new consul arrived.

6. After Pompey had fled from the field, his men scattered immediately.

7. You must not embark before I give you leave.

8. He shall not be accused till he himself is in Rome.

9. The consul said P. Scipio should not be accused before he had returned to Rome.

10. Milo was in the senate till it adjourned.

Exercise 186 [A]

As soon as Demosthenes arrived with his armament before Syracuse, and joined [1] the army of Nicias, the siege was carried on with renewed vigour.[2] At first Nicias' want of energy [3] prevented even Demosthenes from making a direct [4] assault. But at length Nicias was persuaded to allow his men to assault the city in the night time. This attack had an unfortunate result. The Athenians, before they reached the walls of the Achradina, fell into confusion, and were not far from fighting with one another in the darkness. Demosthenes was obliged to sound a retreat. After this Nicias' counsel again prevailed, and they determined to reduce the city by famine.

Exercise 187 [B]

As soon as news reached him of William's [5] landing, Harold hastened southward by forced marches. Flushed [6] by their recent success, his men did not despair of victory, and spent the night before the battle in feasting and drinking. The battle was stubbornly contested [7] all day, and evening was approaching before it was clear which side [8] would win the day. At length, by feigning retreat, William enticed the enemy from their position, and the Norman cavalry made [9] great havoc in the ranks of the Saxon foot. But not until they saw their king fall, pierced through the eye by an arrow, did the Saxons take to flight. After his death they were routed, and fled in all directions.

---

[1] *Intr.* se conjungere cum.
[2] the city was besieged more keenly.
[3] *want of energy*=inertia.   [4] directus.
[5] The Latin forms are *Gulielmus, Haraldus, Normanni, Saxones.*
[6] elati.   [7] ancipiti proelio dimicatur.
[8] utri.   [9] edere.

CUM

Rule 26. **Cum** (= when) **in Primary tenses takes Indicative.**

in Historic ,, ,, **Subjunctive.**

$\left.\begin{array}{l}(=\text{since})\\(=\text{although})\end{array}\right\}$ **always Subjunctive.**

EXAMPLES

(*a*) Cum **potero** reddam.

I will pay it back when I can.

(*b*) Quae cum **cognoscerent**, se recipere in animo habebant

$\left.\begin{array}{l}when\\since\\although\end{array}\right\}$ *they learnt this, they intended to retreat.*

Exceptions.—Cum (= when) may take Historic tenses of the Indicative in certain cases—

(1) *When the clauses are inverted, i.e. when the* cum *clause really contains the principal statement.*

e.g. Jam ver appetebat cum Hannibal ex hibernis **movit.**

Spring was already approaching when Hannibal moved from his winter quarters.

N.B.—If not inverted, this would be 'Hannibal moved from his winter quarters when spring was approaching' (cum ver appeteret).

(2) *When* cum *is frequentative, i.e. is equal to* quoties, *as often as, whenever.* [In this sense use Perfect and Pluperfect.]

e.g. Cum consul abfuerat, seditiosi erant.

They were mutinous whenever the consul was absent.

(3) *When* cum *is equal to* quamdiu, *as long as, or* ex quo tempore, *since.*

e.g. Cum consul aberat tum seditiosi erant.

They were mutinous as long as the consul was awau.

Exercise 188 [A]

1. When spring returns we shall leave winter quarters.

2. Though they knew they would be killed, they advanced.

3. They were already approaching the city when news was brought that reinforcements had arrived.

4. Not knowing what was to be done, they decided to wait for the messengers.

5. I always lived in the country whenever I was able.

6. Knowing, as they did, that there was no hope of safety, they resolved to die bravely.

7. When you return, you will find the city changed.

8. We had scarcely begun our march, when we were ordered to halt.

9. Having approached the city, we halted.

10. Believing that they could hold out, they refused to surrender.

Exercise 189 [B]

1. We will come to meet you when you arrive.

2. Hoping to save the lives of his men, the general gave the signal for retreat.

3. We were at Veii all the time that you were at Rome.

4. They refused to surrender, although they knew they would be conquered.

5. The citizens were almost dead of starvation, when relief arrived.

6. Knowing that the enemy were at hand, we tried to find out when they would attack us.

7. A signal was given whenever a ship approached.

8. Believing, as you do, that there is no hope of safety, why do you remain any longer ?

9. When they came to Athens, they found their friends.

10. Since you think that I have deceived you, why do you not employ another messenger ?

DUM

Rule 27. **Dum (=while [1]) regularly takes Present Indicative, even of Past Time.**

> (= provided that, if only = dummodo) **always Subjunctive.**

> (= until) **follows ordinary rule of Temporal Conjunctions** (Rule 25).

Dum arma **conquiruntur** circiter hominum milia sex ad Rhenum contenderunt.

While the arms were being searched for about 6000 made off for the Rhine.

Oderint dum **metuant.**

Let them hate provided that they fear.

Dum reliquæ naves convenirent ad horam nonam exspectavit.

To allow the rest of the ships to assemble, he waited till the ninth hour.

Mansit dum judices rejecti sunt.

He waited till the judges were rejected.

---

[1] But when ' *while* ' can be turned by ' *as long as*,' dum may take any tense of the Indicative, like quamdiu, etc. *See Rule* 25. *e.g.* Haec feci dum licuit=*I did this while (as long as) I was allowed.*

The difference is that in this case the time of the action of the principal verb and the time of the action of the ' dum ' verb are contemporaneous, *i.e.* begin and end together.

Exercise 190 [*A*]

1. While they were cutting down the wood the enemy came upon them.

2. If only he is accused, without doubt he will be cast into prison.

3. The enemy quietly surrounded us while we were sleeping.

4. Till Camillus be recalled we shall not prosper.[1]

5. As long as the kings ruled in Rome no one enjoyed liberty.

6. None of the enemy were seen while they crossed the hill.

7. They refused to treat for peace until the deserters were given up.

8. We concealed ourselves until they had crossed the river.

9. While you stay I shall stay.

10. Minucius promised that while the dictator was away he would not join battle.

Exercise 191 [*B*]

1. While we were wasting time the Gauls caught us up.

2. He was kept in prison until the king should return victorious.

3. While the conspirators gathered round Caesar, Antonius was led aside by Trebonius.

4. Do not ask him while he is angry.

5. Provided he reaches Rome in time, he will stand for the consulship.

6. Milo said he had stayed in the senate till it was dismissed.

7. While these were holding their conference the Gauls were seen to be stealthily advancing.

8. Deserters kept coming in till Manlius' army was very small.

9. We shall conquer if only we can entice them to battle.

10. He refused to fight till reinforcements came.

---

[1] rem prospere gerere.

Exercise 192 [A]

CUM AND DUM

1. It was decided not to leave winter quarters till spring was approaching.

2. They knew that they could defend the town, provided that provisions did not run short.

3. While provisions held out they resisted all attacks.

4. They were compelled to raise the siege until fresh forces arrived.

5. They were both harassed by the enemy, and were also afraid that their own men would desert.

6. Men generally [1] show themselves brave when danger threatens their country.

7. When I hear what has taken place I will write to you.

8. They were ordered to remain in the camp until the enemy gave them an opportunity of joining battle.

9. We must retreat, he said, especially as the enemy have received fresh forces.

10. No one left his post while the battle lasted.

11. If only the allies can hold out a little [2] longer, we shall be able to renew the fight.

12. The soldiers refused to leave their posts, although the signal for retreat had been given.

---

[1] vulgo, plerumque.   [2] paulo.

Exercise 193 [B]

1. While the consul was absent the danger was increasing.

2. Since the enemy were only two miles distant, we were not allowed to wander out of camp.

3. He took it ill when I asked him to repay the money I had given him.

4. When the priests had returned without accomplishing anything, the Romans sent the women to appease Coriolanus.

5. Although Pompeius took part only in the end of the war, he obtained more glory from it than Crassus.

6. The majority advised him to engage while the troops were still fresh.

7. When our messenger has returned we shall understand better what the enemy intend to do.

8. When men are assembled in great numbers they fall easily into riot.

9. Although I am anxious for peace, I am annoyed at this fresh insult.

10. If only they give up their arms, we shall come to an agreement.

11. When the war is finished the tribune will bring Caesar to trial.[1]

12. It was about noon when the Senate assembled.

---

[1] *bring to trial*=reum aliquem facere, *or* nomen alicujus deferre.

Exercise 194 [A]

Both Demosthenes and the common soldiers were greatly
disheartened at this defeat, though Nicias seemed almost to
have expected it. He now proposed that the siege should be
abandoned, since the gods refused [1] their assistance, and they
repeatedly met with disaster. But while they were still
disputing [2] the Syracusans took away from them their last
means of flight. In several engagements in the harbour they
destroyed the whole Athenian fleet. Now all were eager to
retreat, while it was still possible, towards their allies in the
western part of the island. But the superstition [3] of Nicias
deterred them from setting out till the new moon had risen;
and meanwhile deserters had betrayed their plans to the
Syracusans, who blocked the pass by which alone they could
hope to reach the interior.

Exercise 195 [A]

At length, on the day appointed, they marched several miles
until they came to the fatal pass. When they found this
beset by the enemy, and all their attacks made no impression, [4]
they first tried to discover some other path by which they
could ascend the mountains; then, almost in despair, they
determined to make a dash [5] for the coast, for this purpose
dividing their forces into two divisions. Demosthenes was

---

[1] denegare.

[2] de re disceptatur.

[3] nimia religio.

[4] *effected nothing.*

[5] per medios hostes perrumpere.

speedily overtaken and surrounded. Nicias met the enemy while crossing a river on the sixth day after he had left Syracuse. But, since his men had found no water to drink for many hours, they could not be restrained from rushing into the water, even when it was red with the blood of their comrades. All order being thus lost,[1] Nicias surrendered at discretion.[2] He and Demosthenes, being condemned to death, died by poison; the rest of the Athenians were kept in the stone quarries[3] at Syracuse.

Exercise 196 [A]

After surmounting all these obstacles, and so signally defeating the Gauls, Hannibal was all but destroyed, not in open fight, but by ambuscade. He had almost reached the top of the Alps, when some old men came to him in the guise of envoys. The misfortunes of others, they said, had been a warning to them, and they preferred to make trial of the friendship rather than the might of the Carthaginians, and were ready to do whatever he wished. Hannibal, considering that he must not rashly either trust or slight[4] them, accepted them as guides, but followed with his army in fighting order.[5] The moment[6] they entered a narrow pass, the enemy sprang out of their ambuscade on all sides, and assailed him both in front and in rear, both from a distance and at close quarters.

---

[1] confusis signis et ordinibus.

[2] nullis conditionibus latis.

[3] lautumiae.

[4] aspernari.

[5] 'prepared for battle.'

[6] 'as soon as.'

Exercise 197 [A]

When the Athenians had attempted without success to capture the island of Sphacteria, an assembly was called to discuss what steps should be taken. At this assembly Cleon, who was only a private citizen, and wholly inexperienced in war, declared that they would never be able to take the island while they employed such generals. 'Under my command,' he said, 'I am sure that the enemy would not resist [1] us for twenty days.' There is no doubt that he said this only to slight the other generals; but the Athenians at once assigned to him the control of the campaign, and he set out at once for the seat of war. Here, aided by fortune, he accomplished what he had undertaken, contrary to the expectations of all, and within twenty days returned to Athens in triumph.

Exercise 198 [B]

It was already dawning when the general gave the signal, promising a great reward to the first man who [2] climbed the

---

[1] Non fore ut hostes resistant. This periphrasis is used to express the Fut. Inf. of Verbs that have no Fut. Inf. The same periphrasis may be used for the Fut. Inf. Passive of any Verb; *e.g.* sperant fore ut urbs capiatur.

[2] In such phrases the Superlative must be transferred to the Relative clause—'*the man who first . . .*' So for '*he sent the most faithful slave he had,*' the Latin idiom is, '*he sent the slave whom he had the most faithful.*' Also '*the only man who*'='*the man who alone*' (solus or unus).

walls. No one indeed resisted them as they entered the city, where the walls had been broken down, or climbed the walls by ladders. As soon as the shouting showed that the city had been taken the Asiatics all left their posts, and sought refuge in the citadel. The general allowed his men to plunder the town, partly because he was incensed with the inhabitants, and partly because the soldiers had hitherto always been restrained from plundering captured cities, and he wished them at last to have some reward for their valour. He was indeed accused of having done it to satisfy a grudge.

Exercise 199 [B]

A certain man dreamed that he saw an egg hanging from the top of his bed; and when he had been the next day to consult a friend what the meaning of this dream might be, the friend told him that he would find a great quantity of gold hidden under his bed. After he had been digging for several hours he found a large quantity of gold surrounded with silver. Therefore he sent his friend a small part of the silver. The man, being vexed that he had received so small a reward, sent a messenger to ask whether he could not give him part of the yolk[1] of the egg; for (he said) inasmuch as the gold was covered with silver, the god had intended to show him the gold by the yolk and the silver by the rest.[2] But for my part I am not persuaded that this story is true.

---

[1] vitellus.　　　　　　　　[2] reliqua pars.

Exercise 200 [B]

This man, although he had been banished from his country
on a false charge, did not cease, as often as opportunity
was offered, to help her to the best of his ability. He was
not the man to put his own prosperity before that of[1] the
State; and he used to say that when his countrymen needed
him they would recall him; till that time should arrive he
was willing to remain in exile. Soon an occasion was offered
him to show his devotion.

A conspiracy was formed by some desperate men, who killed
the chief magistrates, and assumed supreme power. In this
crisis the citizens remembered the exile, and sent messengers
to ask him to come to their help. He forgot all the wrongs
which he had suffered, and by his arrival brought safety to
the State which had treated him [2] so unjustly.

Exercise 201 [B]

Rutilius was not fit to be made governor of a province. On
his departure from Asia, while visiting Ephesus, a city whose
inhabitants worship Diana, he had robbed the temple of that
goddess. And he did many other such things as would offend
all Romans of the old character. And as often as he committed a theft he had a jest to justify[3] it by. He said he

---

[1] Omit '*that of*' in Latin.   [2] '*used.*'   [3] excusare.

always took readily the little golden cups which the statues of gods held in their outstretched hands. And when his companions asked him whether he did not expect some day to be punished, he said the gods would not punish a man who, after praying to them for benefits, took the first gift which they offered him. When he was old he did just the same things as [1] he had done when a young man. When on the point of death he said, ' One thing I have been repenting for a long time [2]— that I did not take the golden cloak which Jupiter wears in his temple in Messenia. I could have given him a woollen one for it.'

---

[1] eadem quae.

[2] Jampridem, jamdudum take the Present for the English Perfect, the Imperfect for English Pluperfect. ' Jampridem miror ' = ' *I have long been wondering.*' ' Jampridem mirabar ' = ' *I had been for a long time wondering.*'

CONDITIONAL SENTENCES

Rule 28.

A. Open Conditions, *i.e.* those in which we assume the condition without implying anything as to its fulfilment.

INDICATIVE in both clauses.

Any tense possible according to the sense.

> Si hoc facis, peccas.
> *If you do this, you do wrong.*
>
> Si hoc $\begin{cases} \text{facies} \\ \text{feceris} \end{cases}$ peccabis.
> *If you do this* (*Fut.*), *you will do wrong.*
>
> Si hoc fecisti, peccavisti.
> *If you did this, you did wrong.*

B. Conditions in which it is implied that the fulfilment of the condition is **improbable but possible.**

PRESENT (or PERFECT) SUBJUNCTIVE in both clauses.

> Si hoc facias, pecces.
> *If you* $\begin{cases} \text{did} \\ \text{were to do} \end{cases}$ *this, you would do wrong.*

C. Impossible Conditions, *i.e.* those in which it is implied that the fulfilment of the condition is impossible.

> (1) Relating to **Present** time, or to **continuous** action in **Past** time.
>
> IMPERFECT SUBJUNCTIVE in both clauses.
>
>> Si hoc faceres, peccares.
>> *If you were doing this, you would be doing wrong.*
>> (implying '*but you are not doing it.*')
>> or, *If you had been doing this, you would have been doing wrong.*
>
> (2) Relating to **Past** time.
>
> PLUPERFECT SUBJUNCTIVE in both clauses.
>
>> Si hoc fecisses, peccavisses.
>> *If you had done this, you would have done wrong.*
>> (implying '*But you did not do it.*')

The tense and mood are generally the same in the protasis (*i.e.* the *if* clause) and the apodosis (*i.e.* the conclusion). But in C the condition may obviously relate to *past* time and so be Pluperfect, while the conclusion relates to *present* time and is therefore Imperfect.[1]

> *e.g.* Si hoc fecisses, nunc felix esses.
> *If you had done this, you would now be happy.*

The apodosis need not always be a statement, but may be a command or wish, *e.g.* Ne veneris nisi jussero. Moriar si me facti poenitet.

The English Present is often used for what is really a Future action. In Latin the Future or Fut. Perf. **must always** be used in these cases, *e.g.* Si id feceris (*or* facies), peccabis = '*If you do this, you will do wrong.*'

FURTHER EXAMPLES OF CONDITIONALS

A. Parvi sunt foris arma, nisi est consilium domi.
> *Arms are worth little abroad, unless there is wisdom at home.*
Si te hic offendero, moriere.
> *If I meet you here, you shall die.*
Non si tibi ante profuit, semper proderit.
> *If it helped you before, it will not help you always.*

B. Nonne sapiens, si fame conficiatur, abstulerit cibum alteri ?
> *Would not a wise man, if he were being starved, take food from another ?*

C. Non pacem peterem, nisi utilem crederem.
> *I should not be asking for peace, if I did not think it advantageous.*
Si Camillus tale fecisset, non nobis exemplo esset.
> *Had Camillus done such a thing, he would not be an example to us.*

---

[1] Moreover, in Impossible Conditions, if the verb of the apodosis is possum, debeo, oportet, or a gerundive (or any verb expressing *obligation* or *possibility*), it is regularly put in the Indicative.

> *e.g.* Si patriam perdidisset, interficiendus erat.
> *If he had betrayed his country, he should have been put to death.*

Exercise 202 [A]

1. If you are able to do this, you ought to do it at once.

2. If I could do this, I would do it at once.

3. They always gave money to the poor, if they seemed to need it.

4. If the prisoners escape, we shall be punished.

5. If I thought you needed my advice, I would try to help you.

6. If they had started at once, they would have caught the enemy off their guard.

7. I should not be here now, if I had listened to the advice of my friends.

8. Do not leave your home unless I bid you.

9. If they were asked for help, they gave it readily.

10. If they had been asked for help, they ought to have given it readily.

11. They were always willing to help us, if we deserved help.

Exercise 203 [B]

1. Never promise if your cannot keep your word.

2. If once [1] we reach the camp, we shall be safe.

3. If the river were not so deep, we might have crossed it on foot.

4. They would have shown themselves more prudent if they had landed their forces immediately.

5. You would be wrong if you thought that I did this on purpose.

6. If a man cannot restrain his temper, he is a burden to his friends.

7. Whether he praises or blames you, you know that you have acted rightly.

---

[1] Expressed by Fut. Perf.

8. If reinforcements had come, the enemy would have been compelled to raise the siege.

9. If they take up arms against their country, they will deserve to be condemned to death.

10. If he saw a man suffering wrongfully, he always tried to help him.

11. If only we had kept silence, we should not now be suffering such misfortunes.

Exercise 204 [*A*]

1. If he had not mocked me, I should perhaps have forgiven him.

2. They may hate me, if only they fear me.

3. If Caesar had thrown a bridge over the Rhine, the Germans could easily have been subdued.

4. If we attack the enemy at once, there is no doubt that we shall conquer them.

5. If he were my own brother I should condemn him none the less.

6. Had not Publius Scipio promised to accompany him, the war would never have been entrusted to Lucius Scipio.

7. But for the imposition of a tribute, the Macedonians would be more prosperous now than under their own kings.

8. If a man has wronged me, I take my revenge on him by law, not by violence.

9. When once Italy is reached, I will lead you straight to Rome.

10. Unless a man uses bribery, it is of no advantage to him to stand for the consulship.

11. Whether you go to Rome or remain here,[1] I shall not leave the city.

---

[1] *whether* . . . *or* . . . in double Conditions seu . . . seu (sive).
whether . . . *or* . . . in double Questions utrum . . . an . . .

Exercise 205 [B]

1. Poets starve at Rome unless rich men relieve them.

2. If we march straight to Rome we shall feast to-night in the Capitol.

3. In former times if a man showed himself capable of ruling, he was generally elected consul.

4. Whether this news is true or false, we must remain where we are.

5. I should certainly have brought you the news in time had I been able.

6. If the enemy make an attack at once, I am afraid we shall not be able to resist them.

7. Were I to make such a request of you, you would be rightly angry.

8. When once you return home you will find many friends.

9. If I had never been poor I should not now enjoy my riches.

10. If Gracchus aimed at royal power he was rightly put to death.

Exercise 206 [A]

1. We will take the place of the front rank if they are cut down.

2. If I were on the spot I should know what ought to be done.

3. Unless you remind him, he will have forgotten in three days.

4. Were he able to be present, he would certainly now be speaking for this bill.

5. If he should be present to-morrow, he would speak for this bill.

6. If Fabius had had more influence in the state, Varro would never have been elected consul.

7. If he does anything contrary to the law, punish him.

8. If a man does anything contrary to the law, he must be punished.

9. He would be arrested, if any one caught sight of him.

10. He would be in prison now, if only we could have arrested him.

Exercise 207 [B]

1. If they have conspired against the state, they deserve to be punished.

2. If they had not conspired, they would still be living in the city.

3. If once you reach the shore, you will be able to embark.

4. Had you listened to my advice, you would have kept your riches.

5. If they repent of their crime, they will be forgiven.

6. Unless you spare this man, you will be an object of hatred to all.

7. If he had consulted his own interests, he would not have lost the friendship of Caesar.

8. If we were to send help to the Carthaginians, we should incur the anger of the Romans.

9. If they come to see you, tell them to wait until I arrive.

10. You must use your riches well, if you wish to be happy.

11. You ought to have done this, whether you wished to or not.

Exercise 208 [*A*]

'Fellow-soldiers, we have lost many brave men through treachery, and have been abandoned by our friends. But we must not lose heart; and if we cannot conquer, let us choose rather to perish gloriously, than to fall into the hands of barbarians, who will inflict upon us the greatest miseries. If our ancestors had not been willing to encounter the vast forces of the Persians, Greece would now be in the hands of the barbarians. If we show ourselves worthy of them, we too shall benefit our country. The gods, the avengers of perjury, will be favourable to us, and seeing that they are offended by the violation of treaties, they will also follow us to battle, and combat for us.'

Exercise 209 [*B*]

The general delivered this speech before his men : 'You see how great the forces of the enemy are, and how impregnable their position is. If we attack them we shall without doubt suffer a severe defeat. But if, on the contrary, they were to leave their position and attack us, we should have good hopes of victory, for they have to cross a deep river and climb a steep hill, before they can reach our lines.' By these words the general with difficulty persuaded his men to remain within their fortifications ; and his advice was the salvation of the army. For if the Romans had attacked the enemy, who were superior to them both in numbers and position, they would undoubtedly have been conquered.

Exercise 210 [*A*]

After the death of Tib. Gracchus, C. Blosius showed his friendship for him in a marvellous way. For the senate decreed that all who had taken part with[1] Gracchus should be punished. Blosius, when accused before the consuls, excused himself on the ground of his friendship[2] for Gracchus. ' Whether my judges condemn me,' said he, ' or whether they acquit me, I shall still always rejoice that I was the friend of Gracchus. If you, consuls, should bid me save my life by accusing Gracchus, I would not so save it. If I must die, let me die loyal to my friends.' The two consuls hesitated. At last one of them asked Blosius, ' If Gracchus had ordered you to set fire to the temple of Jupiter would you have done it ? ' To which Blosius replied, ' Gracchus would not have ordered it.'

Exercise 211 [*B*]

On receiving news of the approach of Fairfax, the governor of Raglan Castle called together his men, and spoke as follows : ' If all were going well I should not conceive it to be my duty to consult the men whom I command. But since the enemy are already upon us, and we have not collected[3] sufficient provisions, if there should be any here faint-hearted, or any that careth not to fight to the death in his Majesty's cause, let him depart, and be not burdensome to us in the siege. If I am able I will set[4] him safe on the Welsh[5] side of the river.' If the king himself had addressed them the men could not have shown more zeal than they did on hearing this speech, and if there was any there desirous of going he did not dare to confess it.

---

[1] consentire cum. [2] amicitiae excusatione uti.
[3] frumentum comparare. [4] exponere. [5] Celticus.

PRONOUNS AND ADVERBS

TRANSLATION OF ' ANY '

Quisquam (adj. *ullus*) to be used when ' any ' is *exclusive*; *i.e.* with negatives and sentences virtually negative. Sentences are virtually negative (1) when they contain vix, aegre, sine, (2) when they are questions expecting the answer ' no,' (3) when they are comparative, ' he was taller than *any* of his friends.'

Quivis, Quilibet to be used when ' any ' is *inclusive*; *i.e.* when it means *anybody you like*, or *everybody*.

Quis (adj. *qui*) only used after si, nisi, num, ne (and after quo, quanto, with comparatives).

Aliquis only when *some one* may be substituted for *any one* in the English without altering the sense.

TRANSLATION OF ' SOME '

Aliquis and *Quispiam* are the ordinary words.
    Aliquis should be used for ' somebody,' when it means ' a person of consequence.'

Quidam = a certain man, almost the Eng. Indefinite Article. As a rule it *follows* its noun.

Nescio quis = some one or other, no definite person indicated.

Alii . . . alii = some . . . others.

Nonnulli = some, of number, opposed to *none*, and often implying *a considerable number*.

Aliquot = some, of number.

EXAMPLES

Quivis de virtute loquitur, **vix quisquam** virtutem praestat.
Every one talks about virtue, scarcely any one practises it.

Si quid cognovisti, loquere.
If you have learnt anything, speak.

Forsitan dicat **aliquis** . . .
Perhaps some one may say . . .

Hic **nescio quis** loquitur.
There is some one or other talking here.

OTHER PRONOUNS

Quisquis, whoever (adj. *quicunque*).

Ecquis ? Interrog. and Indef. combined,—' any one at all ' ?

Quisnam ? =the Interrog. *quis*.

Quisque, each man.

> Its commonest uses are with superlatives and ordinals ;
> *e.g.* optimus quisque (all the best men), decimus quisque
> (every tenth man, or one in ten), and in combination with
> suus or ipse ; *e.g.* suam quisque salutem petit (each man
> seeks his own safety).

ADVERBS

Unquam (ever) and *usquam* (anywhere) can only be used
according to the rule of *quisquam ; i.e.* with negatives and
virtual negatives.

Quo (anywhither), *quando* (at any time), in the same way
correspond to *quis*.

> *e.g.* **Si quando** peccaveris, ne celaveris **unquam.**
> *If ever you sin, never conceal it.*
> Contrast—Ne **semper** celaveris =
>
> $$Do\ not\ be \left\{ \begin{matrix} ever \\ always \end{matrix} \right\} concealing\ it.$$

Alicubi (somewhere), *aliquando* (some time, once upon a time),
aliquantum (some quantity), *aliquamdiu* (for some time),
correspond to *aliquis*.   The syllables *ali* always correspond
to the Eng. *some*, and these words must not be used for
the Eng. *any*, except when it stands for *some*.

Nonnunquam (sometimes) corresponds to *nonnulli*.

Exercise 212 [A]

1. If all the best men have perished, who is left to rule the state ?

2. If he ever saw his men suffering hardships, he tried to help them himself.

3. The order was given that each man should see to his own safety.

4. It is of the utmost importance to us to find out if any one has been here during our absence.

5. The horse has been lost for a long time, and no one can find it anywhere.

6. He said that no one had ever persuaded him to take bribes.

7. If the city is taken, I do not suppose the enemy will spare any of the citizens.

8. Having remained within their lines for some time, our men at last sallied out against the enemy.

9. A philosopher has said that fire is the origin of all things.

10. There is no doubt that a considerable number of the enemy are trying to attack us in the rear.

Exercise 213 [B]

1. On my return I was told that some one had come to see me.

2. I returned as quickly as possible, but could not find any one in my house.

3. Did any one ask you what ought to be done ?

4. If any one were to say that there was no hope, he would be killed by the citizens.

5. I am willing to send any one at all to find out what is going on.

6. Some one or another has said that a long life is the greatest misfortune.

7. For some time it was asserted that all our best troops were lost.

8. There is no doubt that they perished, but their bodies have never been found anywhere.

9. When I return to Rome I shall find out if any one has bought my house.

10. An order was given that whoever plundered the houses should be put to death.

Exercise 214 [*A*]

[*Exercises* 214–222 *are for revision.*]

If after so great a victory the Gauls had immediately pursued the fugitives, Rome would certainly have been taken, so astonished and terrified were the citizens at the return of those who had escaped from the battle. The Gauls, however, not imagining the victory to be so great as it really was, gave way [1] to feasting and plundering the camp. Accordingly numbers, who wished to leave the city, had opportunity to escape, while those who remained were able to make preparations for defending the city. The latter, quitting the rest of the city, retired to the Capitol, which they fortified by strong ramparts ; for they knew that if the Gauls attacked them they would need all their strength.

---

[1] se dedere, *dat.*

Exercise 215 [*A*]

There can be little doubt that the guides, whether through treachery or ignorance, were mainly responsible for the disaster. If the army had marched by the main road they would have arrived unmolested, and could have joined battle on the following day on equal terms. But following a shorter way across the fields, they found the road blocked on one side by a marsh, and on the other by cliffs. Then the general called together his officers, and said, ' If we advance we shall run the risk of [1] being surprised by the enemy ; on the other hand, if [2] we retreat we shall perhaps arrive too late. Had we only kept to the main road, we should already be approaching the city.' No one replied at once, and before any plan could be determined the cry was raised that the enemy were upon them.

Exercise 216 [*A*]

A young Spartan, named Isadas, distinguished himself [3] particularly in this action. He had neither armour nor clothes upon his body, and he held a spear in one hand and a sword in the other. In this condition [4] he quitted his home with the utmost eagerness, and was the first to enter the battle. He dealt mortal [5] wounds at every blow, and overthrew all who opposed him without receiving any hurt himself.[6] Whether the enemy were dismayed at so strange a sight, or whether the gods preserved him on account of his extraordinary valour, it is certain that no man ever accomplished such marvellous deeds. It is said that after the battle the Ephori decreed him a crown for his valour, but fined him a thousand drachmae for having exposed himself to so great a danger without arms.

---

[1] Use ' in periculum adduci ut.'

[2] sin = '*but if*' (introducing a second and contrary condition). '*If not*,' ' *otherwise*,' without a verb = si minus.

[3] eniteo.   [4] *thus armed.*   [5] mortifer.   [6] ipse incolumis.

Exercise 217 [*A*]

On the very day on which the Senate was deliberating
whether they ought to summon back to Rome the Master of
the Horse, news was brought that he had led out the troops
which had been left in the camp, and in a battle with the
Samnites had suffered a great disaster. The Dictator would
not even wait to learn what the Senate determined, but hurried
back to the camp. The Master of the Horse, summoned before
the tribunal,[1] was asked why he, to whose care the safety of
the Roman people had been entrusted, had without the orders
of the Dictator led into battle the legions which he had been
ordered to keep within the camp. The only reply he could
make was [2] that he had thought he ought to use the legions
which he commanded for the good of the Roman people whenever an opportunity offered.[3]

Exercise 218 [*A*]

An Indian[4] chief was taken prisoner by the Spaniards, and
because he was a man of influence [5] among the tribes they cut
off his hands, with the intention of disabling him [6] from fighting
any more against them. But he, returning home eager to
avenge this wrong, incited his countrymen not to let the
Spaniards think their accustomed valour had forsaken them.
And when they saw the cruelty which the Spaniards had
practised [7] towards him and others his companions, they burnt
their homes, to prevent any one's wishing to return, and fell
upon the Spanish settlement, with minds made up either to
drive the Spaniards out of the town or to perish themselves
in battle. While the battle was being fought the maimed
chieftain himself carried arrows in his mouth with which to
supply the combatants.

---

[1] tribunal (*n.*).   [2] '*he could only answer this.*'   [3] '*was given.*'
[4] Indicus (*subst.* Indus).   [5] Use ' pollere.'
[6] '*that he might not be able.*'   [7] ' *used.*'

Exercise 219 [B]

The Romans, when they heard of the disaster which had befallen Regulus, fitted out a large fleet for the rescue of the survivors; while the Carthaginians, rightly judging that the resolution of the Romans would not be broken by one calamity, also began to build a new fleet to protect them from another invasion. But in vain did they endeavour to reduce Clypea before the Romans could reach it. The small garrison, with surprising courage, repelled all attacks, and held out till the ensuing summer, when the Roman fleet arrived. A naval battle took place off the Hermaean promontory. The Romans gained the day, and took on board the defenders of Clypea who had so well earned their safety.

Exercise 220 [B]

Hanno was now entrusted with the command. If he had followed [1] the example of Hamilcar, the Romans would without doubt have been defeated. But before he had held the command long he proved himself entirely unworthy of confidence. If ever he won a partial success,[2] he was unable to make use of it; and after having won, as he thought, a complete victory, he allowed his camp to be surprised and taken. Under these circumstances the Carthaginians once more offered Hamilcar the command, although they could not expect a man whom they had treated so unjustly before to come to their help. But Hamilcar, still placing his country before all else, consented to take the command. By his strict discipline, by his energy, and by his great influence with the Numidian chiefs, he defeated the enemy in a pitched battle, and recovered a considerable number of cities which had revolted.

---

[1] *used.* [2] ex parte rem prospere gerere.

Exercise 221 [B]

When Ulysses was cast upon [1] the island of Phaeacia, he was treated with all the hospitality which in those days strangers used everywhere to receive. Nausicaa, the king's daughter, was the first person who met him, and she conducted him to her father's palace. The best raiment which the maidens had woven was bestowed upon him; and he enjoyed the most sumptuous feast which his hosts could provide. On the next day games were held, and he was asked to join in [2] them, an honour which he at first refused. But afterwards, stung by the insults of the king's son, the only man who forgot his duty to a guest, he showed that his strength was almost as great now as when he fought against Troy, and he surpassed the Phaeacians [3] in their own sports.

Exercise 222 [B]

If ever a man [4] deserved to be well treated [5] by his fellow citizens it was Tib. Gracchus. Son of a father who had pacified Spain (a work [6] in which a whole series of consuls had failed), and connected by birth with both the conquerors of Africa,[7] he might have easily claimed the first place in the state, if he had been willing to obey the laws without [8] trying to change them. But he had to journey through Etruria to his first province, Spain, and that country, then desolate, devoid of freemen, cultivated by slaves, made such an impression [9] on him that he determined to find a remedy if he perished in the attempt. All the best men of Rome favoured the laws he proposed, and had not a tribune stood in the way he would have accomplished his work with the goodwill of most, if not all.[10]

---

[1] ejectus in.   [2] interesse.   [3] Phaeaces.
[4] Translate ' *Tib. Gracchus, if any other, was worthy,*' etc.
[5] beneficiis afficere.
[6] ' *That which* (id quod) *many other consuls had relinquished without success* ' (re infecta).   [7] uterque Africanus.
[8] ' *and had not* '=nec.   [9] commovere.   [10] ne dicam omnes.

CONCESSIVE CLAUSES

Rule 29. **Concessive Clauses have their verb** (*a*) **in the Indicative when what is conceded is allowed to be a fact ;** (*b*) **in the Subjunctive if it is only conceded as a hypothesis for argument's sake.**

Quamvis, licet, cum, ut are only to be used with SUBJUNCTIVE.

Quanquam is only to be used with INDICATIVE.

Etsi, etiamsi, tametsi may be used with either according to meaning.

EXAMPLES

(*a*) Romani **quanquam** fessi **erant** procedunt.
  The Romans advanced in spite of being tired.
  Cur nolint, **etiamsi tacent**, satis dicunt.
  Though they are silent they show clearly why they are unwilling.

(*b*) Quod turpe est, id, **quamvis occultetur,** tamen honestum fieri nullo modo potest.
  What is base cannot be made honourable, however much it be disguised.

  Rectum est, **etiamsi** nobis indigna **audiamus,** iracundiam repellere.
  It is right to restrain our passions, even though we should hear things that we resent (*things unworthy of us*).

Exercise 223 [A]

1. Although they were not convicted of treason, they inflicted great injury on the state.

2. Even if you denied this, no one would believe you.

3. However [1] great the numbers of the enemy may be, we must not despair.

4. Knowing, as they did, that their plans were discovered, they still pretended to be innocent.

5. I am willing that you should do this, though I should not have done it myself.

6. Although the general had won many successes, he was disliked by his troops.

7. I am resolved to tell the truth, even if my enemies threaten me with death.

8. Although Caesar had already borrowed [2] immense sums, men still trusted him.

9. Although he had deceived me five times, I should still [3] have trusted him.

10. I should be quite contented even if I had to go into exile for a little time.

Exercise 224 [A]

1. Though he were to offer me a great price, I should not sell the farm.

2. We must get to Rome to-day, however [1] many obstacles hinder us.

3. Though I know very well he is guilty, I shall do my best to acquit him.

4. Great though his army may be, he will not risk all on one battle.

---

[1] quamvis.   [2] mutuari.   [3] nihilo minus, *or* nihilo secius.

G

5. Even if he were chieftain of all Gaul, I would not spare him.

6. Though he was the richest man in all this country,[1] he gave little money to the poor.

7. Though the gods are on our side, we shall need the sword.

8. Though they were my best legions, I should send them back to Pompey.

9. Caesar sent back the two legions Pompey had sent him, though they were the best he had.

10. However great my peril was, I should not try to avoid it in such a cause.

Exercise 225 [B]

1. Any one can remain silent, even if he is angry.

2. They had resolved to remain silent, however many tortures might be inflicted upon them.

3. They held out for some time, although they knew that there was no hope of safety.

4. Believing, as I do,[2] that you wish to serve me, yet I cannot accept your help.

5. I should never believe you, although you bound yourself by an oath.

6. At this crisis the allies deserted, though they had promised to remain faithful.

7. We shall still be soldiers, even if the army is disbanded.

8. The battle raged fiercely for a long time, although we were greatly inferior to the enemy in numbers.

9. You ought not to say such things in the presence of others, however true you may believe them to be.

10. Although he tried to conceal his indignation, there is no doubt that he was annoyed at this.

---

[1] regio. [2] =although I believe.

Exercise 226 [B]

1. Although they had long been living in a foreign land, they observed the customs of their ancestors.

2. They refused to do this, though it was to their own advantage.

3. We will not yield to the enemy, however large their forces may be.

4. Although they were inferior to the enemy in numbers, they held their ground resolutely.

5. Clever as he was, he could not deceive us.

6. I cannot trust him, in spite of his promising to keep his word.

7. Although they were so poor, we could not offer them help.

8. Great as a general's power may be, he is always responsible to the government.

9. Even should they be brought to trial, they would without doubt be acquitted.

10. They were led out to execution,[1] in spite of the general's promise to spare their lives.

---

[1] ad necem.

Exercise 227 [A]

Although Lucullus had won many successes, he was unable
to bring the war with Mithridates to a close. The king,
after defeating Triarius in a pitched battle at Zela, had
retreated to the mountains, satisfied with his success, and
Lucullus gave orders for pursuit. But however desirous he
might himself be of capturing the king, he found his men
unwilling to follow him. Most of them had been absent
from Italy for nearly twenty years, and since Lucullus had
taken the command, they had suffered great hardships.
Lucullus, though a good general, had none of that geniality
which wins the affection of soldiers, and moreover he had
been living in great luxury, though his soldiers often suffered
from want. The result was that the army agreed to defend
Pontus from Mithridates, but positively refused to undertake
a new campaign.[1]

Exercise 228 [A]

Though the army opposed to Caesar had been much more
numerous he would nevertheless have come out of this
campaign victorious. The discipline and experience of his
soldiers were such that, although fortune might be adverse,
they never lost heart. This appeared especially in the war
round Dyrrhachium. Though the lines which they had con-
structed with so much trouble were assailed and the defenders
driven out of them, there was no panic, nor did the soldiers
scatter in flight in all directions over the country; but those
who survived the defeat kept together, and retreated [2] along
the road which led into the mountains. Next day Caesar had
again an army, which, though [3] diminished, was prepared to
face all dangers manfully.

---

[1] *war.*   [2] *retreated in close order.*

[3] Of the Concessive Conjunctions *quamvis* is most frequently used
where the verb is omitted.

Exercise 229 [B]

However men may differ as to Napoleon's character, there can be no doubt that he acquired a wonderful influence over [1] his soldiers. If they sometimes grumbled at his orders in private,[2] yet, when he led them to battle, there was not a man who was not ready to risk his life for him. They did this,[3] although it was evident that he for his part never tried to spare the lives of his men, but was resolved to crush the enemy, however great the losses on his own side [4] might be. Thus it happened that France came off victorious in so many conflicts, although she was opposed by many powerful enemies at the same time.

Exercise 230 [B]

The determination of the Athenians remained unshaken, in spite of the desertion of so many of the Greek States. They readily granted to the Spartans the supreme command of the forces by sea as well as by land, although they themselves furnished two-thirds of the entire fleet. The great Themistocles tried to inspire the other Greeks with some of the enthusiasm which he had aroused in the Athenians. Had he not displayed as much wisdom as valour, the cause of Greek freedom would have been lost. By his advice the confederates [5] bound themselves to resist to the death, and in case of success [6] to consecrate to the Delphian god a tenth part of the property of all Grecian States which had surrendered to the Persians of their own accord.

---

[1] apud. [2] say ' *secretly*.'

[3] Translate ' idque ' (omitting ' *they did* '). Cf. καὶ ταῦτα.

[4] *of his own men.* [5] *allies.* [6] *if things happened well.*

COMPARATIVE CLAUSES

Rule 30. **When the Comparative Clause is meant to state an actual fact its verb is in the Indicative; but when it is a purely imaginary comparison the verb is in the Subjunctive.**

In the first case the commonest words of comparison used are : sicut (just as), perinde ac (exactly as), aeque ac (as much as), aliter ac (otherwise than), alius ac (different from), idem ac (the same as).

In the second case the commonest are : velut, quasi, tanquam (si).

EXAMPLES

Poenas dedit **sicut meritus est.**
He was punished as he deserved.

Absentis Ariovisti crudelitatem **quasi** coram **adesset** horrebant.
They dreaded the cruelty of Ariovistus in his absence just as if he had been present.

Virtus **eadem** in homine **ac** deo **est.**
Virtue is the same in man as in God.

Exercise 231 [_A_]

1. He behaved just as if he were mad.

2. He was rewarded just as he deserved.

3. He fought as if the safety of the State depended on him alone.

4. I foresaw it all, just as it happened.

5. As you thought, his only object was [1] to deceive us.

6. He governs the State, not as circumstances demand, but as if he were setting an example to the rest of mankind.

7. He is not quite so devoted to us as you think.

8. His performance does not agree with his promise.

---

[1] id solum egit ut.

9. While [1] I value my own safety a great deal, I value that of the State a great deal more.

10. I envy you as being free from all cares of State.

11. As might be expected [2] in such times, it was long doubtful which side would conquer.

12. As often happens, he was tired of his task before he had finished it.

Exercise 232 [B]

1. They rushed into the river as if they were mad.

2. Our men have been defeated, just as I foretold.

3. It is our duty to treat others just as we wish them to treat us.

4. It was observed that he often turned round as if some one were pursuing him.

5. Considering their difficult position,[3] they acted as wisely as they could.

6. Seeing is a different thing from believing.

7. There is no doubt that we have less leisure than our ancestors.

8. Their actions were not always in accordance with their promises.

9. They joined battle, as if they had no fear of defeat.

10. The Greeks were not distinguished by the same virtues as the Romans.

11. He threw himself into the river, as if he really wished to save his enemy.

12. As was to be expected at such a crisis,[3] the general was the only man who remained unmoved.

---

[1] Contrast the clauses by ut . . . ita, or by cum . . . tum. These should often be used for *both . . . and* or *not only . . . but also*, where one sentence is to be emphasised more than the other.

[2] 'ut' only. Cf. satis impavidus ut in re trepida, '*keeping presence of mind as much as could be expected in such a panic.*'

[3] ut in tanto discrimine.

Exercise 233 [A]

At the battle of Zama Hannibal showed the same resolution
and the same skill in drawing up his line as he had shown
fourteen years before at the battle of Cannae. But fortune
was against him, and he went into the battle as if he himself
knew it. The elephants, which before had often been a source
of safety to the Carthaginians, now frightened by the shouting
of the Romans, turned upon their own army, and threw the
first line into confusion. The mercenaries formed [1] the first
line, and, as they fell back, the Carthaginians, drawn up in
the second line, would not admit them through their ranks,
and even charged them as if they were the enemy. This
was not contrary to Hannibal's expectations. He ordered the
third line, his veterans brought from Italy, to charge and
drive the disorderly rabble off the field. Then at length the
battle with the Romans was renewed.

Exercise 234 [A]

The messengers, as they had been commanded, informed the
people that in three days they must leave their homes and
depart to another place. These at first made no answer, as if
they did not understand what was demanded of them. But the
chieftain, who under the circumstances showed great presence
of mind, asked the messengers to explain more clearly the
reason for this demand. The latter replied that they were
only acting in accordance with the orders they had received.
Then from the whole village arose loud cries and groans, as
if they had undergone sentence of death ; and one and all
crowded around the messengers, with as much fury and indignation as they could have shown if those men had themselves
been responsible for their sufferings.

---

[1] consistere in.

Exercise 235 [B]

Antiochus had invaded Egypt at the beginning of spring. But it happened just as some of his followers had foretold. As soon as he approached Alexandria a Roman ambassador, Popilius, met him, and handed him a letter from the Senate. The king read it, and replied that he would call his friends to a council and consider it ; but Popilius with his staff drew a line round [1] the king, and bade him not move from the spot before he had given him an answer. Nor did he reply to any of the questions which the king asked him, but stood silent as if he did not hear ; until the king, frightened by the ambassador's boldness, promised to do what the Senate decreed. In like manner, wherever Romans went, they acted as if to them belonged the empire of the world.

Exercise 236 [B]

On hearing that he had been proscribed by Antony, Cicero fled for refuge to his villa,[2] which was close by the sea, and got on board a ship with the intention of crossing over into Macedonia. He put out several times, but was driven back by adverse winds, and at last returned to his villa, declaring that he would die in the country which he had so often saved. He went to bed, and slept well considering his critical position. His slaves, however, as if foreseeing his danger, aroused him, and placing him in a litter carried him through the woods towards the sea. He was soon overtaken by the soldiers, who had been sent in pursuit of him ; and when they came up he forbade his slaves to offer any resistance, and stretching his neck out of the litter bade the soldiers complete their work.

---

[1] circumscribere.   [2] villa.

ORATIO OBLIQUA

Rule **31.** In Latin it is much commoner than in English to report a long speech not in the exact words of the speaker, but in the Indirect form, or **Oratio Obliqua.** Each clause in this will be either an Indirect Statement, or an Indirect Command, or an Indirect Question, or a clause dependent on one of these ; and the mood and tense must be determined by the rules already given.[1]

But observe—

(1) The Oratio Obliqua being continuous, the verb of ' saying ' which introduces it is not to be repeated before each clause, and a verb of command or questioning may be understood from one of saying and *vice versâ*.

(2) Where a command comes in the middle of Oratio Obliqua the *ut* is not expressed, though if it is a prohibition the *ne* must be expressed.

(3) Questions in Oratio Obliqua may be expressed by the Infinitive when they are asked for rhetorical purposes, and not to obtain an answer, and are practically equivalent to negative statements. Questions which in the direct form are in the 1st or 3rd Person are generally rhetorical.

e.g. the following are rhetorical questions : ' *Am I a coward that I should fly without striking a blow ?* ' ' *Is freedom a possession to be lightly esteemed ?* ' (Num libertatem parvi aestimandam esse ?)

---

[1] For Indirect Statement, see pp. 38, 42 ; for Indirect Command, p. 62 ; for Indirect Question, p. 88 ; for clauses dependent on these, p. 96 ; and for the Sequence of Tenses, p. 2.

(4) All *pronouns* representing the 1st and 2nd Persons must be changed into the 3rd Person.

e.g. ego, meus, nos, noster, become se, suus.[1]

tu, tuus, vos, vester, become ille, illius, is, ejus, etc.

hic and iste become ille and is.

Adverbs require similar changes :

hodie becomes illo die.

hic becomes ibi.

nunc becomes jam or tunc.

The following example will illustrate these points :

' The general asked his men why they hesitated, and urged them to advance at once. He reminded them that everything depended on their bravery, and declared that if they shirked the battle they would disgrace him and their country. Was it credible, he demanded, that he was addressing the same men who had so often defeated the enemy ? '

' Imperator suos interrogavit cur haesitarent : statim progrederentur, omnia enim in illorum virtute esse posita ; quodsi pugnam detrectassent illos dedecori fore et sibi et patriae. Num credibile esse se eosdem adloqui qui hostem toties vicissent ? '

Notice here that the English verbs ' urged,' ' reminded,' ' declared,' ' demanded,' are all understood in Latin from the one introductory word ' interrogavit ' ; that the command ' progrederentur ' is expressed without the *ut ;* and that the Infinitive ' esse ' represents a rhetorical question.

Notice also that the Pluperfect ' detrectassent ' stands for the Future Perfect of the Direct Speech.

---

[1] Se and suus represent either the speaker alone or the speaker and the people addressed, where the speaker identifies himself with them.

ORATIO RECTA	ORATIO OBLIQUA
Quod si veteris contumeliae oblivisci *vellem,* num etiam recentium injuriarum, quod *me* invito iter per provinciam per vim *tentavistis,* memoriam deponere *possum* ?	His Caesar ita respondit : Quod si veteris contumeliae oblivisci *vellet,* num etiam recentium injuriarum, quod *se* invito iter per provinciam per vim *tentavissent,* memoriam deponere *posse* ?

But if I were willing to forget the old insult, can I also put aside the memory of more recent wrongs, inasmuch as against my will you forced a way through the Roman province ?

N.B.—Here, as the form of the conditional *si vellet* shows, the infinitive *posse* implies negation, and the question is rhetorical.

ORATIO RECTA	ORATIO OBLIQUA
Ariovistus me consule cupidissime populi Romani amicitiam *appetiit :* cur *hunc* tam temere quisquam ab officio discessurum *judicat* ? *Mihi* quidem *persuadetur,* cognitis *meis* postulatis, eum neque *meam* neque populi Romani gratiam repudiaturum. Quod si furore atque amentia impulsus bellum *intulerit,* quid tandem *veremini* ? aut cur de *nostra* virtute aut de *mea* diligentia *desperatis* ?	Dixit—*Ariovistum se* consule cupidissime populi Romani amicitiam *appetisse :* cur *illum* tam temere quisquam ab officio discessurum *judicaret* ? *Sibi* quidem *persuaderi,* cognitis *suis* postulatis, eum neque *suam* neque populi Romani gratiam repudiaturum. Quod si furore atque amentia impulsus bellum *intulisset,* quid tandem *vererentur* ? aut cur de *sua* virtute aut de *ipsius* diligentia *desperarent* ?

During my consulship Ariovistus most earnestly coveted the friendship of the Roman people. Why does any one suppose that he will so hastily cast off his allegiance ? For my part I am convinced that when he is acquainted with my demands he will not slight either my favour or that of the Roman people. But if under the impulse of rage and madness he does wage war upon us, why, I ask, are you afraid ? or why do you doubt either our courage or my diligence ?

ORATIO RECTA

Si pacem populus Romanus cum Helvetiis *faciet,* in eam partem *ibunt* atque ibi *erunt Helvetii* ubi eos *constituisti*; sin bello persequi *perseverabis, reminiscere* veteris incommodi populi Romani. Quod improviso unum pagum *adortus es* cum ii, qui flumen *transierant* suis auxilium ferre non possent, ne ob *hanc* rem *tuae* magnopere virtuti *tribueris* neve *nos despexeris.*

ORATIO OBLIQUA

Is ita cum Caesare egit : si pacem populus Romanus cum Helvetiis *faceret,* in eam partem *ituros* atque ibi *futuros Helvetios,* ubi eos *Caesar constituisset*; sin bello persequi *perseveraret, reminisceretur* veteris incommodi populi Romani. Quod improviso unum pagum *adortus esset* cum ii, qui flumen *transiissent,* suis auxilium ferre non possent, ne ob *eam* rem *suae* magnopere virtuti *tribueret,* neve *se ipsos despiceret.*

If the people of Rome make peace with the Helvetii, the Helvetii will go to that part of the country which you have assigned to them, and will remain there. But should you persist in harrying them with war—remember the former disaster which befell the Roman people. As to the fact of your having fallen unexpectedly upon a single canton, when those who had crossed the river could not bring help to their friends, do not on this account think too highly of your own valour, or treat us with scorn.

Exercise 237 [A]

Put into Oratio Obliqua after a verb in a Historic tense :—

1. Deliver up to me the hostages I demanded.
2. Why did they refuse to follow him ?
3. I do not wish to betray these men who are under my protection.
4. Do you suppose that you alone know this ?
5. If you do this, all men will praise you.
6. If they had followed us, they would have reached [1] the city in safety.
7. Let us advance to attack the enemy.
8. Follow me, fellow-soldiers, and we shall easily overcome the enemy.
9. We ought not always to consult our own interests.
10. They were prevented by a storm from reaching the harbour.
11. To-day we have won a great victory.

Exercise 238 [B]

1. Why did you persuade the allies to revolt ?
2. Let us depart at once, and never return to this place.
3. I told you before what the result of the battle would be.
4. Give me what I asked you for, and I will depart.
5. When do you suppose that the reinforcements, for which we are waiting, will arrive ?
6. We have stormed the walls, but the citadel is not in our hands.
7. Friends, let us not despair of safety.
8. You ought to have sent us help more quickly.
9. Was he mad to say such things ?
10. If this is true, I refuse to help you any longer.
11. Unless help had arrived, all the citizens would have died of starvation.

---

[1] perventuros fuisse. The Future Participle with fuisse always represents the English *would have* . . . in Indirect Statement.

Exercise 239 [A]

Put into Oratio Obliqua after a verb in a Historic tense :—

1. Why have you invaded my country ?
2. Return to your own country.
3. The Carthaginians attacked us and 700 of their own men, 200 of ours, were killed.
4. Let us not forget the wrongs of our allies, but avenge them speedily.
5. You have shown to-day more valour than they.
6. When we return to Rome we will inquire into this.
7. I cannot help you now. If you come to-morrow I will consider what I can do.
8. Three days ago we could have left the camp, now we are compelled to stay here whether we will or not.
9. Camillus, your fellow-citizens beg and pray you to return and save the state.
10. If you stay in my house you will certainly be attacked by these men.

Exercise 240 [B]

1. Where can we stay to-night ?
2. I am not sure that I shall reach you in time.
3. The two legions which I had I have sent to Pompey.
4. Here there is no safety either for me or for you.
5. If he kept his word he would be here now.
6. Let us all remember that liberty depends for us on this one battle.
7. Never give away your money to a man you do not know.
8. It is not easy, my friend, to think of the interests of [1] your fellow-citizens and at the same time of your own.
9. Is my friend to be neglected because he is away ?
10. Why should I humour a man who is my father's freedman ?

---

[1] consulere, *dat.*

Exercise 241 [A]

Labienus was the next to speak, and he expressed contempt for Caesar's forces. They must not imagine, he said, that this was the army which conquered Gaul and Germany. He was present himself at the battles fought in those countries, and was not rashly stating facts beyond his knowledge.[1] A very small fraction of that army survived. Many had been destroyed by pestilence, many had gone home. Had they not heard that regiments had been manufactured [2] at Brundisium out of the wounded that had been left behind ? The forces which they saw before them were raw recruits, and most of them came from colonies beyond the Po. Moreover the flower of the army had perished in the two engagements at Dyrrhachium. He himself finally would swear never to return to the camp unless victorious; let all the rest follow his example.

Exercise 242 [A]

According to the historian Livy,[3] Appius declared to the assembled Senate that he wished he was deaf so that he might not hear the disgraceful counsels which were that day dishonouring the Roman name. He greatly regretted, he said, their change of temper ; it was very different from the temper of former days. Whither had their pride and courage fled ? Had they not once boasted that they would have opposed Alexander himself if in the period of their youth he had dared to invade Italy ? Let them not now deliver up to Lucanians and wretched Greeks [4] what their fathers had won by the sword.

---

[1] *which he had not ascertained.*   [2] *made.*

[3] Apud Livium scriptum invenimus.

[4] Graeculus, the diminutive expressing contempt.

Exercise 243 [A]

The terms of peace, heavy though they were, were only such as they expected under the circumstances ;[1] and Hannibal dragged down with his own hands from the rostrum an orator who was recommending the continuance of the war. The people were indignant with Hannibal for thus infringing upon their liberty of speech ; but Hannibal replied that they must forgive him if, after serving thirty-six years in the camp, he had forgotten the manners of the forum. Livy relates that the terms agreed upon by Scipio and the Carthaginian government were then referred to the Senate at Rome, and were accepted by them, both because they felt that they were sufficiently severe, and also because they feared that if they rejected them the Carthaginians would renew the war.

Exercise 244 [A]

The general then summoned a council of war and spoke thus : (Or. Obl.) ' We must now decide whether it is to our advantage to hold our position or to retreat while we still have the opportunity. The reinforcements, which we have so long expected, have not arrived ; and for my part I believe we are no match for the enemy. But I know we can trust the courage and endurance of our men, and if it is your wish, I am prepared to hold out as long as possible. Tell me plainly your opinion, for I shall do nothing without your approval.' When the general had finished his speech, many different opinions were expressed ; but at length it was decided that, considering the numbers of the enemy, it would be wiser to retreat and not to run the risk of a severe defeat.

---

[1] in tali re.

Exercise 245 [A]

Caesar, when the report of the Senate's action reached him, addressed his soldiers. He told them what the Senate had done, and why they had done it. ' For nine years he and his army had served their country loyally, and had won many victories. They had driven the Germans over the Rhine; they had made Gaul a Roman province ; and the Senate had now broken the laws of the state, and had deposed the tribunes because they spoke in his defence. They had declared that the state was in danger, and had called Italy to arms, when he himself had in nowise injured them.' The soldiers whom Pompey supposed disaffected, declared with one consent that they would follow their commander and the tribunes. In all the army only one officer proved false.

Exercise 246 [A]

When Sulla had overcome his enemies and assumed supreme power, he assembled the Senate and demanded with the utmost eagerness that Caius Marius should at once be declared an enemy to the state. No one dared to oppose him until Scaevola, on being questioned, refused to express an opinion. When, however, Sulla repeatedly asked him in a threatening voice to give his opinion, at length he replied, (*Or. Obl.*) ' You may show me the troops of soldiers with which you have surrounded the senate house ; you may threaten me with death again and again ; but you will never compel me to say that Marius, by whom the Roman state was saved, is an enemy to Rome.'

Exercise 247 [A]

There are men in our times who seem to desire not only to change the laws (which[1] perhaps would be a laudable desire[2]), but to upset the whole state.[3] I was listening to one such yesterday as he addressed a crowd of artisans in the forum. (*Or. Obl.*) ' Who is it,' he asked them, ' that oppresses us ? Who is it for whom we pile up wealth, while we want ourselves money to buy food ? You yourselves can answer (the question), nor is there any need for me to tell you. Our senators have the power to prevent good laws being carried, and M. Crassus buys the consulship every year for himself and his friends. Fellow-citizens,[4] there is only one remedy—let us drive them from the city. Let us teach them by fire and bloodshed how great a wrong they have done to the people.'

Exercise 248 [A]

Three days after the setting out of the troops from Rome the gloomy intelligence arrived that the enemy, after having utterly routed the Roman army on the 12th of March, were now in possession of the city of Corioli, and all the territory and other property of the allies. (*Or. Obl.*) ' I am the only man,' said the messenger, ' who has survived the battle. The enemy, flushed with recent victory, are coming in, and must[5] even now be not more than three miles from the city. So savage is their temper, that I am sure no one, however old and infirm, will be spared.' Having heard this the Senate determined at once to send envoys to meet the enemy on their approach, with the intention of suing for peace.

---

[1] id quod.　　　[2] *worthy of praise.*　　　[3] rempublicam evertere.
[4] A Vocative in the middle of a speech will usually be simply omitted in Oratio Obliqua.
[5] Use ' sine dubio.'

Exercise 249 [B]

He had now won a decisive victory, and it seemed certain
that the campaign would shortly be brought to a successful
issue, when all his hopes were dashed to the ground [1] by the
refusal of his troops to continue the war.　They declared that
they were worn out with the hardships of the campaign, and
that the prospect [2] of bringing the war to an end seemed as
distant as ever.　Why, they asked, must they leave their
country and all that was dear to them and undergo every kind
of suffering that their general might win the glory of a barren
victory ?　They asserted that, even if they pursued the enemy,
they would be unable to overtake them in their mountain fast-
nesses, while even the victories which they had already won
had been purchased at the cost of much Roman blood.

Exercise 250 [B]

The general replied that no one could be more anxious than
himself to consult the interests of his men ; but he reminded
them how foolish it was to lose the advantages of a victory
wellnigh assured.　They must not think, he said, that he had
undertaken this campaign merely in the hope of winning glory
for himself.　They would share equally with him in the fruits
of victory, and if once the enemy were crushed, they might
return home enriched with spoils taken from the enemy.　He
also pointed out that though the enemy were seeking refuge
in the mountains, they had not yet reached them, and that if
an immediate advance were made, it would be easy to overtake
them before they reached a place of safety.

---

[1] perdo.　　　　　　　　　　[2] spes.

Exercise 251 [B]

Turn into Oratio Obliqua after a Historic tense :—

Do not believe what is commonly asserted in the city,
that I am seeking the consulship for the sake of a province
and the wealth that many of our senators steal from the
subject states of Rome. Can you think that I, who was once
the dear friend of Cato, am so changed in mind ? Indeed, I
had rather give up all hope of office than involve myself in
such disgrace. I have heard recently that the publicani of
Cilicia asked our friend Cicero to give them his legionaries
to collect the taxes with. He refused at first, but afterwards
was prevailed upon. If they were not Romans the very
soldiers would refuse to take part in such cruel work. But
let us try to devote ourselves to philosophy, and forget evils
which we cannot cure.

Exercise 252 [B]

On this night the king gathered round him his little band
of followers, and in a few words said farewell to them.
(*Or. Obl.*) ' Gentlemen,' [1] he said, ' your fortune has so long
been linked with mine that the word which I speak to-night
nothing but the last necessity forces me to utter. If there
were yet a hope, I would still make use of your loyalty and
your aid. Do not think that I value these lightly. You are
the few who, having enjoyed with me the times of prosperity,
refused to desert me in adversity. And for this I thank you.
But permit me now to think of your safety, for the sake of
which I shall to-morrow give myself up. Why should I destroy
you with myself ? When the rebels have me in their hands
they will perhaps leave you free to escape whither you will.'

---

[1] Omit the Vocative. See note 4, p. 191.

Exercise 253 [B]

Hearing of these immense numbers, Robert Guiscard assembled a council of his principal officers. (*Or. Obl.*) 'You behold,' said he, ' your danger : you see how urgent [1] it is. The hills are covered with arms and standards ; and the Emperor of the Greeks is accustomed to wars and triumphs. Union is our only safety.[2] Only bid me, and I am ready at once to yield the command to a worthier leader.' The acclamation even of his foes assured him at this perilous moment of their confidence ; [3] and he thus continued, (*Or. Obl.*) ' Let us trust in the reward of victory, and let us not leave cowards the means [4] of escape. Burn your vessels and your baggage, and give battle on this spot.' This resolution was unanimously approved, and Guiscard awaited in battle array the approach of the enemy. Perhaps he was not conscious that on the same ground Caesar and Pompey had formerly disputed the empire of the world.

Exercise 254 [B]

Turn into Oratio Obliqua after a Historic tense :—

I might have gone to Spain, where I should have had my brother to share my labours, and Hasdrubal instead of Hannibal for my foe. But hearing as I sailed along the coast of the arrival of the enemy in Gaul, I landed immediately, sent on my cavalry before, and moved my camp up to the Rhone. I am anxious to try whether Carthage in the last [5] twenty years has produced a new race of citizens, or whether these are the same men whom we held so cheap when we let them go from Eryx. Would that this contest were for honour merely, not for very life ! But you are fighting for Italy itself, and for your homes ; nor is there another army in your rear to bar the enemy's way if you fail [6] to conquer him. Let each one of you consider that the Senate is watching him, and that the fate of Rome depends upon his valour.

---

[1] Use verb.   [2] *our safety depends on our union.*
[3] *Even his private enemies showed by their applause that they trusted him.*   [4] locus or facultas.   [5] his.   [6] Use nisi.

Exercise 255 [A]

Meanwhile the Carthaginians, knowing the weakness of
their naval force at Lilybaeum, and fully conscious that the
place would not hold out unless they sent help, resolved to
despatch troops at once. Hannibal, son of Hamilcar, was
despatched with all haste to Sicily with fifty ships and 10,000
troops. He moved his fleet among the Aegatian islands
opposite to Lilybaeum, waiting the moment when he should
be able to pass the rocks and reefs that girt the harbour. At
length a favourable wind sprang up. He set sail, and, massing
his troops on deck to be ready for an engagement, with a
boldness that deserved success he made his way safely through
the narrow entrance. In the meanwhile the Roman ships
remained at anchor close by, the sailors looking on aghast at
his rashness, and expecting to see him dashed against the rocks.

Exercise 256 [B]

The fight was fierce and tumultuous. The assailants were
repulsed in their first attack, and several of their bravest
officers were shot down in the act of storming the fortress
sword in hand. The assault was renewed with greater success.
The Indians were driven from one post to another. They
disputed their ground inch by inch,[1] fighting with the utmost
fury. Most of their veterans were cut to pieces, and after a
long and bloody battle Philip and Canonchet, with a handful
of surviving warriors, retreated from the fort and took refuge in
the thickets of the neighbouring forest. The victors set fire to
the wigwams and forts ; the whole was soon in a blaze ; many of
the old men, the women, and the children, perished in the flames.

---

[1] pedem gradatim rettulerunt.

THE ORDER OF WORDS

IN THE SIMPLE SENTENCE

1. Normal Order. A word receives most emphasis when placed at the beginning or end of a sentence, therefore in an ordinary Latin sentence place the Subject first and the Predicate last.

N.B.—By the Predicate we do not mean necessarily the *Verb*. When the verb *esse* is used with Adjectives or Participles it need not take the last place.

2. The middle of a single sentence must be arranged on this principle : Expressions which naturally qualify the subject (generally adjectives or adjectival expressions) must be grouped near the subject, expressions which qualify the predicate (objects, adverbial and prepositional expressions) must be grouped before the verb.

3. Before the subject, however, will naturally come any words which connect with the preceding sentence; *e.g.* relatives, expressions of time, etc. It is exceedingly important to remember that Latin sentences do not usually follow one another without *some* expressed connection. In English we constantly leave the connection to be understood from the general sense.

Thus a Latin simple sentence, in which there is no need

to emphasise particular words, will usually be arranged in this order :

> (1) Connecting words.
> (2) Subject.
> (3) Attributes of Subject.
> (4) Objects and attributes of the Objects.
> (5) Adverbial expressions qualifying Predicate.
> (6) Predicate.

Postero die mane | [1] Servilius consul cum omnibus copiis | flumen quam celerrime transit.

Early next day the consul Servilius with all his forces crosses the river as speedily as possible.

Quibus rebus auditis | dux hostium, vir magna belli peritia, | suos ex castello se recipere jubet.

When he heard this news the leader of the enemy, who had gained experience in many wars, ordered his men to leave the fort.

4. Special Emphasis. To emphasise any special word it must be placed out of its usual position. The Predicate is most emphasised by being placed first, the Subject by being placed last or nearly last. Any other word will be emphasised by taking either of these positions. An attribute separated from its noun, or an adverb separated from its verb, is thereby emphasised.

> **Habet** senectus magnam auctoritatem.
> *Old age* **certainly has** *great influence.*
> Hac clade periit **libertas.**
> **It was liberty that perished** *in this disaster.*

---

[1] The above sentences are divided by lines into (1) Connecting words, (2) those parts which naturally go with the subject, (3) those that go with the predicate. The connection in thought between two sentences is most frequently one of time or place ; *e.g. postero die* in the first sentence.

Recte igitur deos esse diximus.
We were right in saying *that there are gods.*

Exempla proponamus illi **optima.**
Let the examples we set before him be the best.

In English also we can sometimes emphasise by order ; *e.g.* ' *A friend* I am unwilling to accuse.' But we more often put the emphatic words in a clause by themselves, as in the last three examples given above. Compare ' *It is not often that* a rich man envies the poor' with the Latin ' *Haud saepe* invidet pauperibus dives,' where the necessary emphasis on ' not often ' is given by position.

5. **Attributes,** etc. An adjective more often follows than precedes its noun, and a slight emphasis is often given by placing it first.

e.g. Vir bonus ac sapiens.
A good and wise man.
Bonum ac sapientem virum fingimus.
It is the good and wise man that we are describing.

Nouns in apposition generally follow the noun to which they are attached. If they precede it they are thereby emphasised.

e.g. Lemnos insula = the island of Lemnos.
Insula Lemnos = the *island* Lemnos (as opposed to the *town*).
Servilius consul = the consul Servilius.
Consul Servilius = Servilius *when consul,* or *as consul.*

Where there is both an attribute and some defining phrase (a case or a prepositional phrase) put the latter between the attribute and the noun.

e.g. Multa **tua** erga me beneficia.
Your many kindnesses to me.
Filius patri similis.
A son like his father.

THE COMPOUND SENTENCE

6. The Compound sentence consists of a Principal Clause
and Subordinate Clauses. The Subordinate Clauses all stand
in some relation to the principal verb or its subject, being
equivalent to nouns, adjectives, or adverbs ; and they will for
the most part fall into the places that these would have
occupied if the sentence had been simple. Compare, for
instance, the following sentences :

SIMPLE.	COMPOUND.
Quibus rebus auditis,	Quae cum audiisset,
Iberorum dux,	Iberorum dux,
vir magna belli peritia,	qui bellorum peritissimus erat
collectis omnibus copiis,	cum omnes copias collegisset,
impediendi causa Romanos,	ne Romani celerius advenirent,
pontem	pontem rescindi
rescindit.	jubet.

Hearing this, the Iberian leader, a man of great experience in warfare, collected all his forces, and broke down the bridge in order to delay the Romans.

When the Iberian leader, who had had great experience in warfare, heard this, he collected all his forces, and ordered the bridge to be broken down, so as to delay the Romans' advance.

The main principle therefore of the Compound Sentence is
that the subordinate parts of the sentence are **enclosed** between
the subject, which must stand near the beginning, and the
principal verb, which will most frequently come at the end.
The order of clauses will therefore naturally be as follows :

(1) Any clause which connects with the previous sentence.
(2) The subject followed by any attributive clauses which
belong to it.

(3) Any clauses which naturally belong to the Predicate—
(*a*) Adverbial clauses of *time*, etc. ; (*b*) Object clauses, such as Acc. and Inf., Indirect Questions or Commands.

(4) The Predicate.

Quod cum vidisset dux, quia quid hostis paret nescit, paullum moratur.

Seeing this, the general delayed a little time, because he did not know what the enemy was preparing to do.

Reliquis diebus Caesar, ne qui inermibus militibus impetus fieri posset, omnem eam materiam, quae erat caesa, conversam ad hostem conlocabat.

During the remaining days Caesar piled up facing the enemy all the timber that had been cut, so that no attack might be made on his men when unarmed.

Tamen Senones, quae est civitas imprimis firma et magnae inter Gallos auctoritatis, Cavarinum, quem Caesar apud eos regem constituerat, interficere publico consilio conati, cum ille praesensisset ac profugisset, usque ad fines insecuti regno domoque expulerunt.

Nevertheless the Senones, who are the strongest and most influential tribe among the Gauls, tried to kill Cavarinus, whom Caesar had made king among them, and when he found out the plot and fled, pursued him as far as their boundaries, and drove him from his kingdom and home.

But these principles will be modified by many considerations of (*a*) Emphasis, (*b*) Logical Arrangement, (*c*) Sound. No system of rules can take the place of observation in reading, but the following suggestions may be added.

(*a*) **Emphasis.** As in the Simple Sentence, the beginning and end are emphatic positions, and a subordinate clause may be emphasised by being placed in one of these positions. It often happens that the verb which is grammatically the principal verb is not the important part of the predicate, and in that case it will not come last. This is especially frequent with the verb of ' saying ' that introduces Oratio Obliqua, which is not as a rule kept to the end of the sentence.

e.g. Eo cum de improviso celeriusque omni opinione venisset, Remi, qui proximi Galliae ex Belgis sunt, ad eum legatos miserunt qui dicerent se suaque omnia in fidem atque in potestatem populi Romani permittere.

But Caesar arriving there suddenly and sooner than any one had expected, the Remi, who are the nearest to Gaul of the Belgian tribes, sent him ambassadors to say that they surrendered themselves and all they possessed to the sway and authority of the Roman people.

In this sentence *miserunt* is the principal verb, and *dicerent* the main verb of the subordinate clause, but neither contains the main statement of the sentence, and therefore neither stands last. The object of the sentence is to give the message of the Remi ' se . . . permittere.' It is a common mistake of beginners to think they must write ' legatos qui se . . . permittere dicerent miserunt.'

For the same reason a Purpose Clause or Causal Clause will stand last, if to state the Purpose or Cause is the real object of the sentence ; *i.e.* if it is more emphatic than the statement of the Principal Verb. Compare the following :

> He said it to frighten me.
> *Haec dixit ut me terreret.*
>
> He threatened me with torture to frighten me.
> *Ut me terreret cruciatum mihi minabatur.*

In the first sentence to state the purpose is the object of the sentence. In the second the principal verb contains the main idea.

(*b*) **Logical arrangement.** It is generally essential to clearness that the statement of *circumstances* (*e.g.* time, place, etc.)

should precede the main statement, and statement of *cause* precede the statement of the effect. For this reason a Consecutive sentence will almost always come after the verb it depends on, though grammatically subordinate.

It also tends to clearness to observe the following :

(1) When the principal verb and subordinate verb have the same subject, do not put the subject, as we do in English, inside the subordinate clause; *e.g.* for ' When Caesar heard this, he returned,' say, ' Caesar, cum haec audiisset, rediit.'

(2) In translating complicated English sentences into Latin avoid the frequent change of subject which we allow in English. The change of Active for Passive will often obviate difficulty.

(*c*) **Sound.** If we followed universally the rule of *enclosing* subordinate clauses, we should find three or four verbs sometimes together at the end of the sentence. Avoid this by altering the arrangement of words in one or more of the clauses.

Avoid generally placing together similar terminations (especially *-orum, -arum*). Avoid also a sentence consisting entirely of words of the same length ; *e.g.* such a combination as ' Erat quondam pastor quidam Gygis regis.'

The sound often helps the sense ; *e.g.* where the writer wishes to describe a series of events rapidly following one another he may use a series of short sentences, even without conjunctions.

e.g. Concilium dimittit, Liscum retinet. Quaerit ex solo ea quae in conventu dixerat. Dicit liberius atque audacius. Eadem secreto ab aliis quaerit ; reperit esse vera.

On dismissing the council he detained Liscus and inquired of him privately about those matters that he had mentioned at the meeting. Liscus spoke then more openly and boldly, and by private inquiries from others Caesar found that his statements were true.

7. Pronouns.

(a) The Relative always comes first in its clause where possible.

e.g. These towns, one of which has been burnt.
    Haec oppida, quorum unum incensum est
        (*never* unum quorum).
    Catiline is here, by whose slaves he was killed.
    Adest Catilina cujus ab servis interfectus est
        (not ab cujus servis).

So quamobrem, qua de causa, quas inter urbes, etc.

But if the relative is used substantivally, the preposition will precede it as a rule—inter quos, ex quibus, etc.

(b) Many adjectives (especially superlatives) and words in apposition are attracted into the Relative clause in Latin contrary to English usage.

e.g. The beautiful city of Corinth, which was destroyed by
    L. Mummius.
    Corinthus quae urbs pulcherrima ab L. Mummio diruta est.

(c) Observe that cases of se, suus, ipse, quisque in the same sentence generally stand next one another.

    e.g. Suae quisque fortunae faber.
        Each man is the maker of his own fortune.
        Sceleris sui sibi conscius.
        Conscious of his guilt.

SPECIAL VOCABULARIES

N.B.—*In these Vocabularies the principal parts of Irregular Verbs are given where they first occur, but are not as a rule repeated afterwards. Verbs of the First Conjugation are distinguished from verbs of the Third by the mark I. Where the construction is not given verbs govern the accusative.*

Exercise 2

go, **eo, ire, ivi, ĭtum.**
city, **urbs, urbis,** *f.*
buy, **ĕmo, emĕre, ēmi, emptum.**
bread, **pānis, -is,** *m.*
see, **vĭdeo, -ēre, vīdi, vīsum.**
home, **dŏmus, -us,** *f.*
friend, **amĭcus, -i.**
ask for, **rŏgo,** I.
peace, **pax, pācis,** *f.*
send, **mitto, mittĕre, misi, missum.**
run, **curro, -ĕre, cŭcurri, cursum.**
fast, quick, **cĕler;** *adv.* **cĕlĕrĭter.**
catch, take, capture, **căpio, -ĕre, cēpi, captum.**
horse, **ĕquus, -i,** *m.*
tired, weary, **fessus, dēfessus.**
sword, **glădius, -i,** *m.*
kill, put to death, **interfĭcio, -ĕre, -fēci, -fectum;** **occīdo, -ĕre, occīdi, occīsum.**
give, **do, dăre, dĕdi, dătum.**
king, **rex, rēgis.**
son, **fīlius, -i.**
204

Exercise 3

retreat, **se rĕcĭpĕre, -cēpi, -ceptum;** **pĕdem rĕferre, rettuli** or **rētuli, relatum.**
avoid, **vīto,** I.
battle, **pugna, proelium.**
hinder, **impĕdio,** 4.
march, *n.* **ĭter, ĭtĭnĕris,** *n.*
march, *v.* **ĭter făcio;** **contendo, -ĕre, -di, -tum.**
learn (=discover), **cognosco, -ĕre, -nōvi, -nĭtum.**
plan, **consĭlium,** *n.*
advance, **prō-grĕdior, -i, -gressus;** **prōcedo, -ĕre, -cessi, -cessum** (so conjugate **cēdo** and all its compounds).
camp, **castra, -orum,** *n. pl.*
accuse, **accūso,** I.
work, *v.* **lăbōro,** I.
work, *n.* **lăbor, -ōris,** *m.*; **ŏpus, -eris,** *n.*
become, **fīo, fĭĕri, factus sum.**
rich, **dīves, -ĭtis.**
arms, **arma,** *n. pl.*
think, **pŭto,** I.
coward, **ignāvus.**

brave, strong, fortis, vălĭdus.
poor (a poor man), pauper, -eris.
consul, consul, -ŭlis.
ought, dēbeo.
praise, laudo, I.

Exercise 4

help, ĭŭvo, -are, jūvi, jūtum,
   acc. ; subvĕnio, -ire, -vēni,
   -ventum, *dat.*
sick, aeger, -ra, -rum.
suffer, pătior, -i, passus.
pain, dŏlor, -ōris, *m.*
plain, campus, -i, *m.*

Exercise 5

safe, tūtus.
stay, remain, măneo, -ēre,
   mansi, mansum.
save, servo, I.
whole, tōtus, omnis.

Exercise 6

so great, tantus.
such, tālis.
so many, tot (an *indecl. adj.*).
so often, tŏties.
so (with *adv.* and *adj.*), tam.
so (= in such a way,) ĭta.
so (= to such an extent), ădeo.

———

conquer, defeat, vinco, -ĕre,
   vīci, victum.
be afraid, fear, tĭmeo.
our men, nostri [omit *men*].
escape, effŭgio, -ĕre, -fūgi.
fierce, fĕrox ; *adv.* fĕrōciter.
danger, pĕrīcŭlum.
ship, nāvis, -is, *f.*
deep, high, altus.

river, flūmen, -ĭnis, *n.* ; flŭvius,
   -i, *m.*
cross, transeo, -ire, -ii, -ītum.
despise, despĭcio, -ĕre, -spexi,
   -spectum.
fear, mĕtus, -ūs, *m.* ;
   tĭmor, -ōris, *m.*
dare, audeo, -ēre, ausus.
storm, tempestas, -tātis, *f.*
arise, co-ŏrior, -iri, -ortus.

Exercise 7

enough, sătis.
snow, nix, nĭvis, *f.*
set out, prŏficiscor, -i.
   profectus.
easily, făcĭle.
tree, arbor, -ōris, *f.*
fall, cădo, -ĕre, cĕcĭdi, cāsum.
lie, jăceo, -ēre, jăcui.
return, rĕdeo, -ire, -ii, -ītum.
courage, virtus, -tūtis, *f.*
climb, ascendo, -ĕre, -di, -sum.
follow, sĕquor, -i, secūtus.

Exercise 8

arrive, advĕnio, -ire, -vēni,
   -ventum.
full, plēnus.
sea, măre, -is, *n.*
book, lĭber, -ri, *m.*
fly, fŭgio, -ĕre, fūgi, fŭgĭtum.
again, rursus.
idle, cowardly, ignāvus.

Exercise 9

leave, relinquo, -ĕre, -līqui,
   -lictum.
home, homewards, *acc.* of dŏmus,
   -ūs, *f.*

H

Exercise 10

defend, dēfendo, -ĕre, -fendi, -fensum.
walls, -mūri, *m.* ; moenia, *n. pl.*
alone, sōlus.
law, lex, lēgis, *f.*
speak, lŏquor, -i, lŏcūtus.
die, mŏrior, -i, mortuus.
hunger, fămes, -is, *f.*
hurt, laedo, -ĕre, laesi, laesum.

Exercise 11

citizen, cīvis, -is.
messenger, nuntius, -i.
go away, abeo (like *eo*).
cold, frīgus, -ŏris, *n.*
seem, vĭdeor, -ēri, vīsus.
ditch, trench, fossa.
soldier, mīles, -ĭtis.

Exercise 12

weapon, tēlum.
throw, jăcio, -ĕre, jēci, jactum.
place, lŏcus, -i, *m.*
shield, scūtum.
repel, rĕpello, -ĕre, reppŭli, rĕpulsum.
call, appello, I.

Exercise 13

few, pauci.
bear, fĕro, ferre, tŭli, lātum.

Exercise 14

mule, mūlus, -i, *m.*
lead, dūco, -ĕre, duxi, ductum.
laden, -ŏnĕratus.

gold, aurum.
long (*of time*), dĭu ; longer, diūtius.
burden, ŏnus, -ĕris, *n.*
compel, cōgo, -ĕre, coēgi, coactum.
carry, porto, I.
by chance, cāsu, forte.
follow, sĕquor, -i, sĕcūtus.
admire, mīror, I.
kindness, bĕnĕfĭcentia, hūmānitas, -tātis, *f.*
try, cōnor, I. followed by *Inf.*

Exercise 15

hardly, vix.
reinforcements, supplēmentum, nŏvae cōpiae.
resolve, constĭtuo, -ĕre, -ui, -ūtum.
resist, rĕsisto, -ĕre, -stĭti, *dat.*
attack (onset, charge), impĕtus, -ūs, *m.*
almost, paene, prŏpe.
at length, tandem.
joy, gaudium, laetĭtia.
temple, templum, aedes, *f.* [*sing.* only].
gift, dōnum.
go, se conferre.
god, deus, dei.

Exercise 16

hill, collis, -is, *m.*
throw away, abjĭcio, -ĕre, -jēci, -jēctum.
some . . . others, ălii . . . ălii.
exhausted, confectus lăbōre.
hide, cēlo, I.

Exercise 17

hostage, **obses, -ĭdis,** *c.*

near, **prŏpe,** *acc.*

army, **exercĭtus, -ūs,** *m.*

night, **nox, noctis,** *f.*

Exercise 18

banish, **expello, -ĕre, -pŭli, -pulsum.**

bring, **affĕro, afferre, attŭli, allatum;** (of persons)**adduco.**

take away, **aufĕro, auferre, abstŭli, ablātum.**

money, **pĕcūnia.**

friendship, **ămīcĭtia.**

sell, **vendo, vendĕre, vendĭdi, vendĭtum.**

buy, **ĕmo.**

silver, **argentum.**

Exercise 19

Greek, **Graecus.**

general, **dux, dŭcis; impĕrātor, -ōris.**

betray, **prōdo, -ĕre, -dĭdi, -dĭtum.**

present, **dōnum,**

tempt, **tempto, I.**

receive, **accipio, -ĕre, -cēpi, -ceptum.**

reward, **praemium.**

upright, **prŏbus.**

send back, **reddo** (like *prodo*).

punish, **pūnio.**

Exercise 20

Words which take Prolative Infinitive

be able, **possum, posse, pŏtui.**

ought, **dēbeo.**

be accustomed, **sŏleo, sŏlēre sŏlitus.**

dare, **audeo, audēre, ausus.**

wish, am willing, **vŏlo, velle, vŏlui.**

not to wish, be unwilling, **nōlo, nolle, nōlui.**

prefer, **mālo, malle, mālui.**

desire, **cŭpio, cŭpĕre, -ivi, -ītum.**

determine, **stătuo, constĭtuo.**

begin, **incĭpio; coepi, -isse.**

cease, **desĭno, desĭnĕre** [for perfect use **destiti**].

try, **cōnor, I.**

teach, **dŏceo, -ēre, dŏcui, doctum.**

learn, **disco, discĕre, dĭdĭci.**

compel, force, **cōgo.**

allow, **sĭno, -ere, sīvi, sĭtum.**

seem, **vĭdeor.**

Also passives of all verbs of saying, thinking, take Prolative Infinitives.

---

hope, **spēro, I.**

believe, **crēdo, -ĕre, -dĭdi, -dĭtum.**

command, **impĕro, I.,** *dat.*

obey, **pāreo,** *dat.*

country (=native land), **patria.**

for, on behalf of, **pro,** *abl.*

true, **vērus.**

pitch a camp, **castra pōno, -ĕre, pŏsui, pŏsĭtum;** or **castra mūnio.**

lie, **mentior, -iri, mentītus.**

go to the help of, **subvĕnio,** *dat.*

Exercise 21

punish, pūnio; poenā afficio,
-ĕre, -fēcī, -fectum.
benefit, prōsum, prōdesse,
prōfui, *dat.*
barbarians, barbări.
pleasant, jūcundus.
disgraceful, turpis.
foolish, stultus.
wise, săpiens, -entis.

Exercise 22

complain, quĕror, -i, questus.
useless, inūtilis.
of (=concerning), de, *abl.*
rule, rĕgo, regno, I.
difficult, hard, diffĭcilis.
man (as opposed to boy or
woman), vir.

Exercise 23

persuade, persuădeo, -ēre,
suasi, -suasum, *dat.*
master (of pupils), măgister,
-tri; (of slaves), dŏmĭnus, -i.
often, saepe.
useful, ūtĭlis.
against one's will, unwilling,
invītus, *adj.*

Exercise 24

army, exercĭtus, -ūs, *m.*
give up, surrender, trādo, -ĕre,
-dĭdi, -dĭtum.
summon, call, arcesso, -ĕre,
arcessivi, arcessītum;
convŏco, I.
collect, collĭgo, -ĕre, -lēgi,
-lectnm.

Exercise 25

state, cīvĭtas, -tātis, *f.*
drive out, expel, expello.
elect, creo, I.
demand, posco, -ĕre, pŏposci;
impĕro, I.
bring (of persons), dūco;
(of things), fĕro.
chief, princeps, -ĭpis.
seize, răpio, -ĕre, răpui,
raptum.
set on fire, ūro, -ĕre, ussi,
ustum; incendo, -ĕre, -di,
-sum.
set free, lībĕro, I.

Exercise 26

stumble, lābor, -i, lapsus.
fall down, collābor.
attack, aggrĕdior, -i, -gressus;
adorior, -iri, -ortus; (of a
city, camp, etc.), oppugno, I.
advance, prōgrĕdior.
enter, march in, ingrēdior.
return, regredior; rĕdeo (like
eo).
go out, egredior; exeo (like
eo).
be afraid, vĕreor.
die, mŏrior, -i, mortuus, *Fut.
Part.* morĭturus.
delay, mŏror, I.
exhort, hortor, I.
gate, porta.
halt, consisto, -ĕre, -stĭti.
mile, mille passūs; two miles,
duo mīlia passuum.
reach, pervenio ad.
take by storm, expugno, I.

Exercise 27

open, ăpĕrio, -ire, aperui,
    apertum.
call to, appello, I.
approach, appropinquo, I.
winter, hĭems, hiĕmis, *f.*
winter beginning, ineunte
    hiĕme.
at my house, ăpud me.
sleep, dormio.
early, māne [*lit.* in the morning].
bring an answer, responsum
    rĕfĕro.
call for, appello, I.

Exercise 28

wood, silva.
small, parvus.
youth, jŭvĕnis.
rampart, vallum.
fortify, mūnio.
resist, rĕsisto, -ĕre, -stiti, *dat.* ;
    sustĭneo, -ĕre, -tinui,
    -tentum, *acc.*

Exercise 29

silence, sĭlentium.
lead out, ēdūco.
town, oppĭdum.

Exercise 30

gladly, lĭbenter.
save, conservo, I.
foot, pēs, pĕdis, *m.*
at the king's feet, ad pĕdes rēgis.
found (a city), condo, -ĕre,
    -dĭdi, -dĭtum. From the
    foundation of Rome, ab urbe
    condita.

spring, vēr, -is, *n.*
bury, sĕpĕlio, -ire, -ii, or īvi,
    sĕpultum.

Exercise 31

some, nonnulli.
lead back, rĕdūco.
pursue, sĕquor.

Exercise 32

at a distance, prŏcul.
await, exspecto, I.

Exercise 33

eat, ĕdo, -ĕre, ēdi, ēsum.
keep, servo, I.
wounded, saucius, vulnĕratus.
only, sōlum, mŏdo, tantum.
give up, dēdo, -ĕre, -dĭdi,
    -dĭtum.
soon, mox, brĕvi (*sc.* tempore).
take away, aufĕro. (See 18.)
from (out of), ex ; (away from),
    ab ; (down from), de.

Exercise 34

break down (*trans.*), rescindo,
    -ĕre, -scĭdi, -scissum.
bridge, pons, -tis, *m.*
arrival, adventus, -ūs, *m.*
immediately, stătim, extemplo.
therefore, ĭtăque (first word),
    ĭgĭtur (second word).
come down, descendo, -ĕre, -di,
    -sum.
seek, pĕto, -ĕre, -ivi, -ītum.
corn, frūmentum.
repair, rĕfĭcio.

Exercise 35

scout, explōrator, spĕcŭlator.
slowly, grădătim, lente.
tell (=announce), rĕfĕro,
nuntio, I.
to the other side of, across,
trans.
provisions, commeātus, -ūs, *m.* ;
food, cĭbus, -i, *m.*
strong, firmus, vălĭdus.

Exercise 36

country (as opposed to town),
rus, rūris, *n.*
Athens, Athēnae, *f. pl.*
Syracuse, Sўrăcūsae, *f. pl.*
Carthage, Carthāgo, -ĭnis, *f.*
summer, aestas, -tātis, *f.*
next, proxĭmus.
month, mensis, -is, *m.*

Exercise 37

long, longus.
Sicily, Sĭcĭlia.
Greece, Graecia.
new, nŏvus.
Corinth, Cŏrinthus, -i, *f.*

Exercise 38

severe, grăvis.
within, intrā, *acc.*
help, auxĭlium.
delay, cunctor, I. ; mŏror, I.
sail, nāvĭgo, I.
set sail, nāvem solvo, -ĕre,
solvi, sŏlūtum.
perish, pereo, -ire, -ii, -ĭtum.
farm, fundus, -i, *m.*

wage war, bellum gĕro, -ĕre,
gessi, gestum.
harbour, portus, -ūs, *m.*
Florence, Flōrentia.
dawn, prīma lux.

Exercise 39

beautiful, pulcher, -ra, -rum.
sunset, sōlis occāsus, -us, *m.*
companion, cŏmes, -ĭtis.
on the following day, postĕro
die, postrīdie.
about, *adv.*, circĭter,
evening, vesper, -ĕri, *m.* (Locative vesperi or e).
be distant, absum.
broad, lātus.
deep, altus.
from which, whence, undĕ.

Exercise 40

road, via.
for a short time, paulisper.
shore, ōra, lītus, -ŏris, *n.*
every day, quŏtīdie.
beginning, ĭnĭtium.

Exercise 41

shout, clāmor.
by day, interdiu.
song, cantus, -ūs, *m.*
explore, explōro, I.
yard, passus, -ūs, *m.*
come between, intercēdo, -ĕre,
-cessi, -cessum.
accordingly, ĭgĭtur [second
word].
dark, obscūrus.

boat, **linter, -tris,** _f._
get ready, equip, **păro,** I.
up the river, **adverso flūmĭne.**
without the knowledge of—use
inscius.

Exercise 42

The following words govern the Ablative :

get possession of, **pŏtior,** 4.
enjoy, **fruor, -i, fruitus.**
perform, **fungor, -i, functus.**
use, **ūtor, -i, usus.**
feed on, **vescor, -i.**
lean on, **nītor, -i, nixus (nisus** in the sense of _striving)._
relying on, **frētus.**
contented with, **contentus.**
endowed with, **praedĭtus.**
worthy of, **dignus.**
unworthy of, **indignus.**
there is need of, **ŏpus est.**
I have need of help, **opus est mihi auxilio.**
booty, **praeda.**
disease, **morbus, -i,** _m._
body, **corpus, -ŏris,** _n._
weak, **infirmus.**
lot, **sors, -tis,** _f._
duty, **offĭcium.**
undertake, **suscĭpio.**
difficulty, **difficultas, -tātis,** _f._
tall, **altus.**
wing, **āla.**

Exercise 43

like, **sĭmĭlis.**
build, **aedĭfĭco,** I.
height, **altĭtūdo, -ĭnis,** _f._

on the march, **ex** or **in ĭtĭnĕre.**
beat, **caedo, -ĕre, cĕcīdi, caesum.**
Babylon, **Babylon, -ōnis,** _f._
wise, **săpiens.**
wisdom, **săpientia.**
bow, **arcus, -ūs,** _m._
Rhone, **Rhŏdănus, -i,** _m._
many times (with _comp._), **multis partibus.**

Exercise 44

Verbs followed by Acc. and Inf.

think, **pŭto,** I. ; **existĭmo,** I. ; **arbitror,** I. ; **reor, rēri, rātus.**
believe, **crēdo.**
be sure, **pro certo hăbeo.**
perceive, **sentio, -ire, sensi, sensum.**
understand, **intellĕgo, -ĕre, -lexi, -lectum.**
notice, observe, **ănĭmadverto, -ĕre, -verti.**
learn, ascertain, **cognosco, -ĕre, -nōvi, -nĭtum.**
know, **scio.**
not to know, **nescio.**
hear, **audio.**
say, **dīco.**
assert, declare, **affirmo,** I.
inform, tell, **certiorem făcio.**
    See p. 43, note 2.
announce, report, **nuntio,** I., **rĕfero.**
relate, **narro,** I.
cry out, **clāmo,** I.
deny, say not, **nĕgo,** I.
reply, **respondeo, -ēre, -spondi, -sponsum.**

Ex. 44—*contd.*

pretend, sĭmŭlo, I.
men say, it is said, fĕrunt.
it is agreed, well known,
    constat.
promise, prōmitto, polliceor.
hope, spēro, I.
threaten, mĭnor, I.

———

strike a camp, castra mŏveo.
ready, părătus.

Exercise 45

be at hand, adsum.
yield, cēdo, -ĕre, cessi, cessum.
disaster, clādes, -is, *f.*
sustain (=receive), accipio.
a Gaul, Gallus.
Gaul, Gallia.

Exercise 47

deceive, dēcipio, fallo, -ĕre,
    fĕfelli, falsum.
arrival, adventus, -ūs, *m.*

Exercise 48

state, cīvĭtas, -tātis, *f.*
attack, charge, impĕtus.
charge, impĕtum făcio.
finish, confĭcio.
leader, dux, dŭcis.

Exercise 49

as soon as possible, quam
    primum.
traitor, prōdĭtor, -ōris, *m.*
rightly, jūrĕ.
prisoner, captīvus, i.
legion, lĕgio, -onis, *f.*

Exercise 50

come up, arrive, advĕnio.
reward, praemium.
surround, cingo, -ĕre, cinxi,
    cinctum ; circumvĕnio.
ago. See p. 32.

Exercise 51

old man, sĕnex, sĕnis.
complain, quĕror, -i, questus.
wife, uxor, -ōris.
field, ăger, -ri, *m.*
sit, sĕdeo, -ēre, sēdi, sessum.
supper, cēna.
be hungry, ēsŭrio, 4.

Exercise 52

run out, prōcurro. *Perf.* -curri
    or -cucurri.
pass, saltus, -ūs, *m.* ;
    angustiae, *f. pl.*
purposely, de industriā.
abandon, rĕlinquo.
guilty, nŏcens, -entis.
at the same time, simul.
kingdom, regnum.
forum, fŏrum.

Exercise 53

besiege, beset, blockade, ob-
    sĭdeo, -ēre, -sēdi, -sessum.
fail, defĭcio.
greatly, magnŏpĕre.
order, jussum.
territories, fīnes, -ium, *m.* [finis,
    in singular = boundary].
nevertheless, tămen [usually not
    first word].
withdraw, discēdo.

Exercise 54

engage in battle, join battle, **proelium committo.**

dismiss, disband, **dīmitto.**

draw up in line of battle, **instruo, -ĕre, -struxi, -structum.**

withstand, **sustineo.**

line of battle, **ăcies,** *f.*, 5.

escape, *n.*, **fŭga.**

all to a man, **omnes ad unum.**

Exercise 55

review an army, **recenseo, -ēre, -ui.**

thick, **densus.**

cloud, **nūbes, -is,** *f.*

any (in negative sentences), **ullus.**

mortal, **mortālis.**

by name [called], **nōmĭne.**

appear, **vĭdeor.**

capital, **căput, -ĭtis,** *n.*

world, **orbis terrarum.**

practise, **stŭdeo.**

art of war, **ars mīlĭtāris.**

speak the truth, **vēra lŏquor.**

Exercise 56

clever, **callĭdus.**

offence, **noxa, delictum.**

give evidence, **testĭmōnium dīco.**

accuser, **accūsātor.**

anger, **īra.**

make angry, **lăcesso, -ere, -ivi, -ītum.**

swear, **jūro,** I.

Exercise 57

value, think worth, **aestĭmo,** I.

liberty, **lībertas.**

cheap, worthless, **vīlis.**

at a low price, **vili.**

at a high price, highly, **magni.**

of no value, **nĭhĭli.**

cost, **stare** (*dat. of person*).

sesterce, **sestertius, -i,** *m.*

care a straw for, **flocci facio.**

slave, **servus. -i.**

talent, **tălentum.**

virtue, **virtūs, -tutis,** *f.*

Exercise 59

waste time, **tempus tĕro, -ĕre, trivi, trītum.**

confidence, **fĭdūcia.**

too much, **nĭmis,** *adv.* ; **nĭmius,** *adj.*

too little, very little, **părum,** *adv.*

boldness, **audācia.**

loss, **dētrīmentum.**

surrender (*intrans.*), **se trādere, se dēdere ; in dēdĭtionem vĕnire.**

strength, **rōbur, -ŏris,** *n.*

still, **adhuc.**

keep, **conservo,** I.

old (of former times), **antīquus.** (living or lasting long), **vĕtus, -ĕris.**

most, **plērique.**

show (of qualities), **praesto, -stare, -stiti.**

where in the world, **ŭbi gentium.**

live (=dwell), **hăbĭto,** I.

Exercise 60

eloquence, ēlŏquentia.
nation, gens, gentis, *f.*
lose, āmitto.
hope, spes, *f.*, 5.
country (native land), patria.
    (district), rĕgio, fīnes.
    (land), terra.
    (opp. to *town*), rus.
send to help, submitto, *acc.* and *dat.* ; *e.g. copias Caesari submittit.*

Exercise 61

The following couples of verbs, one governing Dat. and the other Acc., are especially to be noted:

help, support, succurro, -ĕre, -curri, -cursum (*dat.*), subvĕnio (*dat.*), jŭvo (*acc.*).
please, plăceo (*dat.*), jŭvo (*acc.*).
advise, suādeo, suāsi, suāsum (*dat.*), mŏneo (*acc.*).
command, impĕro (*dat.*), jŭbeo (*acc.*).
hurt, harm, nŏceo (*dat.*), laedo, -ĕre, laesi, laesum (*acc.*).
heal, mĕdeor (*dat.*), sāno, I. (*acc.*).
marry (woman as subject), nūbo, -ĕre, nupsi, nuptum (*dat.*).
    (man as subject), dūco (*acc.*).

The following govern the Dative:

believe, trust, credo.
obey, pāreo.

spare, parco, -ĕre, pĕperci, parsum
pardon, ignosco, -ĕre, -nōvi, -nōtum.
envy, invĭdeo.
to be angry with, īrascor, iratus.
restrain, tempĕro, I.
to be devoted to, stŭdeo.
favour, făveo, făvi, fautum.

Also all compounds of sum—

adesse, to be present at.
interesse, to take part in.
praeesse, to be in command of.
deesse, to fail, to be wanting to.
superesse, to survive.
prōdesse (prosum), to be advantageous, of service to.

And a large number of verbs compounded with preps. and bene, male, satis, re :

satisfy, sătisfacio.
put in command of, praeficio (*acc.* and *dat.*) ; *e.g.* Labienum legioni praefecit.
entrust, committo, *acc.* and *dat.*
wage war on, infĕro bellum.
declare war against, bellum indīco.
to press hard upon, insto, instĭti.
prefer, antĕpōno (*acc.* and *dat.*); *e.g.* anteponit rus urbi.
throw in the way of, objicio (*acc.* and *dat.*).
threaten, mĭnor, I. ; *e.g.* mortem mihi minatur.
hold out against, resist, rĕsisto.

wealth, riches, dīvĭtiae.
cause, causa.
disease, morbus, -i, *m.*
meet, obviam eo, *dat.*
enemy (public), hostis.
   (private), ĭnĭmīcus.

Exercise 62

French, Galli.
legion, lĕgio.
countrymen   (= fellow-countrymen, fellow-citizens), cīves.
judge, jūdex, -ĭcis.
torture, crŭciatus, -ūs, *m.*
exact from, impero, *acc.* and
   dat.; e.g. naves sociis imperat.
slavery, servĭtus, -tūtis, *f.*
agriculture, agricultūra.

Exercise 63

advice, consĭlium.
safety, sălus, -ūtis, *f.*
in the hands of, in pŏtestate.
Persians, Persae.
Athenians, Athēnienses.
the others, the rest, cēteri,
   rĕlĭqui.
trust, confīdo, -ĕre, confīsus
   sum, *dat.*

Exercise 64

form a plan, consĭlium căpio
   or ineo.
secretly, clam, *adv.*
rout, fundo, -ĕre, fūdi, fūsum.

Exercise 65

fight a battle, proelium facio.
suddenly, sŭbĭto.
take to flight, terga verto, -ĕre,
   verti, versum.
drive down, dēpello.

Exercise 66

robber, latro, -ōnis.
strong (of positions, etc.),
   firmus.
approach, ădĭtus, -ūs, *m.*
block, obsĭdeo, -ēre, -sēdi,
   -sessum.
cut down, succīdo, -ĕre, -cīdi,
   -cīsum.
storm, take by storm, expugno, I.

Exercise 67

crop, sĕgĕs, -ĕtis, *f.*
ripen, mātūresco.
   ripe, ready (early), mātūrus.
guide, dux.
horseman, ĕques, -ĭtis.
take prisoner, căpio, captīvum
   facio.
on the march, ex / in } ĭtĭnĕre.
discover, find (find what one is
   looking for), rĕpĕrio, -ĭre,
   repperi, repertum.
   (find by chance), invenio.
   (find out, learn, of *facts*),
   cognosco.
children, lībĕri.
midnight, mĕdia nox.
German, Germānus.

Ex. 67—contd.

in safety, incŏlŭmis, *adj.*
cattle, pĕcus, -ŏris, *n.*
marsh, pălūs, -ūdis, *f.*

Exercise 68

letter, litterae, *f. pl.*
hold, occupy, occŭpo, I.
recall, rĕvŏco, I.
order, jussum.
cruel, saevus, crūdēlis.
cruelty, saevĭtia,
   crūdēlitas.
massacre, slaughter, caedes,
   -is, *f.*
fleet, classis, -is, *f.*

Exercise 69

England, Brĭtannia.
Englishman, Brĭtannus.
France, Gallia.
Frenchman, Gallus.
French (*adj.*), Gallĭcus.
on account of, ob, propter.
priest, săcerdōs, -dōtis.
weapon, tēlum.
iron (*adj.*), ferreus.
club, clāva, fustis, -is, *m.*
by this means, hoc mŏdo.
shed, effundo, -ĕre, -fūdi,
   -fūsum.
blood, sanguis, -ĭnis, *m.*
blow, ictus, -ūs, *m.*
violence, vīs, *f.*

Exercise 70

knight, ĕques, -ĭtis.
wound, vulnĕro, I.
charge, impĕtum facio in, *acc.*
squadron, āla, turma.

emperor, imperātor.
open (a way, etc.), pătĕfăcio.
thereupon, quo facto.
back, tergum.
rise, surgo, -ĕre, surrexi,
   surrectum.

Exercise 71

almost, paenĕ, fĕrē.
criminal, guilty, nŏcens.
majority, mājor pars.

Exercise 72

lie, mentior.
press hard, prĕmo, -ĕre, pressi,
   pressum.
I am hard pressed, lăbōro, I.

Exercise 73.

arrow, săgitta.
archer, săgittārius, -i.
hold one's ground, in lŏco
   perstare.

Exercise 74

let slip, dīmitto.
opportunity, occāsio, -ōnis, *f.*,
   făcultas, -tātis, *f.*
despise, sperno, -ĕre, sprēvi,
   sprētum.

Exercise 75

ask, rŏgo, *two accusatives;* pĕto
   (*ab* or *ex*)
pray, beg, ōro, I., prĕcor, I.
demand, flāgĭto, I., postŭlo, I.,
   posco, -ĕre, pŏposci.

urge, exhort, encourage, **hortor,**
  I., **admŏneo.**
command, **impĕro,** I., *dat.* ;
  jŭbeo,-ēre, jussi, jussum, *acc.*
decree, ordain, **ēdīco.**
advise, **mŏneo,** *acc.* ; **suādeo,**
  dat.
persuade, **persuādeo,** *dat.*
forbid, **vĕto,** -are, -ui, -itum.

---

street, **via.**
attempt (battle), **tempto,** I.
friendship, **ămīcĭtia.**
baggage, **impĕdīmenta,** *n. pl.*
devote oneself to, **stŭdeo,** *dat.*
halt, **consisto,** -ĕre, -stiti.
vanguard, **primum agmen.**

Exercise 76

bring help, **auxilium ferre,**
  dat.
serious, severe, **grăvis.**
people of town, **oppĭdāni.**

Exercise 77

break down, **rescindo,** -ĕre,
  -scĭdi, -scissum.
Rhine, **Rhēnus,** -i, *m.*
cavalry, **ĕquĭtes,** -um.
infantry, **pĕdĭtes,** -um.
caution, carefulness, **dīlĭgentia.**
off one's guard, **imprŏvĭdus,**
  incautus.
send back, **rĕmitto.**
determination, **constantia.**
lay down, **dēpōno,** -ĕre, -pŏsui,
  -pŏsĭtum.
council, **concĭlium.**
thereupon, **deinde, quo facto.**

assemble (*intr.*), **convĕnio.**
  (*tr.*), **convŏco,** I.
prepare for battle, **arma**
  expĕdio.

Exercise 78

stand for, be a candidate for,
  pĕto.
consulship, **consŭlātus,** -ūs, *m.*
to this side of, **citrā,** *acc.*
last, **ultĭmus.**
prayers, **prĕces,** *f. pl.*
plunder, **spŏlio,** I. ; **dīrĭpio,**
  -ĕre, -ripui, -reptum.
induce, incite, **addūco.**
treasure, **thēsaurus,** -i, *m.*
dangerous, **pērĭcŭlosus.**
remain faithful to Caesar, **fĭdem**
  Caesaris sĕquor.
revolt from, **dēfĭcio ab.**
search for, **quaero,** -ĕre, **quae-**
  sivi, quaesītum ; pĕto, -ĕre,
  -ivi, -ītum.

Exercise 79

on the other side of, **ultrā,** *acc.*
Tiber, **Tĭbĕris,** -is, *m.*
cultivate, **colo,** -ĕre, **cŏlui,**
  cultum.
senate, **sĕnātus,** -ūs; **patres.**
appoint, **creo,** I. ; **făcio.**
bring (of things), **fĕro.**
  (of persons), **dūco.**
displease, **displĭceo,** *dat.*
dictator, **dictātor,** -ōris.
toga, **tŏga.**

Exercise 80

hold, **tĕneo,** -ēre, -ui, -tum.
letter, **litterae, ĕpistŏla.**

Ex. 80—*contd.*

read, lĕgo, -ĕre, lēgi, lectum.
thank, grātias ăgo, -ĕre, ēgi,
  actum, *dat.*
faithful, fīdēlis ; *adv.* fīdēliter.
put back, rĕpōno.
wake (*trans.*), excĭto, I.
at first, prīmo.
fortune, fortūna.

Exercise 81

at (near), ad.
guard, custos, -ōdis.
commander, praefectus, -i.
garrison, praesĭdium.
tear, lacrĭma.
assassinate, trŭcīdo, I.
at the same time, sĭmul.
beseech, obsecro, I.

Exercise 82

younger, nātu mĭnor.
supply, praebeo.
pay, stīpendium.
Spartan, Lacedaemŏnius.
ally, sŏcius.
famine, starvation, fămes, -is, *f.*

Exercise 83

forced march, magnum ĭter.
with the intention of, eo consĭlio
  ut.
the former ... the latter, ille ...
  hic.
take up position, consīdo, -ĕre,
  -sēdi, -sessum.
mound, tŭmŭlus, -i, *m.*
long (of time), diu; *comp.*
  diūtius.

within range, intrā conjectum
  tēli.
shoot, mĭtto.
fire back, return fire, tela rējicio.
take to flight, se fŭgae mandare.
wait, mănĕo, -ēre, mansi,
  mansum.

Exercise 84

vainly, frustrā.
behind, pōnĕ, *acc.*
even, ĕtiam [vel used only with
  superlatives].
not even, ne ... quĭdem [with
  emphatic word between].
conceal, cēlo, I.
pass (of time), ago.

Exercise 85

*Datives of purpose or result of
  action*

to be a burden to, ŏnĕri esse.
to sound a retreat, rĕceptui
  cănere, cĕcĭni, cantum.
to be (serve as) a signal, signo
  esse.
to be a disgrace, to disgrace,
  dēdĕcori esse.
to be to the advantage of, to
  benefit, ūsui esse.
to be the cause of, to cause,
  causae esse.
to be an example, exemplo
  esse.
to help, be a help to, auxĭlio,
  subsĭdio esse.
to be a credit to, laudi esse.
to be hateful to, hated by, ŏdio
  esse.

to be (mean) destruction to, **exĭtio esse.**

to be a protection to, **praesĭdio esse.**

to be the salvation of, **sălūti esse.**

to be a proof, **indĭcio esse.**

———

constancy, **constantia.**

negligence carelessness } **neglĭgentia.**

only, merely, **mŏdo, sōlum, tantum.**

Exercise 86

avarice, **ăvārĭtia.**

Exercise 87

banish, **expello.**

free, **līber, -era, -erum.**
    (*vb.*) **lībĕro, I.**

free from, devoid of, **văcuus.**

far from, **prŏcul.**

son of, **nātus.**

descended, **prognatus, ortus.**

abound, **ăbundo, I.**

endowed, **praedĭtus.**

full, **plēnus.**

depart from, **discēdo, excēdo.**

kingly power, **rēgia pŏtestas, regnum.**

exile, **exsul, -ŭlis.**

prison, **carcer, -is, *m.* ; vincula, *n. pl.***

captive, **captīvus, -i.**

fault, blame, **culpa.**
    blame (*vb.*), **culpo, I.**

praise, **laus, -dis, *f.***

willingly, **lĭbenter.**

fruit, **fructus, -ūs, *m.***

flower, **flos, flōris, *m.***

inhabit, **incŏlo, -ĕre, -ui.**

not only... but also, **non sōlum ... sed ĕtiam.**

race, people, **gens, -tis, *f.***

Exercise 88

noble, **nōbĭlis.**

children, **lībĕri.**

desist from, **dēsisto, -ĕre, -stiti.**

siege, **obsĭdio, -ōnis, *f.***

goods, **bŏna, *n. pl.***

angry, in a passion, **īrātus.**

Exercise 89

rightly, **jūrĕ.**

wrongly, **injūriā.**

in the fashion of, **mōre.**

by your leave, **păce tuā.**

by force, **vi** ; by force of arms, **vi et armis.**

with all one's power, **summā vi, pro vĭrīli parte.**

older, **nātu major.**

younger, **nātu mĭnor.**

in a loud voice, **magnā vōce.**

———

disorder, confusion, **tŭmultus, -ūs, *m.***

arm, **armo, I.**

fury, **fŭror, -ōris, *m.***

excel, **sŭpĕro, I.**

talents, **ingĕnium.**

inferior, **infĕrior.**

numbers, **nŭmĕrus, -i, *m.*** [only in *sing.*].

ancestors, **mājōres.**

Exercise 90

care, cūra, dīligentia.
skill, ars, -tis, *f.*
superior, sŭpĕrior.
be superior, praesto.
sorrow, dŏlor, -ōris, *m.*
characters (= letters), littĕrae.
withdraw, go away, ăbeo,
    discēdo.
smile, rīsus, -ūs, *m.*
    (*vb.*) subrīdeo, -ēre, -rīsi,
    -risum.
here, hic ; (of motion), huc.
act, ago, me gĕro.

Exercise 91

loss, damnum.
decide the contest, rem dēcerno,
    -ĕre, -crēvi, -crētum.
by name, called, nōmine.
separate, sējunĝo, -ēre, -junxi,
    -junctum.
turn round (*trans.*), converto.
turning round (*intr.*), conver-
    sus.
in turn, singŭli, *adj.*, in vĭcem.

Exercise 92

mention above, suprā com-
    memŏro, I.
golden, aureus.
apple, mālum.
garden, hortus, -i, *m.*
nymph, nympha.
remarkable, mīrus, insignis,
    praeclārus.
beauty, pulchrĭtūdo, -ĭnis, *f.*,
    forma.

distant, longinquus.
surround, cingo, -ĕre, cinxi,
    cinctum.
on all sides, ab omnibus
    partibus, undĭque.
moreover, praetĕreā.
guard, custōdio.
by day . . . by night, interdiu
    . . . noctu.

Exercise 93

conspire, conjūro, I.
conspiracy, conjūrātio, -ōnis, *f.*
delay, mŏra.
centre, mĕdia or intĕrior pars.
on his arrival, adventu ejus.
    [If *he* refers to the subject
    of sentence say qui cum
    advenisset.]
the rest of, rĕlĭqui, cētĕri, *adj.*
under arms, armati, in armis.
join, *trans.*, conjungo; *intrans.*,
    se conjungĕre cum.
invasion, incursio, -onis, *f.*
borders, fines, -ium, *m.*

Exercise 94

about, de, *prep.*
watch, vĭgĭlia.
caution, dīligentia.
until late in the night, usque ad
    multam noctem.
take up, sūmo, -ĕre, sumpsi,
    sumptum.

Exercise 95

Sicily, Sĭcĭlia.
meanwhile, intĕrea, intĕrim.

attack (of a disease), afficio, -ĕre, -fēci, -fectum.

carry off (= destroy), dēleo, -ēre, -ēvi, -ētum ; confĭcio.

sustain, encourage, confirmo, I.

attend to, stŭdeo, *dat.* ; cūro, I., *acc.*

in every way, omni mŏdo.

tent, tăbernăculum.

abandon a siege, raise a siege, obsĭdionem rĕlinquo, obsidione dēsisto.

feel, sentio, -ire, sensi, sensum.

Exercise 96

husband, vir, măritus, -i.

give up hope, spem abjĭcio.

rush out, effundor, -i, -fusus.

to meet, obviam, *dat.*

win a victory, victoriam rĕporto, I., rem prospĕre gĕro.

temple, templum.

great quantity of, multus.

Exercise 97

scarcely, vix.

sow, sĕro, -ĕre, sēvi, sătum.

autumn, auctumnus, -i, *m.*

gather, collĭgo, -ĕre, -lēgi, -lectum.

harvest, messis, -is, *f.*

undertake, suscĭpio.

check, cŏhĭbeo.

Exercise 98

disturbance, tŭmultus, -ūs, *m.* ; mōtus, -ūs, *m.*

excite, excĭto, I.

cover, ŏpĕrio, -ire, -ui, -pertum; (shelter), tĕgo, -ĕre, texi, tectum.

sometimes, nonnunquam, interdum.

fall down, delābor, -i, -lapsus.

further, longius, ultrā.

urge on, urgeo, ursi.

wolf, lŭpus, -i, *m.*

press upon, threaten, insto, *dat.*

suffering, dŏlor, -ōris, *m.* [also indignation, resentment].

prey, praeda.

Exercise 99

write, scrībo, -ĕre, scripsi, scriptum.

change, mūto, I.

Exercise 100

hasten, prŏpĕro, I. ; festino, I.

desire, stŭdium, ămor, cŭpīdo, -inis, *f.*

desirous, anxious, cŭpĭdus.

suffer, pătior, -i, passus.

reading, lectio, -onis, *f.*

win, ădĭpiscor, -i, adeptus.

honour, hŏnōs, -ōris, *m.* ; fāma.

offer an opportunity, făcio pŏtestatem, do occāsionem.

Exercise 101

forage, *vb.*, pābŭlor, I.

n. pābŭlum.

consult, consŭlo, -ĕre, -sului, -sultum, *acc.*

consult interests of, consulo, *dat.*

disgraceful, turpis.

Ex. 101—*contd.*
devote oneself to, **stŭdeo,** *dat.*
in all directions, **passim.**

Exercise 102

lead on, induce, **addūco.**
waste time, **tempus tĕro.**

Exercise 103

face, **obeo,** *acc.*
fit for, **aptus ad, ĭdōneus ad.**
harm, injury, **damnum, incommŏdum.**
send for, **arcesso, -ĕre, -īvi,
-ītum.**
one needs, **ŏpus est.**
officer, **lēgatus, praefectus.**
citadel, **arx, arcis,** *f.*
fill, **compleo, -ēre, -plēvi,
-plētum.**
merchandise, **merces,** *pl.*
pardon, **vĕnia.**

Exercise 104

story, **fābula.**
strange, **mīrābĭlis.**
pay, **solvo.**
found, **condo.**
colony, **cŏlōnia.**
all agree, **constat inter omnes.**
play, **lūdo, -ĕre, lusi, lusum.**

Exercise 105

lawful, **fas** [indeclinable].
go to bed, **cŭbĭtum eo.**
on behalf of, **pro,** *abl.*

Exercise 106

strike terror into, inspire with
terror, **injĭcio terrōrem,** *dat.*
bring into danger, **in pĕrīcŭlum
addūco.**
give ground, **cēdo.**
unexpected, **sŭbĭtus,
inŏpīnatus.**
break (a line), **inclīno,** I.

Exercise 107

invite, **invīto,** I.
Ireland, **Hĭbernia.**
Irish (*adj.*), **Hĭbernicus.**
scatter, **dispergo, -ĕre, -si, -sum,**
trans. [For *intrans.* use the
Passive.]
rebel, **rĕbellis.**
troop (of horse), **turma.**
effect escape, **sălūtem fŭgā
pĕtĕre.**

Exercise 108

at close quarters,} **commĭnus,**
hand to hand,   } *adv.*
at a distance, **ēmĭnus.**
inexperienced, **impĕrītus,** *gen.*
withdraw, **dēdūco,** *trans.*
obstinate, **pertĭnax.**
    obstinately, **obstĭnate.**
    obstinacy, **pertĭnācia.**
recollection, **mĕmŏria.**
prolong, **prōduco, dūco.**
desert, **desĕro (-ĕre, -ui, -tum),
transfŭgio.**
    desert (=revolt from),
    dēfĭcio ab.
    deserter, **transfŭga,
    perfŭga.**

as far as, **usque ad.**
outposts, **stătiones,** *f.*
for fear of this, **hoc tĭmore** (*lit.* through this fear).
as, **pro,** *abl.*
sentinels, **custōdes, vĭgĭliae.**

Exercise 109

interest⎫
rēfert ⎭ it concerns.

These take a Genitive of the person concerned. But instead of the Gen. of pronouns they take *meâ, tuâ,* etc. They may also be qualified by a Gen. of value or neuter adjective :

e.g.⎰maximi interest⎱ = it is of
     ⎱multuminterest⎰

the greatest importance.

They can be followed both by infinitive and indirect question.

family, household, **fămĭlia.**
property, **bŏna,** *n. pl.*
evident, **mănĭfestus.**
remove, **transfĕro.**
population, **pŏpŭlus, multĭtūdo.**
accomplish, **efficio.**
safely, **tūto.**
dismay, **păvor, -ōris,** *m.*

Exercise 110

Interrogative words

who? what? **quis, quid** (*adj.* **qui, quae, quod**). Also **quis-nam.**
which of two? **ŭter, -tra, -trum.**

of what sort? **quālis.**
how great? **quantus.**
how many? **quot.**
how often? **quŏties.**
how? (with *adj.* and *adv.*) **quam.**
how? (= in what manner?) **quō-mŏdo, quemadmodum.**
how long? **quamdiu.**
why? **cur, quārē, quamobrem.**
when? **quando.**
where? **ŭbi, quâ.**
whence? where from? **undĕ.**
whither? where to? **quo.**

———

increase, *trans.,* **augeo, -ēre, auxi, auctum.**
   intrans., **cresco, -ĕre, crēvi, crētum.**
regard as, **hăbeo, dūco.**
cunning, *n.* **sollertia.**
   adj. **sollers.**
panic, **păvor.**
terms, **condĭtiones.**
worthy, **dignus.**

Exercise 112

Words introducing indirect questions

ask, **rŏgo ; interrogo ; quaero, -ĕre, quaesīvi, quaesītum** (*ex*).
know, **scio.**
not to know, **nescio.**
it is doubtful, **incertum, dŭbium est.**
to be doubtful, to doubt, **dŭbĭto,** I.
to ascertain, **cognosco.**

Ex. 112—*contd.*

to deliberate, consult, dēlībĕro, I., consŭlo.

to consider, cōgĭto, I., rĕpŭto, I.

to be of importance, make a difference, interest, rēfert. (See Voc. 109.)

it matters a great deal, multum or magni interest.

Exercise 113

on purpose, de industria.

Exercise 114

old, sĕnex, -is.

happy, fēlix, beātus.

understand, intellĕgo, -ĕre, -lexi, -lectum.

young, jŭvenis.

Exercise 115

to-morrow, cras.

intend, in animo habeo.

late at night, multā nocte.

what news? quid nŏvi?

regiment, cŏhors, -ortis, *f.*

quite, admŏdum.

Exercise 117

go on, happen, *passive of* ăgo.

traveller, viātor.

Exercise 118

prophet } vātes, -is.
prophetess }

piece (of gold), nummus, -i, *m.*

once more, rursus.

price, prĕtium.

Exercise 119

wonder, mīror.

offer, offĕro, offerre, obtŭli, oblatum.

show, ostendo, -ere, -di, -sum, or -tum.

Exercise 120

add, addo, -ĕre, -dĭdi, -ditum.

moved (by anger), commōtus.

sign, signum.

rather, pŏtius.

cut in two, discindo,-ĕre, -scĭdi, -scissum.

augur, augur, -ŭris.

Exercise 121

following, next, proximus.

recover, *trans.*, rĕcipio.

rising ground, ēditus lŏcus.

trick, dŏlus, -i, *m.*

most of them, plērique.

encamp, consīdo, -ĕre, -sedi, -sessum.

Exercise 122

indeed, quĭdem.

once, formerly, ōlim, quondam.

by means of, per.

overcome (by fear), perculsus.

whereupon, quo facto.

Exercise 123

celebrated, praeclārus.

catch sight of, conspĭcio, -ĕre, -spexi, -spectum; conspĭcor, I.

some days after, **aliquot post diebus.**
door, **jāuuạ.**
in astonishment, **attŏnītus.**
be mad, **fŭro, -ĕre** (no Perfect).
adj. **insānus, āmens.**
exclaim, **clāmo, I.**

Exercise 124

custom, **mōs, mōris,** *m.*
schoolmaster, **măgister, -tri.**
without the knowledge of. Use **inscius.**
former . . . latter, **ille . . . hic.**
commit to one's care, **mando, I.,** *acc.* and *dat.*
rod, **virga.**
such . . . as, **talis . . . qualis.**
drive, **ăgo.**
severe, **grăvis.**
punishment, **poena, supplicium.**

Exercise 125

panic, **păvor.**
in silence, **sīlentio.**
decree, **dēcerno, -ĕre, -crēvi, -crētum.**
clothe, **vestio.**
stroke, **mulceo, mulsi, mulsum.**
beard, **barba.**
strike, **percŭtio, -ĕre, -cussi, -cussum.**

Exercise 126

visit, **vīso, -ĕre, -si, -sum.**
unlike, **dissĭmilis.**
discuss, **dissĕro, -ĕre, -ui, -tum** (**de**).
fortunate, **fēlix.**

happy, **beātus.**
whoever, whatever, **quisquis, quicquid,** or **quicunque, quaecunque, quodcunque.**

Exercise 127

piety, duty (natural affection), **piĕtas.**
ox, **bōs, bŏvis,** *c.*
drag, draw, **trăho, -ĕre, traxi, tractum.**
cart, **carrus, -i,** *m.*
both, **ambo.**
prove, **dēmonstro, I.**
liable to, **obnoxius,** *dat.*
misfortune, **res adversae.**
honourable (of things), **hŏnestus.**
honourable (of persons), **prŏbus.**
indeed, **rēvērā.**

Exercise 128

Impersonal Verbs

A

me **mĭseret,** I pity.
me **taedet,** I am tired of.
me **pŭdet,** I am ashamed of.
me **paenitet,** I am sorry for, I repent.
The above 'verbs of feeling' may take a Genitive for a further object; *e.g.* me **paenitet crudelitatis,** I am sorry for my cruelty.

B

me **dĕcet,** it is becoming to me.
me **ŏportet,** it is my duty, I ought.

Ex. 128—*contd.*

C

mihi plăcet, I am pleased, it seems good to me, I am resolved.

mihi lĭcet, I am allowed, I may.

mihi accĭdit, it happens to me.

mihi contingit, it happens to me (generally of *good* fortune).

All the verbs B and C may be followed by an Infinitive. C may be followed by a Subjunctive.

(For **interest, rēfert,** see Voc. 109.)

Exercise 129

of one's own accord, **suā sponte.**
parent, **părens.**
deed, **factum.**

Exercise 130

cowardice, **ignāvia.**
kind, **bĕnignus.**
    kindness, **benignitas, bĕnĕvolentia, bĕnĕfĭcium** (= act of kindness).
towards (of feelings), **ergā,** *acc.*
staff (= officers), **lĕgati.**

Exercise 131

Words followed by Genitive

remember, **mĕmĭni** (sometimes *acc.*).
forget, **oblīviscor** (sometimes *acc.*).
recall, recollect, **rĕmĭniscor** (sometimes *acc.*).

remind, **admŏneo,** *acc.* and *gen.*
accuse, **accūso,** I., *acc.* and *gen.*
pity, **mĭsĕreor.**
mindful, **mĕmor,** (*adj.*).
forgetful, **immĕmor,** (*adj.*).
ignorant of, **inscius, impĕritus.**
skilled in, **pĕrītus.**
experienced in, **expertus.**
anxious to, desirous of, **cŭpĭdus.**
eager for, **ăvĭdus.**
unaccustomed to, **insuetus.**
recollection, remembrance, **mĕmŏria.**
skill, **perītia.**
desire, **cŭpĭdo, stŭdium.**
knowledge (of things), **cognĭtio.**
    (of persons), acquaintance, **consuētūdo, -inis,** *f.*

———

belonging to other people, **ăliēnus.**
address, **allŏquor, -i, -lŏcūtus.**
absent, **absens.**
necessary, **nĕcessārius.**
past, **praetĕrĭtus.**
for the sake of honour, **hŏnōris causā.**
administer public affairs, **rempublicam admĭnistro,** I.

Exercise 132

spend (life, period of time, etc.), **ăgo.**
treachery, **prōdĭtio.**
powerful, **pŏtens.**
design, **consĭlium.**
give up, abandon, **rĕlinquo,** *acc.* ; **desisto,** *abl.*
swim, **năto,** I.

Exercise 133

now, moreover (continuing a narrative), **autem** (second word).

ship of war, **longa nāvis.**

several, **ălĭquot, complūres.**

turn back (especially with object unaccomplished). **rĕvertor**

proud, **sŭperbus.**

looks, expression, face, **vultus, -ūs,** *m.*

dress, attire, **ornatus, -ūs.**

splendid, **insignis.**

come on board, embark, (**in**) **navem conscendo.**

  embark (*trans.*), **impōno** (*milites,* etc.).

land, disembark (*intr.*), **ēgredior e navi ;** (*trans.*) **expono** (*milites,* etc.).

by chance, **forte, cāsu.**

Exercise 134

need, **ĕgeo, indĭgeo,** *abl.* or *gen.*

  he needs money, **opus est ei pecuniā.**

  be without, lack, **căreo,** *abl.*

kindly, **bĕnigne.**

hold on course, **cursum tĕnēre.**

Exercise 135

lately, **nūper.**

inhabitant (of country), **incŏla.**

  (of city), **cīvis.**

  (of town), **oppĭdānus.**

garment, **vestis, -is,** *f.* ; **vestī-mentum.**

stream, **rīvus, -i.**

a certain (= Indefinite Article), **quidam.**

want, **cŭpio.**

flow, **fluo.**

rise, **ŏrior.**

outside, **extrā.**

district, **rĕgio, -onis,** *f.*

Exercise 136

with the intention of, **eo consilio ut.**

wreck (of ship), **frango, -ĕre, frēgi, fractum.**

to be shipwrecked, **ejicĭor in lītus (or litŏre).**

Exercise 137

key, **clāvis, -is,** *f.*

elders, **patres.**

give an opinion, **sententiam fero.**

wake, arouse, **excĭto,** I.

at least, **certē, saltem.**

Exercise 138

recognise, **agnosco, -ĕre, -nōvi, -nĭtum.**

mob, **turba, multitūdo.**

in nowise, **haudquāquam.**

drag, **trăho.**

magistrate, **măgistratus, -ūs.**

detain, **rĕtĭneo.**

Exercise 139

sister, **sŏror.**

village, **vīcus.**

entrance, **ōs (ōris),** *n.,* **ostium, adĭtus, -ūs,** *m.*

cavern, **spēlunca.**

Ex 139—*contd.*
limb, membrum.
form, forma, figūra.
colour, cŏlor.
skin, cŭtis, -is, *f.*
tinge, tingo, -ĕre, tinxi, tinctum.
green, vĭrĭdis.
set before, offĕro, prōpōno.
touch, tango, -ĕre, tĕtĭgi, tactum.
torment, torture, crŭcio, I.
sad, gloomy, tristis.
tear, lacrĭma.

Exercise 140

accustomed to, assuētus ad, assuēfactus ad.
healthy, sānus.
light, lux, lūcis, *f.*
flock, grex, grĕgis, *m.*
sound, sŏnus, -i, *m.* ; sŏnĭtus, -ūs, *m.*
wander, văgor, I.
stupefied, stŭpĕfactus.
excessive, nĭmius.
heat, cǎlor.
thus, sic, hoc mŏdo.

Exercise 141

check, restrain, cŏhĭbeo.

Exercise 142

short, brĕvis.
quiet, tranquillus.
set, post, dispōno ; collŏco, I.
chosen, picked, dēlectus.
fall on, incĭdo, -ĕre, -cĭdi, -cāsum (in).

Exercise 143

insolence, arrŏgantia.

Exercise 144

refuse, rĕcūso, I.
theft, furtum.
put in prison, in vincŭla conjĭcio.
admit, admitto.
fit to, dignus qui, *subj.*
launch, dēdūco.
patiently, aequo animo.

Exercise 145

shirk, vĭto, I., detrecto, I.

Exercise 146

suitable, ĭdōneus.
rashly, tĕmĕre.
towards evening, sub vesperum.
take place of, relieve, succēdo, *dat.*
disabled, confectus.
ladder, scāla.
scale, ascendo.
elephant, ĕlĕphantus, -i, *m.*
in front of, prō.
bring up, admŏveo.

Exercise 147

prepared to, părātus, *Inf.*
oppose, bar way of, hinder, obsto, obsisto, *dat.* ; impĕdio, *acc.* ; prŏhĭbeo, *acc.*
build, aedĭfĭco, I.
in two days, bĭduo.
for two days, biduum.
opposite bank, altera rīpa.

landing, ēgressus, -us.
up the river, in adversum flūmen, adverso flumine.

Exercise 148

Carthaginian, Poenus (adj. Pūnicus).
cold, frīgidus.
   (noun), frīgus, -ŏris, n.
desolate, dēsertus.
especially, praesertim.
want, inŏpia.
hardship, lăbor.
terrible, terrĭbĭlis.
downwards, deorsum.
rest, se rĕfĭcĕre.
encourage, confirmo, I.

Exercise 149

see to (undertake) the building of a house, curare (suscipere) aedificandam domum.
accuse of, accūso, I. (with Gen. of crime).
treachery, prōdĭtio.

Exercise 150

until (with nouns), usque ad.

Exercise 151

delay, mŏror, I. : cunctor, I.
winter quarters, hīberna, n. pl.
hold a levy, dēlectum (4th decl.) habeo.

Exercise 153

get out, evado, -ĕre, -si, -sum.
pass, defile, saltus, -ūs, m. ;
   angustiae, fauces, f.

narrow, angustus.
in vain, frustrā, nēquicquam.
both, ŭterque.
clothes, vestis, -is, f.
open, apertus.
plain, campus, -i, m., plānĭties, f. 5.
still (=even), etiam.

Exercise 154

fair terms, aequae condĭtiones.
send under the yoke, sub jŭgum mitto.
treaty, foedus, -ĕris, n.
clothes, vestis, -is, f., vestītus, -ūs, m.

Exercise 156

not yet, nondum.
assault (on town), oppugnatio.
departure, prŏfectio.

Exercise 157

standards, signa, n. pl.
overtake, assĕquor, consĕquor.

Exercise 158

invade, invādo, -ĕre, -vāsi, -vāsum (in acc.).
return, rĕdĭtus, -ūs. m.

Exercise 159

peasant, agrĭcŏla, m.
vineyard, vīnētum.
dig up, effŏdio, -ĕre, -fōdi, -fossum.
deceive, dēcĭpio, fallo.
fertile, fertĭlis.

Ex. 159—*contd.*

produce, ēdo, -ĕre, -ēdĭdi, ēdĭtum.

regret, me paenitet, *gen.*

vine, vītis, -is, *f.*

excellent, ēgrĕgius.

disobey, disregard, neglĭgō, -ĕre, -lexi, -lectum.

Exercise 160

because, quod, quia.
[*Use* quia *for actual cause only, and therefore with Ind., except in Indirect Statement.*]

since, quŏniam, quando, cum [cum *always with Subj.*].

on the ground that, for the reason that, proptĕreā quod.

this being so, in this state of affairs, quae cum ita sint, essent.

rejoice, be glad, gaudeo, -ēre, gāvīsus (*quod*).

it is for the good of, ex ūsu est, usui est, *dat.*

condemn to death, capitis damno, I.

Exercise 161

late, sēro, *adv.*

sound the retreat, rĕceptui cănĕre.

exile (person), exsul, -ŭlis.

exile (state), exsĭlium.

treason, mājestas.

Exercise 162

triumph, triumphus, -i, *m.*

fall (of city), use căpio.

be disliked by, displĭceo, *dat.*

pride, sŭperbia.

equal, pār, păris.

chariot, currus, -ūs, *m.*

white, albus.

sacred, săcer, -ra, -rum.

Jupiter, Juppiter, Jŏvis.

finally, postrēmo, dēnĭque.

spoils, spŏlia, *n. pl.*

Apollo, Apollo, -ĭnis.

too much, nimius, nimis (*with gen.*).

Exercise 163

contrary to, contra.

be brought to trial, put on trial, reus sum.

law of nations, international law, jus gentium.

oppress, opprĭmo, -ĕre, -pressi, -pressum.

unjust, injustus.

any, *adj.* in negative sentences, ullus.

govern, rĕgo.

Exercise 164

fall on, căpio.

oracle, ōrăculum.

untouched, intĕger, -ra, -rum.

protect, servo, I.

gulf, sĭnus, -ūs, *m.*

except, praeter.

holy, săcer, -cra, -crum.

Exercise 165

plague, pestis, pestĭlentia.

survive, sŭpersum.

set sail, navem solvo.

meet with, obtain, **nanciscor, -i, nactus.**

favourable, **sĕcundus.**

west, **occĭdens.**

towards, **ad.**

Exercise 166

gaze at, **specto, I.**

warrior, **jŭvĕnis.**

each of two, **ŭterque** [each army = **ŭterque exercitus**].

one . . . other (of two), **alter . . . alter.**

choose, **delĭgo, -ĕre, -lēgi, -lectum.**

prevail, **sŭpĕro, I.**

spear, **hasta.**

slip, **lābor.**

deadly, **mortifer, fūnestus.**

rush, **rŭo, -ĕre, rui, ruitum.**

rush forward, **prōruo.**

be born, **nascor, -i, natus.**

carry off, **abripio, -ĕre, -ui, -reptum.**

Exercise 167

carelessness, **neglĭgentia.**

surprise, **opprĭmo.**

in front, **a fronte.**

waggon, **plaustrum.**

artillery, **tormenta, _n. pl._ ; ballistae.**

Exercise 168

Verbs and phrases to be followed by quin.

non dŭbĭto quin.

non est dŭbium quin.

quis dubitat quin? (virtual _neg._).

fĭĕri non potest quin, it is impossible that . . . not.

facere non possum quin, I cannot help . . .

minimum abest quin, be within a very little of (always _impersonal_).

nĭhil praetermitto quin, leave nothing undone to.

nēmo est quin sciat, there is nobody who does not know ; everybody knows ; all the world knows.

———

do wrong, **pecco, I.**

be on one's side, **făveo, _dat._ ; ab aliquo stare.**

keep word, **fĭdem praesto.**

Exercise 169

birth, race, **gĕnus, -ĕris, _n._**

scorn, **contemno, -ĕre, -tempsi, -temptum.**

by force of arms, **vi et armis.**

multitude, **plebs, plēbis, _f._**

Exercise 170

Verbs of hindering and preventing, which may be followed by quominus, _and when neg. by_ quin.

hinder, **impĕdio,** _acc._; **obsto,** _dat._

prevent, **prŏhĭbeo** (which prefers _Inf._).

deter, **deterreo.**

refuse, **rĕcūso, I.** (also with _Inf._ in _neg._ sentences).

Ex. 170—contd.

it was due to you that . . . not,
per te stetit quominus.

Alps, **Alpes,** *pl.*
weigh anchor, **ancŏras tollo.**

Exercise 171

pass a law, **lēgem jŭbeo.**
threat, **mĭnae.**
destroy, **dēleo.**
supply, **praebeo ;** *acc.* of thing,
  dat. of person.
tribune, **trĭbunus (plebis).**

Exercise 172

hesitate, **dŭbito,** with *Inf.*
Salamis, **Salamis** (*acc.* -**ĭna.**).

Exercise 173

make an assault, **oppugno,** I.
report, **rĕfĕro ; nuntio,** I.
cause panic, **păvōrem injĭcio,**
  dat.
base, **turpis.**

Exercise 174

the salvation of. Cf. Ex. 85.
again and again, **ĭdentĭdem.**
with great loss, **plŭrimis**
  āmissis, magnā strāge.
offer a prayer to, invoke, **prĕcor,** I.
drown, **submergo,** -**ĕre,** -**mersi,**
  -**mersum.**
contrary to expectation, **praeter**
  spem, ŏpīnionem.
repulse, **repello.**

Exercise 175

provoke, **lăcesso.**
ambassador, **lēgatus.**
violate, **viŏlo,** I.
take part in, **interesse,** *dat.*
vow, **jūro,** I.
with the help of the gods, **cum**
  dis.
avenge, **ulciscor,** -**i, ultus.**
for some time, **aliquamdiu.**
be amazed, **mīror,** I.

Exercise 176

as many as, **tot . . . quot.**
neighbour, neighbouring,
  vīcīnus.
to the last, **ad ultĭmum, ad**
  extrēmum.
shut up, **claudo,** -**ĕre,** -**si,** -**sum.**
survive, **superesse,** *dat.*
independence, freedom, **lĭber-**
  tas.

Exercise 177

greet, **sălūto,** I.
stretch out, **porrigo,** -**ĕre,** -**rexi,**
  -**rectum.**
despatches, **litterae.**
read through, **perlĕgo,** -**lēgi,**
  -**lectum.**
draw a circle round, **circum-**
  scrībo.
rod, **virga.**

Exercise 178

shed (tears), **effundo.**
jealousy, **invĭdia.**
hatred, **ŏdium.**

to be most important, **maximi interesse** (Voc. 109).

Exercise 179

elated, **ēlātus.**
departure, **discessus, -ūs,** *m.* ; **prŏfectio.**
more. (See Synonyms.)
boast, **jacto,** I.
transfer, **transfero.**
land forces, **terrestres copiae.**
make straight for, **recto cursu pĕto.**
ravage, **pŏpŭlor,** I. ; **vasto,** I.
unconquerable, invincible, **invictus, indŏmitus.**

Exercise 180

a cry was raised, **clāmatum est.**
give battle to, **proelium committere cum.**
centre (of army), **mĕdia ăcies.**
wing, **āla.**
on both sides, **utrimque.**
foremost ranks, **prīmi ordines.**
flank, **lătus, -ĕris,** *n.*
soldier of the line, **lĕgionarius miles.**

Exercise 181

bring forward (a law), **fero.**
common people, **plebs, plēbis.**
satisfy, **indulgeo, -ēre, -si, -tum.**
aim at, **peto.**
kingship, **regnum, rēgia pŏtestas.**
deliver a speech before, **ōrātionem hăbēre ăpud.**

lessen, diminish, **dīmĭnuo.**
iniquitous (unjust), **inīquus.**

Exercise 182

before, **antequam, priusquam.**
after, **postquam.**

> N.B.—Ante, prius, post, *may be separated from* quam *by the principal verb and other words. See the last example.*

until, **dum, dōnec, quoad.**
whilst, as long as, **donec, quoad.**
as soon as, **sĭmŭlac.**
as often as, **quŏties.**
since, from the time when, **ex quo tempore.**

Exercise 183

man, **compleo.**
raise a shout, **clāmōrem tollo.**
advance standards, **signa fero.**
pass, **praetereo.**

Exercise 184

finish, complete, **perfĭcio.**
address, **contiōnor ăpud.**
take the field, **exercitum ēdūco.**
in close order, **confertus, conferto agmine.**

Exercise 185

stand firm, **resisto.**
province, **prōvincia.**
resign the consulship, **abire (se abdĭcare) consŭlatu.**
field (of battle), **ăcies.**

Ex. 185—*contd.*
give leave, jŭbeo.
adjourn, be dismissed, dīmittor.

Exercise 186

armament, classis.
prevail upon, persuădeo.
result (*n.*), ēventus.
 (*vb.*), evenio.
unfortunate, infēlix.
fall into confusion, perturbor, I.
with one another, inter se.
darkness, těnebrae.
reduce, rědīgo.

Exercise 187

south, měrīdies, -ēi, *m.*
despair, spem abjicio.
feast, ĕpŭlor, I.
drink, bĭbo, -ěre, bĭbi.
win the day, vinco.
feign, sĭmŭlo, I.
entice, ēlĭcio, -ěre, -cui, -citum.
havoc, strāges, -is, *f.*
pierce, transfīgo, -ěre, -fixi, -fixum.

Exercise 189

relief, auxĭlium.

Exercise 190

come upon, incĭdo in.
cut down, succīdo, -ěre, -cīdi, -cīsum.
without doubt, sīne dŭbio.
quietly, unobserved, clam.
recall, rěvŏco. I.
prosper, rem gěro prospěre.
treat for, ago de.

Exercise 191

keep, detain, rětĭneo.
victorious, victor.
conspirator, conjūratus.
gather round, cingo.
in time, ad tempus, tempori.
hold a conference, collŏquor.
stealthily, furtim.
lead aside, dēdūco.

Exercise 192

raise a siege, desistere obsidione.
run short, fail, deficio.
hold out (of provisions), suppeto.
harass, lăcesso.
renew, rědintegro, I. ;
 rěnŏvo, I.

Exercise 193

wander, văgor, I. ; erro, I.
be annoyed at, taken ill, aegre fero.
repay, reddo.
without accomplishing anything, re infectă.
appease, pāco, I.
take part in, interesse. Cf. Ex. 61.
credit, laus, -dis, *f.*
fresh, intěger.
riot, tŭmultus, ūs, *m.*
insult, injūria, contŭmēlia.
come to an agreement, consentio, -ire, -sensi, -sensum.
noon, měrīdies.
bring to trial, reum făcio.

Exercise 194

disheartened, mĕtu commōtus.
defeat, clādes, -is, *f.* ;
incommŏdum.
propose, censeo, -ēre, censui
[*acc.* and *inf.* or *subj.*].
meet with, pătior, -i, passus.
still, adhuc.
possible, translate by facio or
fiĕri pŏtest.
western part, pars quae ad oc-
cāsum sōlis spectat.
interior, pars intĕrior.

Exercise 195

appoint, constituo.
fatal, fūnestus.
in despair, re or sălūte despe-
rata ; spe abjectā.
for this purpose, ad hoc.
in two divisions, bĭpartīto.
red, rŭber, -bra, -brum.
poison, vĕnēnum.
Syracuse, Syracusae.

Exercise 196

obstacle, difficultas.
surmount, sŭpĕro, I.
so signally, tantā strāge.
ambuscade, insĭdiae. In the
last sentence use ex insidiis
invadĕre.
open fight, pitched battle, justum proelium, ăcies.
in the guise of, mōre.
warning, exemplo esse. Cf.
Ex. 85.
make trial of, expĕrior.

considering, calculating, rătus
(reor).
rashly, tĕmĕre, inconsulte.
slight, aspernor, I.
narrow, angustus, artus.

Exercise 197

without success, to no purpose,
frustrā, nēquicquam.
private citizen, prīvātus.
wholly, altogether [*vith neg. and
virtual neg.*], omnīno.
seat of war, sēdes belli.
assign, attrĭbuo.
control of campaign, chief command, totius belli summa,
summa imperii.
in triumph, victor. [Triumphus
= the triumphal procession of
a Roman general.]

Exercise 198

dawn, illūcescit, illuxit.
break down, prōruo.
seek refuge in, fly for refuge to,
confŭgio ad.
incensed with, īratus, *dat.*
partly, partim.
hitherto, adhuc.
grudge, resentment, invĭdia.

Exercise 199

dream, *vb.* somnio, I. ; somnio
vĭdeo [= to see in a dream].
dream, *n.* somnium.
egg, ōvum.
hang, *intr.* pendeo.
        trans. suspendo.
mean, indicate, signĭfĭco, I.

Ex. 199—*contd.*

bed, cŭbīle, *n.*
dig, fŏdio.
I for my part, ĕquĭdem [*use only with 1st pers. sing.*].
be vexed, aegre or mŏleste fero.

Exercise 200

charge, crīmen, -ĭnis, *n.*
prosperity, advantage, commŏdum.
to the best of his ability, pro vīrīli parte.
devotion, stŭdium.
desperate, perdĭtus.
assume, ūsurpo, I.
supreme power, summa impĕrii.
crisis, discrīmen.
wrong, injūria.

Exercise 201

fit to, aptus, dignus qui (a consecutive clause).
governor of a province, prōconsul.
worship, cŏlo.
rob, spŏlio, I. ; diripio.
offend, displĭceo, *dat.*
character, mōres, *pl.*
commit, admitto.
theft, furtum.
thief, fūr, fūris, *m.*
jest, jŏcus, -i, *m.*
justify, excūso, I.
cup, pōcŭlum.
statue, stătua.
stretch out, extendo, porrĭgo.
benefit, bĕnĕficium.
now for a long time, jāmprīdem, jāmdudum.

cloak, pallium.
military cloak, săgum.
wear, *pass.* of induo, vestio.
woollen, lāneus.
wool, lāna.

Exercise 203

on foot, pedibus.
restrain, mŏdĕror, I., *dat.*
prudent, prūdens.

Exercise 204

mock, irrīdeo, *dat.*
throw bridge over, pontem facio in, *abl.*
straight, recto ĭtinere, dīrecto.
subdue, subĭgo, in pŏtestatem rĕdĭgo.
none the less, nĭhĭlōmĭnus.
tribute, trĭbūtum, vectīgal, -ālis, *n.*
impose, impōno.
prosperous, fēlix.
wrong, injūriam facio, *dat.*
revenge oneself on, poenas sūmo de ; ulciscor, *acc.*
bribery, ambĭtus, -ūs, *m.*
it is no advantage, minime prōdest.

Exercise 205

poet, poeta.
relieve, sublĕvo, I.
capitol, căpĭtōlium.
in former times, antīquĭtus.
capable of, aptus ad.
false, falsus.
certainly, certo, sĭne dŭbio.
starve, făme pereo.

Exercise 206

take place of, succēdo, *dat.*
cut down, occīdo.
front rank, prima ăcies.
remind, admŏneo.
bill, rŏgātio.
influence, auctōritas.
have influence, văleo.
arrest, comprehendo, -ĕre, -di,
-sum.

Exercise 207

object of hatred. (See Ex. 85.)
incur, subeo.

Exercise 208

lose heart, despēro, animum
dēmitto.
fall into hands of, in pŏtestatem
venire.
gloriously, (cum) summa laude.
inflict ... on some one, aliquem
afficere, *abl.*
avenger, ultor.
perjury, laesa fĭdes.
be favourable to, făveo. *dat.* ;
sto ab aliquo.
violate, vĭŏlo, I.
be offended at, aegre fero.
misery, suffering, dŏlor.

Exercise 209

impregnable, inexpugnābilis.
steep, praeruptus.
lines, munītiones, munīmenta.
siege works, ŏpera, *n. pl.*

Exercise 210

marvellous, mīrus.
before the consuls, apud con-
sules.
condemn, condemno, I. ;
damno, I.
acquit, absolvo.
loyal, fĭdēlis.

Exercise 211

go well, prōficio.
faint-hearted, tĭmĭdus.
to the death, usque ad mortem.
burdensome (cf. Ex. 85), mŏlestus.
speech, ōrātio.
confess, confĭteor.
side (of river), rīpa.

Exercise 212

suffer hardship, lăbōro.
bribe, pĕcūnia.
philosopher, phĭlŏsŏphus.
origin, ŏrīgo, -ĭnis, *f.*

Exercise 213

in my house, apud me.
misfortune, mălum.

Exercise 214

fugitive, fŭgĭtīvus.
imagine, reor, dūco.
really, rēvērā.
rest, reliqua pars.

Exercise 215

ignorance, inscientia.
responsible for, auctor.

I

Ex. 215—contd.
main road, **via, certum iter.**
unmolested, **incŏlŭmis.**
on equal terms, **aequo Marte,
aequā contentione.**
cliff, **rūpes, -is,** *f.*

Exercise 216

named, by name, **nomine.**
particularly, **praeter omnes.**
overthrow, **sterno.**
sight, **spectācŭlum.**
extraordinary, **ēgrĕgius.**
crown, **cŏrōna.**
fine, **mulcto aliquem,** *abl.*
expose oneself to, **se objĭcĕre,**
   dat. **; occurro,** *dat.*
eagerness, **stŭdium.**
dismayed, **perterritus, pavore
perculsus.**
marvellous, **mīrus.**

Exercise 217

master of the horse, **măgister
equitum.**
without the orders of, **injussu.**

Exercise 218

cut off, **dēsĕco.**
accustomed, **sŏlĭtus.**
settlement, **cŏlōnia.**
with minds made up, **obstĭnātis
animis.**
maimed, **saucius.**

Exercise 219

fit out, **instruo.**
rescue, **rĕdūco.**

survivor, **sŭperstes, -ĭtis,** *or*
   verb **sŭperesse.**
break, **frango.**
reduce, **rĕdĭgo.**
naval, **nāvālis.**
off, *prep.* **contrā.**
promontory, **prōmontōrium.**
take on board, **in navem ex-
cipio.**
defender, **dēfensor.**
earn, **mĕreo, mĕreor.**

Exercise 220

hold a command, **impĕrium
obtĭneo.**
prove oneself, **se praebēre.**
confidence, trust, **fĭdes.**
complete, **certus, mănĭfestus.**
treat, **ūtor.**
place before, prefer, **antĕpōno.**
   Cf. Ex. 61.
consent, **vŏlo.**
strict, **sĕvērus.**
discipline, **disciplīna.**
energy, **stŭdium.**
influence with, **auctōritas apud.**
pitched battle, **justum
proelium.**
recover, **rĕcĭpio.**

Exercise 221.

treat, **afficio.**
hospitality, **hospĭtium.**
host, guest, **hospes.**
everywhere, **ŭbīque.**
raiment, **vestis, -is,** *f.*
weave, **texo, -ĕre, texui,
textum.**
sumptuous, **magnĭfĭcus, lautus.**

hold games, lŭdos cĕlĕbro, I.
stung, commotus, lăcessītus.
provide, praebeo.
bestow, dono, I.
surpass, supero, I.
sports, ludi.

Exercise 222

pacify, pāco, I.
connected by birth, cognatus,
 natu conjunctus.
claim, ūsurpo, I.
first place, princĭpātus, -ūs, *m.*
devoid of, nūdatus, văcuus.
remedy, rĕmĕdium.
attempt, cōnatus, *or use verb.*
with the goodwill of. Use
 apprŏbare.
Spain, Hispania.

Exercise 223

convict of treason, damno
 mājestatis.
inflict injury, injūriam inferre,
 dat.
innocent, insons, -tis.
quite, sătis.

Exercise 224

to do one's best to, id ăgĕre ut.
risk, perīclĭtor, I.

Exercise 225

remain silent, tăceo.
bind (by oath), obstringo.
in the presence of, cōram.
oath, jusjurandum.
disband, dimitto.
indignation, ira, dŏlor.

Exercise 226

foreign, externus.
observe customs, instĭtūtis
 ūti.
be responsible, translate by
 'I must give an account,'
 rătionem reddo.
government, magistratūs, ei
 qui rempublicam admini-
 strant.
resolutely, obstinate, summa
 constantia.

Exercise 227

bring to a close, conficio.
satisfied, contentus.
geniality, cōmĭtas.
win affection, stŭdium
 concĭliare.
luxury, luxus, -ūs, *m.*
want, inŏpia.
the result is that, ēvĕnit ut.
positively, absolutely (with
 negative words), omnīno.
undertake, suscipio.

Exercise 228

diminish, dimĭnuo, *trans.*
more numerous, mājor.
come out, prove, ēvădo, -ĕre,
 -si, -sum.
experience, ūsus, -ūs, *m.*;
 pĕrītia.
in close order, conferto agmine.
face, obeo, *acc.*
adverse, adversus, inīquus.
trouble, lăbor.

Exercise 229

differ, inter se differre.
grumble at, quĕror˙˙de, aegrē fero.
risk one's life, pĕrīculum căpĭtis sŭbire.
crush, opprĭmo ; prōflīgo, I.
acquire, acquīro, nanciscor.

Exercise 230

unshaken, immōtus.
readily, lībenter.
two-thirds, duae partes.
inspire, injicio aliquid alicui.
enthusiasm, stŭdium.
the cause was lost. Use actum est de.
display, praesto.
consecrate, vŏveo.
desert, deficio.
grant, do, mando, I., trado.

Exercise 231

behave, se gĕrĕre.
reward, praemio afficio.
depend on, ponitur in.
foresee, prōvĭdeo.
his object was, id ēgit ut.
be devoted to, stŭdeo, dat.
affairs of state, res publicae.
set an example. (See Ex. 85.)

Exercise 232

rush into, irruo in.
foretell, praedīco.
leisure, ōtium.
distinguished, insignis.

Exercise 233

at the battle of Zama, pugna Zamae facta.
mercenaries, mercēnārii milites.
contrary to expectation, praeter spem, ŏpīnionem.
veteran, veterānus.
disorderly, tŭmultuārius.
rabble, turba.

Exercise 234

show presence of mind, impă-vĭdus esse, se intrĕpĭde gerere.
explain, expōno, ēdo.
cry, clāmor.
groan, gĕmĭtus, -ūs.
undergo sentence, poenam subeo.
crowd round, circumfundor, dat.
sufferings, măla, n. pl.

Exercise 235

consider, dēlībĕro de.
silent, tăcĭtus.
Egypt, Aegyptus, -i, f.
empire, impĕrium.

Exercise 236

proscribe, proscrībo.
put out to sea, ēvĕhor(in altum).
adverse, adversus.
litter, lectīca.
stretch out, porrĭgo.
neck, cervīces, f. plu.
drive back, repello.

considering his critical position,
ut in tanto discrimine.

Exercise 237

be under protection, **fĭdem
sequor.**

Exercise 239

inquire, hold inquiry about,
quaestionem habeo de.
wrong, **injuria.**

Exercise 240

humour, **mōrem gero,** *dat.*
freedman, **lībertus, -i.**

Exercise 241

regiment, **cŏhors.**
(raw) recruit, **tĭro, -ōnis.**
Po, **Pădus, -i,** *m.*
flower (of army), **rōbur, -ŏris,** *n.*

Exercise 242

deaf, **surdus, auribus captus.**
dishonour, disgrace, **dēdĕcŏro,
I.; dēdĕcŏri esse.**
regret, **dēplōro, I.**
change, **mūto, I.**
temper, **animus.**
former days, **tempus prius, sŭ-
pĕrius.**

Exercise 243

drag down, **dētrăho.**
orator, **ōrātor.**
continue a war, **bellum dūco,
produco.**
infringe upon, **dēmĭnuo.**

serve as soldier, **stīpendia
mĕreo** (stipendium = soldier's
pay).
agree upon, fix, **constĭtuo.**
refer, **rĕfero.**
reject, **rējicio, respuo.**
be indignant with, **irascor,** *dat.*

Exercise 244

endurance, **pătientia.**
plainly, **ăpertē, plānē.**
approval, **consensus, -ūs,** *m.*
opinion, **sententia.**
express, **ēdo, fero.**
run risk of, **periculum subeo.**

Exercise 245

depose from tribuneship, **abrŏgare trĭbūnatum,** *dat.*
disaffected, mutinous, **sēdĭtio-
sus.**
with one consent, **consensu.**
loyal, **fĭdēlis.**
prove false, **me infidelem
praebeo.**

Exercise 246

declare an enemy to the state,
hostem dēcerno.
ask repeatedly, **rŏgĭto.**
threatening, **mĭnax.**
senate house, **cūria.**

Exercise 247

in our times, **his tempŏribus,
nostra aetate.**
artisan, **artĭfex, -ĭcis.**
pile up, **congero.**
want (be without), **căreo,** *abl.*

Ex. 247—*contd.*

bloodshed, **cruor, -ōris,** *m.*
every year, **quŏtannis.**
senators, **patres.**
carry (a law), **fero.**

Exercise 248

gloomy, **tristis, fūnestus.**
utterly rout, **prōflīgo,** I.
infirm, **infirmus, invalidus.**

Exercise 249

decisive, **haud anceps.**
be brought to a successful issue, **prospĕrē ēvĕnire.**
barren, **irrītus.**
be purchased at cost of, **stare,** *abl.*
fastness, **castellum.**
dear, **cārus.**

Exercise 250

assured, **explōratus.**
share with, **partior cum.**
enriched, **auctus.**
equally, **aeque, părĭter.**

Exercise 251

recently, **nūper.**
commonly, **vulgo,**
steal, **abripio.**
subject (*adj.*), **subjectus imperio.**
dear friend, **conjunctissimus.**
office, **hŏnōres.**
involve oneself in, **occurro,** *dat.*
disgrace, **dēdĕcus, -oris,** *n.* ; **ignominia.**
tax, **vectīgal.**

philosophy, **philosophia.**
cure, **mĕdeor,** *dat.* ; **sāno,** I. *acc.*

Exercise 252

followers, **cŏmites.**
say farewell to, **jubeo aliquem vălēre.**
last necessity, **ultima nĕcessitas.**
loyalty, **fĭdes,** *f.* 5.
prosperity, **res prosperae.**
adversity, **res adversae.**

Exercise 253

principal officers. (See note, p. 55.)
union, **consensus.**
yield (*trans.*), **concēdo.**
applause, **plausus, -ūs,** *m.*
approve, **prŏbo,** I.
in battle array, **acie instructa.**
dispute, **dēcerto de.**
perilous moment, **discrimen.**

Exercise 254

share, take part in, **partĭceps sum** (*gen.*).
sail along, **lĕgo, praetervĕhor.**
produce, **ēdo.**
hold cheap, **parvi facio.**
let go, **dīmitto.**
would that, **ŭtĭnam.**

   (1) *Present subj.* of future time.
   (2) *Imperfect subj.* of present time.
   (3) *Pluperfect subj.* of past time.

contest, **certāmen.**
watch, **specto,** I.

Exercise 255

fully, **satis.**
weak (of forces), **exĭguus.**
reef, **saxa, scŏpŭli.**
success, **successus, -ūs.**
ride, be at anchor, **in ancŏris
stare.**
make his way in, **se insĭnuare.**
rashness, **tĕmĕritas.**
dash against, **allīdo, -ĕre, -si,
-sum.**

opposite to, **contra, e regione,**
gen.
aghast, **obstŭpefactus.**

Exercise 256

tumultuous, **tumultuosus.**
assailant, **oppugnator.**
fortress, **castellum.**
thicket, **virgultum.**
bloody, **cruentus.**
to be in a blaze, **ardēre.**
wigwam, **căsa.**

PREPOSITIONAL PHRASES

Ad

Gaul lies towards the north.	Gallia vergit ad septemtriones.
A battle fought in the neighbour-hood of Cannae.	Pugna ad Cannas[1] facta.
About 10,000 soldiers.	Ad decem milia militum.
At a fit time, opportunely.	Ad tempus.
They advanced as far as the gate.	Usque ad portam progressi sunt.
On the right.	Ad dextram.
All without exception, all to a man.	Omnes ad unum.
Finally, at the extremity.	Ad ultimum, ad extremum.
To speak to the point, to good purpose.	Ad rem loqui.
For the purpose of keeping up hope.	Ad spem servandam.

Apud

In the writings of Caesar.	Apud Caesarem.
At my house.	Apud me.
Among the Gauls.	Apud Gallos.
A speech delivered before the people.	Oratio apud populum habita.

Secundum

To march along the banks of a river.	Secundum flumen iter facere.
To live in accordance with nature.	Secundum naturam vivere.

---

[1] Distinguish carefully—Cannas = *to* Cannae.
  Cannis = *at* Cannae.
  Ad Cannas = *near* Cannae.

Per

To ascertain by means of scouts.	Per exploratores cognoscere.
A man loved for his own merits.	Vir per se ipsum amatus.
It was owing to you that we did not cross the river.	Per te stetit quominus flumen transiremus.
I beseech you by the gods.	Per ego te deos oro.

Sub

To winter under canvas, in tents.	Sub pellibus hiemare.
To halt at the foot of a mountain.	Sub monte consistere.
To send an army under the yoke.	Exercitum sub jugum mittere.
Towards evening.	Sub vesperum.

Praeter

He led his forces past Caesar's camp.	Praeter Caesaris castra copias suas transduxit.
To speak beside the mark.	Praeter rem loqui.
To an extraordinary degree, unnaturally.	Praeter modum.
Beyond hope.	Praeter spem.
Contrary to expectation.	Praeter opinionem.
They have no clothing besides skins.	Nihil vestitūs praeter pelles habent.
You do more than all the rest.	Praeter ceteros laboras.

Super

Beyond all others.	Super omnes.

Ab or ā

At a distance of 15 miles.	A milibus passuum quindecim.
In the rear, on the side, etc.	A tergo, a latere.
From sunrise till late in the day.	Ab sole orto usque ad multum diei.
Since the foundation of Rome.	Ab urbe condita.
He was on our side.	A nobis stetit.

Cum

With the help of the gods.	Cum dīs.
To live virtuously	Cum virtute vivere.
Some were tortured and put to death.	Pars cum cruciatu necabatur.
I have to deal with you.	Tecum mihi res est.
He wrote with care.	Cum diligentia[1] scripsit.

De

To throw oneself down from a wall.	De muro se dejicere.
About midnight.	De media nocte.
On purpose.	De industria.
Unexpectedly.	De improviso.
We are ruined, it is all up with us.	Actum est de nobis.

Ex or ē

To dismount.	Ex equo desilire.
To fight on foot or on horseback.	Pedibus aut ex equis pugnare.
In the course of a march.	Ex itinere.
Over against the town.	E regione oppidi.
After the consulship of Cotta.	E Cottae consulatu.
A man miserable after being happy.	Homo miser ex beato.
Since (of time).	Ex quo.
None of the barbarians.	Nulli e barbaris.
For the good of Gaul.	Ex usu Gallorum.
In accordance with the treaty.	Ex foedere.
Partly.	Ex parte.
Favourably, as we wish.	Ex sententia.

---

[1] *Or* magna diligentia.   If there is no epithet 'cum' must generally be used. See Voc. 89.

Pro

Caesar led his troops before the camp.	Caesar pro castris suas copias produxit.
To be sure.	Pro certo habere.
To state as a fact.	Pro certo ponere.
Considering the size of the population.	Pro multitudine hominum.
With your usual prudence.	Pro tua prudentia.
To the best of one's ability, manfully.	Pro virili parte.
According to time and circumstances.	Pro tempore et pro re.
He was a father to me.	Pro parente mihi fuit.
Proconsul, propraetor.	Pro consule, pro praetore (*later as single word*—Proconsul).

Prae

He displayed a dagger.	Prae se pugionem tulit.
I made no secret of having done this.	Hoc me fecisse semper prae me tuli.
They seem cowardly in comparison with the Gauls.	Prae Gallis ignavi videntur.
I do not know where I am for joy.	Prae gaudio nescio ubi sim. (*Only use* prae *in this sense with negatives or* vix).

In

To make a bridge over a river.	Pontem in flumine facere.
To be under arms.	In armis esse.
At present.	In praesenti.
Our safety depends upon you.	Salus nostra in te posita est.
Daily, from day to day (of something increasing.	In dies.
For the future.	In posterum, in futurum.
In turn.	In vicem.

SYNONYMS

About . . (around, of place), **circum, circa.**
(of time or number), **circiter,** *adv.* or *prep.*
(of number), **ad.**
(=concerning), **de**

Again . . (general word), **rursus.**
(a second time), **iterum.**
(again and again), **saepenumero, identidem.**

All . . . (general word), **omnis.**
(with superlatives), **quisque,** *e.g.* **optimus quisque,**
all the best.
(all together, implying connection), **cunctus, uni-
versus ;** *e.g.* **cunctus senatus.**
(the whole, entire), **totus,** *e.g.* **tota provincia.**

Ask . . . (questions), **rogare, interrogare, quaerere (ex).**
(requests), **rogare, petere (ab), poscere, postulare, orare, flagitare.**
Petere is most frequently used of a request addressed to a superior. *Poscere* and *postulare* imply
a claim or demand, made as of right. *Orare* is 'to
beg.' *Flagitare* is used of a vehement or im-
portunate demand.

Bear . . . (carry), **ferre, portare, vehere.**
Vehere is most used of conveying by ship,
carriage, or animals. *Equo vehi*=to ride ; *nave
vehi*=to sail.

(endure), **pati, tolerare, ferre.**
Pati is the most general word. *Tolerare* is 'to
put up with.' *Ferre* is 'to bear bravely.'

Call . . . (summon), **vocare, arcessere.**
(name), **nominare, appellare, vocare.**
(call to, accost, invoke), **appellare.**

Each . . (of any number), **quisque.**
(of two), **uterque.**
(one by one, separately), **singuli;** *e.g.* **singulos interrogavit,** he questioned each separately.

Fear . . . (general word), **timere.**
(often with the idea of respect), **vereri.**
(dread, apprehend future evil), **metuere.**
The nouns *timor*, *metus* correspond to their verbs. *Pavor* is 'panic,' 'trembling with fear.'

Find . . . (a thing or person), **invenire, reperire.**
Reperire most often means finding something lost and searched for.
(find out facts), **cognoscere, comperire.**

Follow . . **Sequor** and compounds.
Consequor, assequor = come up with, reach.
Prosequor = escort.
Subsequor = follow close after, come next.
Persequor = follow up, follow to the end.

Happen . (generally of bad fortune), **accidit.**
(generally of good fortune), **contingit.**
(result, happen as result of something else), **evenit.**

Kill . . . (general word), **interficere.**
(in fighting), **occidere.**
(especially of hunger, poison, etc.), **necare.**
(massacre, implying cruelty), **trucidare.**
(murder), **jugulare.**

Know, Knowledge

(know mentally, *e.g.* languages, sciences, etc. ; know how to do a thing), **scire.**

(know persons), **novisse.**

(learn facts), **cognoscere, comperire.**

(perceive, learn by the senses), **percipere, sentire.**

(understand), **intellegere.**

(recognise persons or things known before), **agnoscere.**

The nouns *scientia* and *cognitio* correspond to *scire* and *cognoscere;* knowledge of persons is to be translated by *consuetudo.*

Land . .

(opposed to sea), **terra.**

(a country, district), **regio, terra.**

(lands), **agri,** *e.g.* **agros, populatus est.**

(native land), **patria.**

(ground soil), **solum.**

Last . . .

(furthest, *i.e.* first or last of a series, in place or time), **ultimus, extremus ;** *e.g.* **extremum oppidum Allobrogum.**

(utmost, extreme), the same words, *e.g.* **ultimum supplicium.**

(immediately preceding), **proximus ;** *e.g.* **proxima nocte.**

(latest), **novissimus ;** *e.g.* **qui novissimus venit, necatur.**

Lose . . .

(wilfully), **perdere.**

(lose by carelessness, etc.), **amittere.**

(let slip opportunity, etc.), **omittere, dimittere.**

Man . . .

(human being, opp. to animals), **homo.**

(opp. to women, children, cowards), **vir.**

Mind . .

(general words), **animus, mens. Animus** is more often used of the emotions, **mens** of the intellect.

(talent, intellect), **ingenium.**

More . . (comparing qualities or acts), **magis**; *e.g.* **magis consilio quam virtute.**

(comparing degree, quantity), **plus**; *e.g.* **valet salus plus quam libido.**

(*rather*, implying preference), **potius**; *e.g.* **consilium potius quam vis postulatur.**

(usually of time or number), **amplius**; *e.g.* **amplius horis quattuor.**

New, Old . That which has lasted a long time is **vetus**, and opposed to **recens**, fresh, newly made.

That which existed in former times is **antiquus**, and opposed to **novus**, new, not having previously existed.

People, Race

(a 'nation' in the political sense), **populus.**

(a race, a people), **gens.**

(a tribe, generally of distant, barbarous tribes), **natio.**

Only use 'genus' for 'race' where it means 'family'; *e.g.* **nobili genere ortus.**

'People' in the sense of 'men generally' (as in 'men say,' 'on dit') is either omitted, or may be translated by *homines*, especially where it means 'mankind generally.'

Power . . (legal, official power), **potestas.**

(political power, not necessarily due to official position), **potentia.**

(influence, importance, often personal influence), **auctoritas.**

(supreme magisterial or kingly power, especially from the military point of view), **imperium.**

(dominion, sway), **ditio, potestas, imperium**; *e.g.* **in potestate Populi Romani esse**, *to be subject to the Romans.*

(royal power), **regnum.**

(tyranny, absolute rule), **dominatus.**

(physical power, strength), **vires.**

See . . . (general word), **videre.**
(catch sight of), **conspicere, conspicari.**
(discern, see clearly), **perspicere,** *pres.* and *imp.*
tenses of **cernere.**
(gaze at), **spectare, intueri.**
For 'see' in the sense of 'understand' *cf.* 'Know.'

Show . . (display, hold out), **ostendere.**
(show off, parade), **ostentare.**
(point out, especially of facts, but also 'to point out
a road,' etc.), **demonstrare.**
(produce, bring out, show up), **exhibere.**
(show qualities), **praestare;** *e.g.* **praestare virtutem,** or **se praebere fortem.**

Speak . . (say something, express thought), **dicere.**
(talk), **loqui.**
(speak to, accost), **alloqui, appellare.**
(address), **alloqui.**
(make a speech), **orationem habere.**

Take . . (general word), **capere.**
(take up, assume; *e.g.* arma), **sumere.**
(undertake; *e.g.* bellum), **suscipere.**
(take with the hand or arrest), **comprehendere.**

Want . . (be without), **carere.**
(need), **egere, indigere** (or use **opus esse**).
(wish for), **velle, cupere.**
(to be wanting, to fail), **deficere.**

Work . . (labour, toil), **labor.**
('a work,' 'works'; most frequently the *result* of
labour), **opus;** *e.g.* **opera,** *military fortifications.*

Notice the following Verbs, which in English may be either Transitive or Intransitive.

	TRANSITIVE.	INTRANSITIVE.
Burn	incendere, urere	ardere.
Change	mutare	mutari.
Collect	colligere, cogere	convenire.
Embark	imponere in navem	conscendere (in) navem.
Increase	augere	crescere.
Join	conjungere	se conjungere cum.
Land	exponere in terram	egredi e nave.
Leave	relinquere	abire, discedere.
Move	movere	se movere.
Return	reddere.	redire.
Scatter	dispergere	dispergi.
Surrender	tradere, dedere	se tradere, se dedere.
Trust	mandare, committere	confidere, credere.
Turn	convertere	converti, se convertere.

MILITARY VOCABULARY

The Army. Men and Officers

legion (*largest number*, 6000), legio.

cohort, regiment (*tenth part of legion*), cohors.

squadron (*of calvary*), turma, ala (*tenth part of* turma).

company (*of infantry*), manipulus (= 200 men).

infantry, pedites, *m. pl.*, peditatus, *m.* 4 (*collective*).

cavalry, equites, *m. pl.*, equitatus, *m.* 4 (*collective*).

army in battle order or line, acies.
    in marching order or column, agmen.

those of military age, juventus (*collective*), qui arma ferre possunt.

light-armed troops (*collective*), levis armatura.

troops ready for battle, expediti.

heavy-armed troops, use legionarii.

archers, sagittarii.

slingers, funditores.

scouts, exploratores, speculatores.

recruits, tirones.

veterans, veterani.

reserves, subsidia.

reinforcements, supplementum, novae copiae.

auxiliary forces, auxilia (= *allies and light-armed troops as opposed to the legion*).

a large force, magnae (*not* multae) copiae.

a small force, exigua manus.

the flower of the troops, robur militum.

camp followers, calones.

---

non-commissioned officers (sergeants, etc.), centuriones.

captains, best translated centuriones.

colonels, best translated tribuni militum.

officers, general's staff, legati.

commander of cavalry, praefectus equitum.

general of division, legatus.

commander-in-chief, imperator.

the command-in-chief, summa imperii.

to appoint some one to chief command, summam imperii alicui deferre.

to give some one command of legion, aliquem legioni praeficere.

to be at the head of a legion, legioni praeesse.

Arms

to take up arms, arma sumere, capere.

to make ready for battle, arma expedire.

to be under arms, in armis esse.

to lay down arms, ab armis discedere.

to throw away arms, arma abjicere.

by force of arms, vi et armis.

missiles, tela.

a shower of missiles, crebra tela, *or* magna vis telorum.

to discharge, shoot, conjicere, mittere.

to return fire, tela rejicere.

within, out of range, intra, extra teli jactum.

to draw a sword, gladium stringere.

to sheath a sword, gladium in vaginam recondere.

artillery (see under *Siege*).

helmet, galea.

shield, scutum.

breastplate, lorica.

sword, gladius.

javelin, pilum.

Enlisting, Serving, Deserting

to enlist men, conscribere.

to hold a levy, delectum habere.

to take the oath of allegiance, in verba jurare alicujus.

to serve a campaign, stipendia merere.

to serve five years, quina stipendia merere.

to review an army, recensere.

to disband, dimittere.

discharged (*honourably*), emeritus.

to avoid military service, militiam detrectare.

a deserter, perfuga, transfuga.

to desert, transfugere, signa relinquere.

mutiny, seditio.

mutinous, seditiosus.

Camp

to choose a site for a camp, castra capere, locum castris (ad castra) idoneum deligere.

to pitch camp, castra ponere, munire.

   to strike, castra movere, promovere (= *advance*), signa convellere.

   to leave undefended, castra nudare.

to remain inactive in, castris se tenere, continere.

winter, summer quarters [castra] hiberna, aestiva.

———

sentinels, vigiliae, custodes, custodiae.

to be on guard, keep watch, excubias (custodias) agere.

watchword, signum, tessera.

pickets, stationes.

rampart, vallum, agger.

Camp—*contd.*

to raise a rampart, vallum exstruere, facere.

trench, fossa.

to make a trench, fossam ducere.

The March

the vanguard, primum agmen.

the rearguard, novissimum agmen, novissimi.

to set out, proficisci.

to march, iter facere, contendere.

forced march, magnum iter.

to advance, progredi, signa movere, signa ferre.

with closed ranks, in order of war, agmine quadrato, confertis ordinibus (*opposed to* solutis ordinibus).

to bring up the rear, agmen claudere.

to build a road, viam munire.

to have one's passage barred, itinere intercludi.

to stop marching, iter intermittere.

to change one's route, wheel, signa convertere.

to halt, consistere.

to station pickets at intervals, custodias disponere.

to reconnoitre, explorare.

to cut off stragglers, palantes excipere.

to climb hill, superare collem.

to transport an army over a river, exercitum flumen trajicere.

baggage, impedimenta.

baggage animals, jumenta.

Commissariat

supplies, commeatus (*sing.*).

corn, corn supply, frumentum, res frumentaria.

to forage, pabulari.

to get corn, frumentari.

to cut off the enemy's supplies, hostes commeatu intercludere, prohibere.

to look after corn supplies, rem frumentariam comparare, rei frumentariae providere.

to procure supplies, parare, suppeditare frumentum.

there are supplies in abundance, commeatus suppetit.

abundance of provisions, magna vis commeatus.

War. General Phrases

to proclaim war, bellum indicere.

to make war upon, bellum inferre.

to wage war, bellum gerere (cum).

to prolong, drag on, bellum ducere.

to begin war, belli initium facere.

to finish war, bellum conficere, finem belli facere.

to renew the war, bellum redintegrare.

to conduct a war, bellum administrare.

to ac on the defensive, bellum illatum defendere.

to rebel, revolt, deficere ab.

war materials, apparatus (*sing.*) belli.

Invasion, Inroad

to make an invasion, inroad, incursionem, excursionem facere.

to ravage with fire and sword, omnia ferro ignique vastare.

to plunder, carry off booty, ferre atque agere praedam. (*N.B.* —ferre *of inanimate things,* agere *of cattle. Cf. Greek* φέρειν καὶ ἄγειν.)

to lay waste the country, agros vastare.

Conquest

to subjugate, subigere, in potestatem redigere.

to keep in submission, aliquem in officio continere.

to remain in submission, in officio permanere.

submit, in deditionem venire, *or* in fidem ac potestatem se permittere.

Battle

(1) GENERAL PHRASES

to engage, proelium committere, signa conferre.

to fight (with missiles) at a distance, eminus (telis, jaculis) pugnare.

> *at close quarters, hand to hand,* comminus pugnare.
> *on foot, on horseback,* pedibus, ex equis pugnare.

a skirmish, leve proelium.

a cavalry engagement, proelium equestre.

a battle fought near Cannae, proelium ad Cannas factum.

a pitched battle, justum proelium.

to fight a pitched battle, in acie dimicare, justo proelio contendere.

> *a drawn battle,* aequo Marte (aequis conditionibus) pugnare.
> *a losing battle,* fortunā inclinatā pugnare.
> *a decisive battle,* proelio decertare.

the battle lasted till late in the day, pugnatum est usque ad multum diei.

to win, lose a fight, rem bene, male gerere.

an indecisive battle, proelium anceps.

a favourable battle, proelium secundum.

an adverse battle, proelium adversum.

to be superior in numbers, numero praestare, superiores esse.

to be inferior in numbers, numero inferiores esse.

(2) BEFORE THE BATTLE

to offer battle to the enemy, copiam (potestatem) pugnandi hostibus facere.

to provoke to battle, proelio (ad proelium) lacessere, provocare.

Battle—_contd._

to decline battle, proelium detrectare.

to give the signal to engage, signum proelii (committendi) dare.

to draw up forces in battle order, aciem instruere, copias acie instruere.

to extend the line, deploy, aciem explicare.

to muster, ad signa convenire.

to harangue the men, contionari apud milites, _or use_ cohortari.

to encourage, embolden the men, animos militum confirmare.

(3) DURING THE BATTLE

to attack, aggredi, adoriri, signa inferre (_in_).

    the enemy in front, adversis hostibus occurrere.

    in the rear, hostes aversos (a tergo) aggredi.

to charge, impetum facere in (for _gen., dat., abl. plural_ use forms of _incursio_ instead of _impetus_).

    at full speed, cursu (in hostes) ferri.

    at a gallop, citato equo.

to resist a charge, impetum sustinere.

to come to close quarters, manum conserere, signa conferre cum hoste.

to make an obstinate resistance, hostibus strenue obstare.

to repulse the enemy, hostes pellere, repellere.

the line wavers, acies inclinat, inclinatur.

to form a square, orbem facere.

with close, serried ranks, conferti, conglobati, confertis ordinibus.

to break through the enemy's centre, per medios hostes perrumpere.

to dislodge, dejicere (_de_).

to renew the struggle, pugnam redintegrare.

to restore the fortunes of the day, proelium restituere.

to send up reserves, subsidia summittere (_dat._).

fresh troops relieve, come to help of the tired men, integri et recentes defatigatis succedunt, subveniunt.

to be hard pressed, premi, laborare.

to leave the ranks, ab signis discedere.

affairs were in a critical condition, res in summum (extremum) discrimen adducta erat.

(4) AFTER THE BATTLE—ROUT, RETREAT, PURSUIT.

to abandon position, loco excedere.

to sound the retreat, receptui canere.

to retreat, pedem, signa referre, se recipere.

to rout, fundere, fugare.

to utterly defeat, rout, profligare.

utterly routed, fusi fugatique.

to put to flight, in fugam conjicere.

to take to flight, fugae se mandare, terga vertere.

to seek safety in flight, fuga
salutem petere.

to fly for refuge, confugere (*ad*).
   headlong flight, fuga effusa.

to pursue, sequi, persequi.

to overtake, assequi, consequi.

to press hard on fugitives, fugi-
entibus instare.

to cut off the enemy's flight, fugi-
entes excipere.

to let escape, hostes e manibus
dimittere.

(DEFEAT)

to inflict defeat upon, cladem
inferre (*dat.*).
   suffer defeat, cladem accipere.

to cause great slaughter, ingen-
tem caedem edere.

to massacre, trucidare, stragem
facere, stragem edere.

to cut up, annihilate, concidere,
delere.

to be mortally wounded, vulnus
mortiferum accipere.

to inflict a wound upon, vulnus
infligere (*dat.*).

weakened, disabled by wounds,
vulneribus confectus.

with great loss, multis amissis,
magna strage.

(VICTORY)

victory, to win, victoriam re-
portare, hostes proelio vincere.
   let slip a sure victory,
   victoriam   exploratam
   dimittere.
   to raise a shout of victory,
   victoriam conclamare.

the victory cost much blood,
victoria multo sanguine stetit.

the victorious army, exercitus
victor.

triumphant, use victor. (*N.B.—
triumphus is only used of the
triumphal procession allowed
by the state to a victorious
general.*)

a success, res bene (*or* prospere)
gesta.

Siege

garrison, praesidium.

*a town with strong natural
position,* oppidum natura loci
munitum.

commander, governor, praefectus.

to besiege, blockade, invest,
obsidere.

to assault, oppugnare.

a siege, obsidio.

assault, oppugnatio.

to take by storm, expugnare, vi
capere.

to reduce by starvation, fame
domare.

*to raise a siege (of relieving
army),* obsidione liberare.

Siege—*contd.*

to abandon a siege, obsidionem relinquere, obsidione desistere.

to raise siege works, opera facere.

to be busy with siege works, in opere versari.

to advance pent-houses, shelters, vineas agere.

to apply scaling ladders, scalas admovere.

battering ram, aries.

artillery, cannon, machinae, tormenta, ballistae.

to break through the lines, munitiones perrumpere.

to man the wall, murum cingere, complere.

to barricade the gates, portas obstruere.

to break down the gates, portas refringere.

a breach, nearest word ruina muri.

to make a breach, partem muri refringere.

to undermine, muros subruere, cuniculum facere.

to drive defenders from the wall, murum nudare defensoribus.

to make a sally, eruptionem facere, erumpere.

to aestroy, raze to ground a town, oppidum evertere, funditus delere.

to plunder, diripere, spoliare.

provisions are running short, res frumentaria (cibus) deficit.

provisions hold out, suppetit commeatus.

Surrender, Terms, Peace

to capitulate, surrender, se dedere, in deditionem venire.

to give up arms, arma tradere.

to receive the surrender of the enemy, hostes in deditionem accipere.

(*to surrender*) *at discretion*, nullis latis conditionibus.

to offer terms of surrender, conditiones ferre.

favourable, hard, terms, aequae, iniquae conditiones.

to treat for peace, agere de pace.

to bring about a peace, pacem componere.

a truce, indutiae.

treaty, foedus.

to make a, foedus facere, ferire, icere.

according to a, ex foedere.

to grant a man his life, aliquem (incolumem) conservare.

their lives were spared, conservati sunt, *or* venia petentibus data est.

to beg for one's life, mortem deprecari.

to exact hostages from the enemy, obsides hostibus imponere.

Naval

man of war, navis longa.

merchantman, transport, navis oneraria.

ram, beak, rostrum.

sails and rigging, vela et armamenta.

mast, mālus.

admiral, commander, praefectus classis.

rowers, remiges.

helmsman, pilot, gubernator.

to embark (*trans.*), (milites) in navem imponere.

    (*intrans.*), (in) navem conscendere.

to disembark (*trans.*), (milites) in terram exponere.

    (*intrans.*), e nave egredi.

to man a ship, navem complere.

to weigh anchor, set sail, ancoram tollere, (navem) solvere, vela dare.

to ride at anchor, ad ancoram deligari, in ancoris stare.

to drop anchor, ancoram jacere.

to sail out to sea, navigare, in altum provehi.

to sail along the coast, oram legere.

to sail with the wind behind, vento secundo provehi.

to round, double a promontory, superare promontorium.

to row, navem remis propellere.

to drift, dejici, deferri.

to bring to land, (navem) appellere.

to make land, portum capere.

to hold on one's course, cursum tenere.

to be shipwrecked, naufragium facere, in litus ejici.

to be wrecked, founder (*of ship*), frangi, deperire.

by land and sea, terra marique.

fleet, have a powerful, navibus plurimum posse.

    to equip, (naves, classem) armare, instruere.

    launch, deducere.

    haul up, subducere.

    repair, reficere.

    build, construct, aedificare.

NAVAL BATTLE

the admiral's ship, navis praetoria.

to fight a naval battle, proelium navale facere.

to clear the decks for action, navem expedire.

the fleets charge, classes concurrunt.

grappling irons, manus ferreae, copulae.

to board a ship, in navem transcendere, navem expugnare.

to sink a ship, navem submergere, deprimere.

to drive on shore, navem in litus agere.

to ram a ship, navem rostro percutere.

GENERAL VOCABULARY

This Vocabulary contains all the words given in the Vocabularies to the separate Exercises. The principal parts of irregular verbs, and the genitive singular and gender of nouns are given.

nn. = noun.　　　　　　*vb.* = verb.

A

abandon, rĕlinquo, -ĕre, -līqui, -lictum.

ability, to the best of his a., pro vīrīli parte.

able, to be, possum, posse, potui.

abound, ăbundare.

about (number, etc.), circĭter, *adv.*

　(of, concerning), de, *prep. abl.*

above, to mention, suprā commĕmŏrare.

absent, to be, absum, -esse, afui.

accept, accĭpio, -ĕre, -cēpi, -ceptum.

acclamation, plausus, -ūs, *m.*

accompany, cŏmĭtari.

accomplish, effĭcio, -ĕre, -fēci, -fectum.

accomplishing anything, without, re infecta.

accord, of their own, sua sponte.

according to (of writers), apud, *prep. acc.*

accordingly, so, ĭgĭtur (*generally second word*) ; ĭtăque (*first word*).

account, on a. of, ob, *acc.*

accuse, accūsare ; insĭmŭlare.

accuser, accūsător, -oris, *m.*

accustomed, sŏlĭtus ; assuētus.

　accustomed to, assuētus ad.

　to be, sŏleo, -ēre, solĭtus sum.

acquaintance (with persons), consuetudo, -dinis, *f.* ; (*with things*), cognitio, -ionis, *f.*

acquire, acquīro, -ĕre, -quisivi, -quisitum ; nanciscor, -i, nactus sum.

acquit, absolvo, -ĕre, -solvi, -solutum.

across, trans, *acc.*

act, ăgo, -ĕre, ēgi, actum ; se gĕro, -ĕre, gessi, gestum.

add, addo, -ĕre, addĭdi, addĭtum.

added, it is, accēdit.

address, allŏquor, -i, -locutus sum ; contionari.

adjourn (be dismissed), dīmittor, -i, -missus sum.

administer public affairs, rempublicam administrare.

admire, mīrari.

admit, admitto, -ĕre, -misi, -missum.

　(confess), făteor, -ēri, fassus sum.

adopt a plan, consilium ineo, -ire, -ii, -itum ; *or* consilium căpio, -ĕre, cēpi, captum.

advance, progrĕdior, -i, -gres-
sus sum ; prōcēdo, -ĕre,
-cessi, -cessum ; signa
fero, ferre, tuli, latum.
advantage, commŏdum, -i, *n.*
to be to the a. of, ex usu
esse ; usui esse.
adverse (*fortune*), adversus ;
iniquus.
adversity, res adversae.
advice, consĭlĭum, -i, *n.*
advise, suādeo, -ēre, suasi,
suasum ; mŏnēre. See
Voc. 61 and Rule 12, p. 64.
affection, ămor, -oris, *m.* ;
stŭdium, -i, *n.*
afraid, terrĭtus.
be afraid, tĭmēre.
after, post, *prep. acc. and adv.* ;
postea, *adv.* ; postquam,
conj.
afterwards, postea *or* post.
again, rursus.
(*a second time*), ĭtĕrum.
again and again, ĭdentĭdem ;
saepenumero.
against, contra, *acc.*
against one's will, invītus.
aghast, obstŭpĕfactus.
age, abhinc. See p. 32.
agree upon (*terms*), constĭtuo,
-ĕre, -stitui, -stitutum.
agreed, it is, constat.
agreement, come to an, consentio, -ire, -sensi, -sen-
sum.
agriculture, agrĭcultūra, -ae, *f.*;
agrorum cultus, -ūs, *m.*
aid, auxĭlium, -i, *n.*
aid, send to the, submitto,
-ĕre, -misi, -missum ; subsĭdio mitto, -ĕre, misi,
missum.
aim at, pĕto, -ĕre, -ivi, -itum.
alarm, terror, -oris, *m.*

alive, vīvus.
all the best men, optimus quisque.
allow, sĭno, -ĕre, sīvi, sĭtum.
allowed, it is, lĭcet. Voc. 128.
ally, sŏcius, -i, *m.*
almost, paene ; fĕre ; ferme.
alone, sōlus.
Alps, Alpes, -ium, *m. pl.*
already, jam.
also, etiam.
altogether, omnīno.
always, semper.
amazed, to be, mīrari.
ambassador, lēgātus, -i, *m.*
ambuscade, insĭdiae, -arum,
f. pl.
amount, any, quantusvis, *adj.*
ancestors, majores, -um, *m. pl.*
anchor, to ride at, sto (stare,
steti, stătum) in ancŏris.
to weigh, ancŏras tollo, -ĕre,
sustuli, sublatum.
to cast, ancoras jăcio, -ĕre,
jēci, jactum.
ancient, antīquus.
in a. times, antīquĭtus (*adv.*).
anger, īra, -ae, *f.*
angry, īratus.
be a. with, īrascor, -i, iratus
sum.
make angry, lacesso, -ĕre,
lacessivi, lacessitum.
announce, nuntiare ; rĕfero,
-ferre, rettuli, relatum.
annoyed at, to be, aegre fero,
ferre, tuli, latum.
answer, respondeo, -ēre, re-
spondi, responsum.
(*nn*)., responsum, -i, *n.*
anxious to, cŭpĭdus.
any one. See p. 164.
Apollo, Apollo, -inis, *m.*
appear, appārēre ; vĭdeor, -ĕri,
visus sum.

appease, plācare.
applause, plausus, -ūs, *m.*
apple, mălum, -i, *n.*
appoint, crĕare.
appointed day, *on the*, die constitutā.
approach, ădĭtus, -ūs, *m.*
  to, apprŏpinquare.
  (*of time*), appĕto, -ĕre, -ivi, -itum.
approval, consensus, -ūs, *m.*
approve, prŏbare.
archer, săgittarius, -i, *m.*
arise, cŏŏrior, -iri, coortus sum.
arm, armare.
armament (=*fleet*), classis, -is, *f.*
arms, arma, -orum, *n. pl.*
  arms, *to take up*, arma sūmo, -ĕre, sumpsi, sumptum.
  under arms, in armis.
army, exercĭtus, -ūs, *m.*
arouse, excĭtare.
arrival, adventus, -ūs, *m.*
arrive, advĕnio, -ire, -vēni, -ventum.
arrow, săgitta, -ae, *f.*
art, ars, artis, *f.*
  of war, ars mīlĭtāris.
artillery, tormenta, -orum, *n. pl.*
artisan, artĭfex, -ficis, *m.*
as if, quăsĭ; tanquam.
ascertain, cognosco, -ĕre, -nōvi, -nĭtum.
ashamed of, *to be*, pŭdet.
ask, *ask for*, rŏgare; interrogare; quaero, -ĕre, quaesivi, quaesitum; peto, -ĕre, -ivi, -itum. See Synonyms.
ask repeatedly, rŏgĭtare.
assail, *assault*, oppugnare.
assailant, oppugnator, -oris, *m.*

assassinate, trŭcīdare.
assault (*on town*), oppugnatio, -ionis, *f.*
assemble, *trans.* convŏcare; *intr.* convĕnio, -ire, -vēni, -ventum.
assembly (*public*), contio, -ionis, *f.*; concilium, -i. *n*,
assert, affirmare.
assign, attrĭbŭo, -ĕre, -ui, -utum.
assist, adjŭvare; subvĕnio, -ire, -vēni, -ventum.
assume, ūsurpare.
assured (*of things*), explōratus.
astonished, miratus; attŏnĭtus.
at. See Rule 5 A, p. 32.
at last, tandem.
Athenian, Athēniensis.
Athens, Athēnae, -arum, *f. pl.*
attack (*onset*, *charge*), impetus, -ūs, *m.*; (for *gen.*, *dat.*, *abl.* plural use forms of incursio, -ionis, *f.*).
  to, aggredior, -i, -gressus sum; adorior, -iri, -ortus sum; impetum făcio (-ĕre, fēci, factum) in, *acc.*
  (*of towns*), oppugnare.
  (*of disease*, *etc.*), affĭcio, -ĕre, -fēci, -fectum.
attempt, cōnari.
attempt (*battle*), temptare.
attend to, cūrare; stŭdēre.
attire, ornātus, -ūs, *m.*
augur, augur, -uris, *m.*
autumn, autumnus, -i, *m.*
avarice, ăvărĭtia, -ae, *f.*
avenge, ulciscor, -i, ultus sum.
avenger, ultor, -oris, *m.*
avoid, vītare.
await, exspectare.
away, *to be*, absum, -esse, afui.

B

back, tergum, -i, *n.*
(*adverb*), retro.
bad, mălus; prāvus.
baggage, impĕdīmenta, -orum,
n. pl.
band, mănus, -ūs, *f.*
banish, expello, -ĕre, -puli,
-pulsum.
bank, rīpa, -ae, *f.*
barbarians, barbări, -orum,
m. pl.
barren (*profitless*), irrĭtus.
base, turpis.
battle, proelium, -i, *n.*; pugna,
-ae, *f.*
  line of, ăcies, -ei, *f.*
  pitched, justum proelium,
    -i, *n.*; ăcies, -ei, *f.*
  there was a battle, pugnatum
    est.
  fight a battle, proelium făcio,
    -ĕre, fēci, factum.
  give battle to, proelium com-
    mitto (-ĕre, -misi, -mis-
    sum) cum, *abl.*
  draw up in battle array, (in)
    ăcie instrŭo, -ĕre, -struxi,
    -structum.
bear, fero, ferre, tuli, latum.
  (of burdens), portare.
  (endure), pătior, -i, passus
    sum.
beard, barba, -ae, *f.*
beat, caedo, -ĕre, cecīdi,
    caesum.
beautiful, pulcher, -chra,
    -chrum.
beauty, pulchrĭtūdo, -inis, *f.*
because, quod; quia. See Rule
    22, p. 124.
become, fio, fieri, factus sum.
becoming, it is, dĕcet.

bed, cŭbīle, -is, *n.*
  go to, cūbĭtum eo, ire, ivi,
    itum.
befalls, it, contingit, -ĕre,
    -tĭgit (*generally good luck*);
    accĭdit, -ĕre, -cĭdit.
before, ante, *prep. acc.*; ante-
    quam; priusquam, *conj.*
    (Rule 25, p. 140); ante
    or antea, *adv.*
  before long, haud multo post.
beg, ōrare; prĕcari.
begin, incĭpio, -ĕre, -cēpi,
    -ceptum; coepi, -isse.
beginning, inĭtium, -i, *n.*
behalf, on b. of, pro, *abl.*
behave, se gĕro, -ĕre, gessi,
    gestum.
behind, post, *acc.*
behold (*catch sight of*), con-
    spĭcari; conspĭcio, -ĕre,
    -spexi, -spectum.
behoves, it, ŏportet.
believe, crēdo, -ĕre, credĭdi,
    credĭtum.
belonging to others, ălĭēnus.
benefit (*nn.*), bĕnĕfĭcium, -i, *n.*
    (*vb.*) prōsum, prodesse,
    profui; usui esse.
beseech, obsecrāre.
beset, besiege, obsĭdeo, -ĕre,
    -sēdi, -sessum.
besides, praetĕrea.
besiege, obsĭdeo, -ēre, -sēdi,
    -sessum.
bestow, dōnare.
betake oneself, se confero,
    -ferre, -tuli, collatum.
betray, prōdo, -ĕre, -dĭdi,
    -dĭtum.
between, inter, *acc.*
bill, rŏgātio, -ionis, *f.*
bind (*by an oath, etc.*), ob-
    stringo, -ĕre, -strinxi,
    -strictum.

birth (*race*), gĕnus, -eris, *n.*
bitterly, vĕhĕmenter.
blame, culpa, -ae, *f.*
blame, to, culpare.
blind, caecus ; ŏcŭlis captus.
block, obstruo, -ĕre, -struxi, -structum.
blockade, obsĭdeo, -ēre, -sēdi, -sessum.
blood, sanguis, -inis, *m.*
bloodshed, caedes, -is, *f.* ; strāges, -is, *f.*
bloody, cruentus.
blow, ictus, -ūs, *m.*
board, to come on, conscendo (-ĕre, -scendi, -scensum) nāvem.
boat, linter, -tris, *f.*
boast, jactare ; prae se fero, ferre, tuli, latum.
boastful, to be, glōriari.
body, corpus, -oris, *n.*
boldness, audācia, -ae, *f.*
book, lĭber, -bri, *m.*
booty, praeda, -ae, *f.*
borders, fīnes, -ium, *m. pl.*
born, to be, nascor, -i, natus sum.
borrow, in aere alieno esse ; aes alienum făcio, -ĕre, fēci, factum.
both, ambo ; uterque.
    both . . . and, et . . . et.
bottom, īmus.
bow, arcus, -ūs, *m.*
boy, puer, -eri, *m.*
brave, fortis ; vălĭdus.
    to show oneself, se praebēre fortem.
bravely, fortĭter.
bravery, virtus, -utis, *f.* ; fortĭtūdo, -dinis, *f.*
bread, pānis, -is, *m.*
break, frango, -ĕre, fregi, fractum.

break (*a law*), vĭŏlare.
    (*a line*), inclīnare.
    down, dīrŭo, -ĕre, -rui, -rutum ; rescindo, -ĕre, -scĭdi, -scissum.
    through, perrumpo, -ĕre, -rupi, -ruptum.
breeze, aura, ae, *f.*
bribe (=*money*), pĕcūnia, -ae, *f.*
bribery, ambĭtus, -ūs, *m.*
bridge, to throw over a river, pontem in flumine făcio, -ĕre, fēci, factum.
bring (*of persons*), adducĕre.
    (*of things, news*), affero, -ferre, attuli, allatum.
    help, auxilium fero, ferre, tuli, latum.
broad, lātus.
brother, frāter, -tris, *m.*
build, aedĭfĭcare.
burden, ŏnus, -eris, *n.*
burden, to be a, ŏneri esse. Voc. 85.
burdensome, mŏlestus.
burn, intr. ardeo, -ēre, arsi ; *trans.* (*set fire to*), incendo, -ĕre, -cendi, -censum ; uro, -ĕre, ussi, ustum.
bury, sĕpĕlire.
but, sed (*first word*) ; autem (*second word*).
    (=*except*), praeter, *prep. acc.* ; nisi, *conj.*
buy, ĕmo, -ĕre, ēmi, emptum.

C

calamity, incommŏdum, -i, *n.* ; călămĭtas, -tatis, *f.*
calculating (*thinking*), rătus.
call, vŏcare. See Synonyms.
    together, convŏcare.
    (*by name*), appellare.

camp, castra, -orum, *n. pl.*
  to keep in, castris tĕnēre.
  to pitch a, castra pōno, -ēre,
    posui, positum.
  to strike a, castra mŏveo,
    -ēre, mōvi, mōtum.
capable of, aptus ad, *acc.*
capital (=*city*), căput, -itis, *n.*
capitol, căpĭtōlium, -i, *n.*
captive, captīvus, -i, *m.*
care for, value. See p. 48.
care, *carefulness*, dīlĭgentia,
  -ae, *f.*
carefully, dīlĭgenter.
careless, neglĭgens.
carelessly, neglĭgenter.
carelessness, neglĭgentia, -ae, *f.*
carry, portare.
  off, aufero, -ferre, abstuli,
    ablatus ; abrĭpio, -ēre,
    -ripui, -reptum.
  (*of a law*), fero, ferre, tuli,
    latum.
cart, carrus, -ūs, *m.*
Carthage, Carthago, -inis, *f.*
Carthaginian, Poenus, -i, *m.* ;
  adj. Punĭcus.
castle, castellum, -i, *n.*
Catiline, Cătĭlīna, -ae, *m.*
catch, căpio,-ēre, cēpi, captum.
  sight of, conspĭcio, -ēre,
    -spexi, -spectum ; con-
    spĭcari.
  up, consĕquor, -i, -secutus
    sum.
cattle, pĕcus, -oris, *n.*
cause (*be the cause of*), causae
  esse. Voc. 85.
  (*see to*), cūrare (Voc. 149) ;
    efficio (-ēre, -fēci, -fec-
    tum) ut.
caution, dīlĭgentia, -ae, *f.*
cavalry, ĕquĭtātus, -ūs, *m.* ;
  equites, -um, *m. pl.*
cavern, spēlunca, -ae, *f.*

cease, dēsino, -ēre (*perf. use*
  destiti).
celebrated, praeclārus.
  the celebrated Plato, Plato ille.
centre, mĕdia pars, -rtis, *f.*
  (*of line*), mĕdia ăcies, -ei, *f.*
certain, *a certain* (=*the indef.
  article*), quīdam.
certainly, certo ; (*at least*),
  certe.
chance, *by*, fortĕ ; cāsu.
change, mūtare.
character, mōres, -um, *m. pl.*
characters (*letters*), litterae,
  -arum, *f. pl.*
charge (*accusation*), crīmen,
  -inis, *n.*
  (*attack*), impĕtus, -ūs, *m.*
charge, *to*, impĕtum făcio
  (-ēre, fēci, factum) in, *acc.*
chariot, currus, ūs, *m.*
cheap, vīlis.
  to hold, parvi (mĭnimi)
    făcio (-ēre, fēci, factum) ;
    parvi aestimare.
check, cŏhĭbēre.
cheer, *to be of good*, bono ănĭmo
  esse.
chieftain, princeps, -cipis, *m.*
children, lībĕri, -orum, *m. pl.*
  (*sometimes* puĕri, -orum,
    m. pl.).
choose, dēlĭgo, -ēre, -lēgi,
  -lectum.
circumstances, *under these*,
  quae cum ĭta sint, essent.
  under the circumstances, u
    in tali re.
citadel, arx, arcis, *f.*
citizen, cīvis, -is, *m.*
city, urbs, -bis, *f.*
claim, ūsurpare.
clear, *it is*, lĭquet ; manifestum
  est.
clearly, manifesto ; certo

cleave, discindo, -ĕre, -scĭdi,
　-scissum.
clever, callĭdus; sollers.
cliff, rūpes, -is, *f.*
climb, ascendo, -ĕre, -scendi,
　-scensum.
cloak, pallium, -i, *n.*
　(*military*), sāgum, -i, *n.*
close, claudo, -ĕre, clausi,
　clausum.
close order, *in*, conferto
　agmĭne.
close quarters, *at*, commĭnus.
clothe, vestire.
clothes, vestis, -is, *f.*; vestītus,
　-ūs, *m.*
cloud, nūbes, -is, *f.*
club, clāva, -ae, *f.*; fustis,-is, *m.*
coast, ōra, -ae, *f.*; lītus, -oris, *n.*
cold (*nn.*), frīgus, -oris, *n.*
　adj., frīgĭdus; gĕlĭdus.
collect, collĭgo, -ĕre, -lēgi,
　-lectum.
colony, cŏlōnia, - ae, *f.*
colour, cŏlor, -oris, *m.*
come, vĕnio, -ire, vēni, ventum.
come out, ēgrĕdior, -i, -gressus
　sum.
　back, regrĕdior, -i, -gressus
　　sum; rĕdeo, -ire, -ii, -itum.
　between, intercēdo, -ĕre,
　　-cessi, -cessum.
　down, descendo,-ĕre,-scendi,
　　-scensum.
　to the help of, subvĕnio
　　-ire, -vēni, -ventum (*dat.*).
　off victorious, ēvādo (-ĕre,
　　-vasi, -vasum) victor.
　upon, incĭdo, -ĕre, -cudi, in,
　　acc.
command, impĕrare; jubeo,
　-ēre, jussi, jussum. See
　Voc. 61 and Rule 11, p. 62.
be in command of, praesum,
　-esse, -fui.

command, *put into command*,
　praefĭcio, -ĕre, -fēci,
　-fectum.
chief command, summa (-ae,
　f.) imperii.
commander, praefectus, -i, *m.*
　See p. 105, note 3.
commit, admitto, -ĕre, -misi,
　-missum.
　(*to one's care*), mandare
　alicui.
commonly, vulgo; plerumque.
　or use constat.
companion, cŏmes, -itis, *m.*
compel, cōgo, -ĕre, coēgi,
　coactum.
complain, quĕror, -i, questus
　sum.
complete (*victory*),certus; haud
　dubius.
conceal, cēlare.
concerns, *it*, attĭnet ad; per-
　tĭnet ad; rēfert; interest.
　Voc., 109.
condemn, damnare.
　to death, căpĭtis damnare.
conditions, condĭtiōnes, -um,
　f. pl.
conduct, dūcĕre.
conference, collŏquium, -i, *n.*
confess, confĭteor, -ēri, -fessus
　sum.
confidence (=*trust*), fĭdes, -ei,
　f.; fĭdūcia, -ae, *f.*
confusion, tŭmultus, -ūs, *m.*
　throw into, perturbare.
connected with (*by birth*), cog-
　nātus; conjunctus nātu.
conquer, sŭpĕrare; vinco, -ĕre,
　vici, victum.
conqueror, victor, -oris, *m.*
consecrate, vŏveo, -ēre, vōvi,
　votum.
consent, vŏlo, velle, volui.
　with one consent, consensu.

consider, cōgĭtare; rĕpŭtare; dēlĭbĕrare.

considering, rătus.

conspiracy, conjūratio, -ionis, *f.*

conspirator, conjūratus, -i, *m.*

conspire, conjūrare.

constancy, constantia, -ae, *f.*

construct, aedĭfĭcare.

consul, consul, -sulis, *m.*

consulship, to stand for, consŭlatum pĕto, -ĕre, petivi, petitum.

consult, consulo, -ĕre, -sului, -sultum; dēlīberare.

   interests of, consŭlo, -ĕre, -sului, -sultum. Voc. 101.

content, contentus.

contest, certamen, -inis, *n.*

continue, prodūcĕre.

continue to march, iter continuare.

contrary to, contra, *acc.*

control (of campaign), summa (-ae. *f.*) impĕrii, *or* summa belli administrandi.

convict, condemnare.

Corinth, Cŏrinthus, -i, *f.*;

corn, frūmentum, -i, *n.*

cost, sto, stare, steti, stătum, Voc. 57.

council, concĭlium, -i, *n.*

counsel, consĭlium, -i, *n.*

countenance, vultus, -ūs, *m.*

country (district), terra, -ae, *f.*; rĕgio, -ionis, *f.*

   (only when opposed to town), rus, ruris, *n.*

   in the, rūri *or* rūre.

   (native land), pătria, -ae, *f.*

courage, virtus, -utis, *f.*

   to show, virtutem praesto, -are, -stiti, -stitum.

course, to hold on his, cursum tĕneo, -ĕre, tenui, tentum.

cover, ŏpĕrio, -ire, operui, opertum.

   (shelter), tĕgo, -ĕre, texi, tectum.

coward, ignāvus.

cowardice, ignāvia, -ae, *f.*

credit, laus, laudis, *f.*

   to be a, laudi esse. Voc. 85.

crime, scĕlus, -eris, *n.*

criminal, nŏcens, -entis, *m.*

crisis, discrīmen, -minis, *n.*

crop, sĕges, -getis, *f.*

cross, transeo, -ire, -ii, -itum; transjicio, -ĕre, trajeci, trajectum.

crowd, turba, -ae, *f.*; multĭtūdo, -dinis, *f.*

crowd round, circumfundor, -i, -fusus sum.

crown, cŏrōna, ae, *f.*

cruel, saevus; crūdēlis.

cruelty, saevĭtia, -ae, *f.*; crudēlĭtas, -tatis, *f.*

crush, prōflīgare.

cry, clāmor, -oris, *m.*

cry out, clāmare.

   (a cry was raised), clāmatum est; clāmor sublatus est.

cultivate, cŏlo, -ĕre, colui, cultum.

cunning (nn.), sollertia, -ae, *f.*; *adj.* sollers.

cup, pōcŭlum, -i, *n.*

cure, sānare; mĕdēri.

custom, mōs, moris, *m.*

   according to, mōre, *gen.*

customary, sŏlĭtus.

customs, instĭtūta, -orum, *n. pl.*

K

cut down, succīdo, -ĕre, -cīdi,
-cisum.
(*kill*), occīdo, -ĕre, -cīdi,
-cisum.
cut off, dēsĕco, -are, -secui,
-sectum.
cut in two, discindo, -ĕre,
-scĭdi, -scissum.

D

danger, pĕrīcŭlum, -i, *n.*
dangerous, pĕrīcŭlōsus.
dare, audeo, -ēre, ausus sum.
dark, obscūrus.
darkness, tĕnebrae, -arum,
f. pl.
dash against (*trans.*), illīdo,
-ĕre -lisi, -lisum.
daughter, fīlia, -ae, *f.*
dawn, prima lux, lucis, *f.*
to, illūcesco, -ĕre, illusit.
day, dies, -ei, *m.*
space of two days, bĭduum,
-i, *n.*
day, every, quŏtīdie ; in dies.
on the appointed, die con-
stĭtutā.
on the following, postĕro die ;
postrīdie.
deadly wound, vulnus (-eris, *n.*)
mortiferum.
deaf, surdus ; aurĭbus captus.
dear, cārus.
death, mors, -rtis, *f.*
to the, usquĕ ad mortem.
to condemn to, căpĭtis damnare.
to face, mortem ŏbeo, -ire,
-ii, -itum.
debt, aes (aeris, *n.*) ăliēnum.
deceive, dēcĭpio, -ĕre, -cēpi,
-ceptum.
decide, constĭtuo, -ĕre, -stitui,
-stitutum.

decide (*contest*), rem dēcerno,
-ĕre, -crevi, -cretum.
decisive, haud anceps.
declare, affirmare.
war, bellum indīcĕre.
decree, ēdīcĕre ; dēcerno, -ĕre,
-crevi, -cretum.
deed, factum, -i, *n.*
deed (*gen. with bad sense*),
făcĭnus, -oris, *n.*
deep, altus.
defeat, clādes, -is, *f.* ; incommŏdum, -i, *n.*
(*vb.*), vinco, -ĕre, vici, victum.
defend, dēfendo, -ĕre, -fendi,
-fensum.
defender, dēfensor, -oris, *m.*
defile, angustiae, -arum, *f. pl.* ;
fauces, -ium, *f. pl.*
delay, mŏra, -ae, *f.*
to, cunctari.
deliberate, dēlībĕrare ; consŭlo,
-ĕre, -sului, -sultum.
delight (=*joy*), gaudium, -i,
n.
delightful, jūcundus.
deliver, trādo, -ĕre, -dĭdi,
-dĭtum.
demand, postŭlare ; flăgĭtare ;
posco, -ĕre, poposci ; impĕrare. See Synonyms.
deny (*say not*), nĕgare.
depart, abeo, -ire, -ii, -itum ;
discēdo, -ĕre, -cessi,
-cessum.
(*change homes*), dēmigrare.
departure, prŏfectio, -ionis, *f.*
depend on, constare in, *abl.* ;
pōnor (-i, positus sum)
in, *abl.*
depose, abrŏgare imperium
(trĭbūnātum) alicui.
deprive, prīvare.
descended, prognatus ; ortus.

desert (*trans*.), deséro, -ére,
    -serui, -sertum ; (*intr*.)
    transfúgio, -ére, -fúgi.
    (*revolt from*), défício, (-ére,
    -féci, -fectum) ab, *abl.*
deserter, transfúga, -ae, *m.* ;
    perfúga, -ae, *m.*
deserve, méréri ; dignus esse.
    Rule 18, p. 110.
deservedly, méríto.
design, consílium, -i. *n.*
desire, stúdium, -i, *n.* ; cúpído,
    -dinis, *f.*
    to, cúpio, -ére, -ivi, -itum.
desirous, cúpídus.
desist from, désisto,-ére, -stiti,
    -stitum.
desolate, désertus.
despair, spem abjício, -ére,
    -jeci, -jectum.
    in, re *or* sálute desperatá
    (*abl. abs.*).
despatches, litterae, -arum,
    f. pl.
desperate, perdítus.
despise, despicio, -ére, -spexi,
    -spectum ; sperno, -ére,
    sprevi, spretum ; con-
    temno, -ére, -tempsi,
    -temptum.
destroy, déleo, -ére, -evi, -etum.
destruction, *to be*, *or mean*,
    exítio esse. Voc. 85.
detain, rétíneo, -ére, -tinui,
    -tentum.
deter, déterrére.
determination, constantia, -ae,
    f.
determine, statuo, -ére, statui,
    statutum ; constituo,-ére,
    -stitui, -stitutum.
devoid of, vacuus ; núdátus.
devoted to, *to be*, stúdére.
devotion, stúdium, -i, *n.*
dictator, dictátor, -toris, *m.*

die, mórior, -i, mortuus sum
    (*fut. part*. moriturus).
differ, inter se differo, -ferre,
    distuli, dilatum.
    greatly from, multum di-
    sto (-stare, -stiti) ab, *abl.*
difference, to make a, interesse ;
    réferre.   Voc. 109.
different from, alius ac *or*
    atque.
difficult, difficílis.
difficulty, difficultas, -tatis, *f.*
dig up, effódio, -ére, -fódi,
    -fossum.
diligence, dilígentia, -ae, *f.*
diligently, dilígenter.
diminish,   dimínuo,   -ére,
    -minui, -minutum.
directions, in all, passim ; in
    omnes partes.
    from all, undíque ; ex omni-
    bus partibus.
disabled, confectus.
disaffected, sédítíosus.
disaster, cládés, -is, *f.*
disastrous, infélix ; fúnestus.
disband, dímitto, -ére, -mísi,
    -missum.
discipline, discíplína, -ae, *f.*
discover, invénio, -ire, -véni,
    -ventum ; répério, -ire,
    -pperi,   -pertum.   See
    Syn., *find*.
discover (*of facts*), cognosco,
    -ére, -nóvi, -nítum ; com-
    perio, -ire, -peri, -pertum,
discretion, at, nullis conditioni-
    bus latis, acceptis.
discuss, disséro (-ére, -serui,
    -sertum) de, *abl.*
disease, morbus, -i, *m.*
disembark (*trans*.), expóno
    -ére, -posui, -positum.
    (*intr*.), e nave egrédior, -i,
    -gressus sum. Voc. 133.

disgrace, dēdĕcus, -oris, *n.* ;
ignōminia, -ae, *f.*
to, dēdĕcŏri esse. Voc. 85.
disgraceful, turpis.
disheartened, mĕtu commōtus.
dishonour, dēdĕcŏrare ; dēdĕcŏri esse. Voc. 85.
disliked, to be, ŏdio esse. Voc.
85.
dismay, păvor, -oris, *m.*
dismayed, păvōre perculsus.
dismiss, dīmitto, -ĕre, -mīsi,
-missum.
disobey (*an order*), neglĭgo,
-ĕre, neglexi, neglectum.
disorder, tŭmultus, -ūs, *m.*
disorderly, tŭmultuarius.
display (*a quality*), praesto,
-are, -stĭti, -stĭtum.
displease, displĭcēre.
disposition, mens, -ntis, *f.* ;
indōles, -is, *f.*
dispute, dēcertare de, *abl.*
(*in conversation*), dissĕro
(-ĕre -serui, -sertum) de,
abl.
distance, at a, prŏcul ; ēmĭnus.
distant, longinquus.
to be, absum, -esse, afui.
distinguished, insignis.
district, rĕgio, -ionis, *f.*
disturb, turbare.
disturbance, tŭmultus, ūs. *m.* ;
mōtus, -ūs, *m.*
ditch, fossa, -ae, *f.*
divisions, in two, bĭpartīto.
do, făcio, -ĕre, fēci, factum.
do one's utmost to, id ăgo
(-ĕre, ēgi, actum) ut.
dominion, impĕrĭum, i, *n.*,
See Syn., *power*.
dominion (*with idea of tyranny*),
dŏmĭnatus, -ūs, *m.*
door, porta, -ae, *f.* ; jānua,
-ae, *f.*

doubt, dŭbĭtare. Rules 16,
p. 88 ; 23, p. 130.
(*without*), sĭne dŭbio.
doubtful, to be, incertum, dŭbium esse.
downwards, deorsum.
drag, draw, trăho, -ĕre, traxi,
tractum.
draw up, instruo, -ĕre, -struxi,
-structum.
dread, formīdo, -dinis, *f.*
dream, somnium, -i, *n.*
to, somniare ; somnio vĭdeo,
-ēre, vīdi, visum.
dress, ornatus, -ūs, *m.*
drink, bĭbo, -ĕre, bĭbi.
drive, ăgo, -ĕre, ēgi, actum.
out, expello, -ĕre, -puli, -pul-
sum.
drive down, or away, depello,
-ĕre, -puli, -pulsum.
back, rĕpello, -ĕre, -puli,
-pulsum.
drown (*trans.*), submergo,
-ĕre, -mersi, -mersum.
due, it is due to you, per te stat
(p. 132).
duty, offĭcium, -i, *n.*
it is one's, oportet.
dwell in, habitare in, *abl.* ; incŏlo, -ĕre, -colui, cultum.

E

eager, ăvĭdus.
eagerness, stŭdium, -i, *n.*
early (*in the morning*), mānĕ.
(*in good time*), mātūrē.
earn, mĕrēre.
easily, făcĭle.
east, sōlis ortus, -ūs, *m.*
ŏriens, -ntis, *m.*
easy, făcĭlis.
eat, ĕdo, -ĕre, ēdi, ēsum.

272

effect, effĭcio, -ĕre, -fēci, -fectum.

effort, lăbor, -oris, *m.*; cōnātus, -ūs, *m.*

egg, ōvum, -i, *n.*

Egypt, Aegyptus, -i, *f.*

elated, ēlatus.

elders, patres, -um, *m. pl.*

elect, crĕare.

elephant, ĕlĕphantus, -i, *m.*

eloquence, ēlŏquentia, -ae, *f.*

embark (*trans.*), impono, -ĕre, -posui, -positum.

   (*intr.*), (in) navem conscendo, -ĕre, -scendi, -scensum. Voc. 133.

emperor, impĕrātor, -oris, *m.*

empire, impĕrium, -i, *n.*

employ, ūtor, -i, usus sum.

encamp, consīdo, -ĕre, -sēdi, -sessum ; castra pōno, -ĕre, posui, positum.

encourage, hortari ; admŏnēre.

end, fīnis, -is, *m.*

   bring to an end, confĭcio, -ĕre, -fēci, -fectum ; fīnire.

endowed, praedĭtus.

endurance, pătientia, -ae, *f.*

enemy (*private*), ĭnĭmīcus, -i, *m.*

   (*public*), hostis, -is, *m.*

energy, stŭdium, -i, *n.*

engage in battle, proelium committo, -ĕre, -misi, -missum.

engagement, certāmen, -minis, *n.*

England, Brĭtannia, -ae, *f.*

Englishman, Brĭtannus, -i, *m.*

enjoy, fruor, -i, fructus sum.

enough (*quite*), sătĭs.

enraged, īrātus.

enter, ingrĕdior, -i, -gressus sum ; intrare.

enthusiasm, stŭdium, -i, *n.* ; ardor, -oris, *m.*

entice, ēlĭcio, -ĕre, -licui, -licitum.

entrance, ōs, oris, *n.*; ostium, -i, *n.* ; ădĭtus, -ūs, *m.*

entrust, committo, -ĕre, -misi -missum ; mandare.

envoy, lēgātus, -i, *m.*

envy, invĭdia, -ae, *f.*

envy, to, invĭdeo, -ēre, -vīdi, -visum.

equal, par.

   (*favourable, or fair*), aequus.

   (*of the same age, contemporary*), aequalis, -is, *c.*

   on equal terms, aequo Marte ; aequa contentione.

equally, aeque ; părĭter.

equip, părare.

err, errare.

escape, fŭga, -ae, *f.*

   to, effŭgio, -ĕre, -fūgi.

especially, praesertim.

esteem. See Voc. 57.

even, ĕtiam.

   not even, ne . . . quĭdem.

evening, in the, vespĕri.

   towards, sub vespĕrum.

ever, unquam. See p. 165.

   (=*always*), semper.

every day, quŏtīdie.

everywhere, ŭbīque.

evidence, testĭmonium, -i, *n.*

   to give evidence, testĭmōnium dīcĕre.

evident, mănĭfestus.

evil, mălum, -i, *n.*

exact from, impĕrare (*dat.* and *acc.*).

example, to be an, exemplo esse. Voc. 85.

excel, sŭpĕrare.

excellent, ēgrĕgius.

except, praeter, *prep. acc.* ;
  nĭsi, *conj.*
excessive, nĭmius.
excite, excĭtare.
exclaim, clāmare.
exhausted, confectus (lăbōre,
  etc.).
exhort, hortari ; admŏnēre.
exile, exsĭlium, -i, *n.*
exile, an, exsul, -ulis, *c.*
expect, exspectare.
expectation, contrary to, praeter
  spem, ŏpīnionem.
expedient, it is, expĕdit.
expel, expello, -ĕre, -puli,
  -pulsum.
experience, perītia, -ae, *f.*
experienced in, expertus ; pĕrītus.
explain, expōno, -ĕre, -posui,
  -positum ;   ēdo,   -ĕre,
  -dĭdi, -dĭtum.
explore, explōrare.
expose (*trans.*), objĭcio, -ĕre,
  -jēci, -jectum.
  oneself to, se objicĕre ; occurro, -ĕre, -curri, -cursum.
express, ēdo, -ĕre, -dĭdi, -dĭtum.
extent, to a great, magna ex
  parte.
eye, ŏcŭlus, -i, *m.*

F

face, vultus, -ūs, *m.*
face death, mortem ŏbeo, -ire,
  -ii, -itum.
fail, dēfĭcio, -ĕre,-fēci, -fectum.
faint-hearted, tĭmĭdus.
fair, aequus.
faithful, fĭdēlis.
faithfully, fĭdēliter.
fall, cădo, -ĕre, cecĭdi, casum.
  (*of a city*), căpior, -i, captus
  sum.

fall down, dēlābor, -i, -lapsus
  sum.
  into or upon, incĭdo (-ĕre,
  -cĭdi) in, *acc.*
  to the lot of, contingit, -ĕre,
  -tĭgit.
  See ' *befall.*'
false, falsus.
falsely, falso.
family, fămĭlia, -ae, *f.*
famine, fămes, -is, *f.*
far, longe.
  too far, longius.
far as, as, usquĕ ad, *acc.*
far off, prŏcul.
farewell, say, jŭbēo (-ēre, jussi,
  jussum) vălēre.
farm, fundus, -i, *m.*
farmer, cŏlōnus, -i, *m.*
fashion of, in the, mōre,
  gen.
fastness, castellum, -i, *n.*
fatal, fūnestus.
fate, fortūna, -ae, *f.* ; fātum,
  -i, *n.*
fated, fātālis.
father, păter, -tris, *m.*
fatherland, patria, -ae, *f.*
fault (*blame*), culpa, -ae, *f.*
favour, făveo, -ēre, făvi, fautum.
favourable (*of things*), sĕcundus ; ĭdōneus.
fear, tĭmor, -oris, *m.* ; mĕtus,
  -ūs, *m.* See Syn.
  to, tĭmēre ; mĕtuo, -ĕre,
  metui. Rule 21, p. 120.
  (*with idea of respect*), vĕrēri.
  through fear of this, hōc
  tĭmore.
feast, ĕpŭlae, -arum, *f. pl.*
  to, ĕpŭlari.
feed, vescor, -i.
feel, sentio, -ire, sensi, sensum.
feign, sĭmŭlare.

fellow-citizen, fellow-country-man, cīvis, -is, *m.*

fertile, fertīlis.

few, pauci.

field, ăger, -gri, *m.*
  of battle, ăcies, -ei, *f.*
  take the, mīlĭtēs ēdūcĕre.

fierce, fĕrox.

fiercely, fĕrōciter.

fight a battle, proelium făcio, -ĕre, fēci, factum.
  with, pugnare contra.
  in the army, stīpendia mĕrēre; *sometimes* mĕrēre *alone.*

fighting order, in, acie (instructā).

fill, compleo, -ēre, -plēvi, -pletum; repleo, -ēre, -plēvi, -pletum.

finally, dēnĭque.

find. See ' *discover.* '

fine, multare.

finish, confĭcio, -ĕre, -fēci, -fectum.
  (*accomplish*), perfĭcio, -ĕre, -fēci, -fectum.

fire, ignis, -is, *m.*
  set on, incendo, -ĕre, -cendi, -censum.
  back, tēla rējĭcio, -ĕre, -jēci, -jectum.

first, at, prīmō.

fit out, instruo, -ĕre, -struxi, -structum.
  for, aptus ad; ĭdōneus ad,*acc.*
  to be, dignus qui. Rule 18, p. 110.

flame, flamma, -ae, *f.*

flank, lătus, -eris, *n.*
  on the, ab lătĕre.

fleet, classis, -is, *f.*

flight, fŭga, -ae, *f.*
  put to, fundo, -ĕre, fudi, fusum; fŭgare.

flight, take to, tergă verto, -ĕre, verti, versum; se fŭgae mandare.

flock, grex, gregis, *m.*

flow, flŭo, -ĕre, fluxi.

flower, flōs, -oris, *m.*
  of army, rōbur, -ŏris, *n.*

flushed (*elated*), elatus; sublatus.

fly, fŭgio, -ĕre, fūgi.

follow, sĕquor, -i, secutus sum (*and compounds*).

following (*of time*), proxĭmus.

follows, as, ĭta; ad hunc modum.

fond of, cŭpĭdus.

food, cĭbus, -i, *m.*

foolish, stultus.

foot, pēs, pĕdis, *m.*
  on, pĕdĭbus.

foot-soldier, pĕdes, -ĭtis, *m.*

for, nam (*first word*), enim (*second word*).
  for the sake of, pro, *abl.*

forage, frūmentum, -i, *n.*; pābŭlum, -i, *n.*
  to, frūmentari; pābŭlari.

forbid, vĕto, -are, vetui, vetītum.

force (*vb.*), cōgo, -ĕre, coēgi, coactum.
  (*nn.*) vis (*acc.* vim, *abl.* vi), *f.*
  by force of arms, vi et armis.

forces, cōpiae, -arum, *f. pl.*
  land, copiae terrestres.

foreign, externus.

foresee, prōvĭdeo, -ēre, -vīdi, -visum.

forest, silva, -ae, *f.*

foretell, praedĭcĕre.

forget, oblīviscor, -i, oblitus sum; immĕmor esse.

forgive, ignosco, -ĕre, -novi, -notum.

form, fĭgūra, -ae, *f.*
  a plan, consĭlium căpio, -ere, cēpi, captum; consilium ineo, -ire, -ii, -itum.
former, sŭpĕrior; prior.
  the former . . . the latter, ille . . . hic.
formerly, antea.
formidable, grăvis; mĕtuendus.
fortifications, mūnīmenta, -orum, *n. pl.*
fortify, mūnire.
fortress, castellum, -i, *n.*
fortunate, fēlix.
fortunately, fēlīciter; prospĕre.
fortune, fortūna, -ae, *f.*
  (*generally bad*), cāsus, -ūs, *m.*
forum, fŏrum, -i, *n.*
found, condo, -ĕre, -dĭdi, -dĭtum.
fountain, fons, -ntis, *m.*
France, Gallia, -ae, *f.*
free, liber, -era, -erum.
  from, văcuus; expers.
  to free, lībĕrare.
freedman, lībertus, -i, *m.*
freedom, lībertas, -atis, *f.*
French, Gallĭcus.
Frenchman, Gallus, -i, *m.*
frequently, saepe.
fresh, intĕger, -gra, -grum.
  (*recent*), rĕcens.
friend, ămīcus, -i, *m.*
friendship, ămīcĭtia, -ae, *f.*
frighten, terrēre.
front, in, a fronte.
fruit, fructus, -ūs, *m.*
fugitive, prŏfŭgus, -i, *m.*
  (*gen. of slaves*), fŭgĭtīvus, -i, *m.*
full, plēnus.
furnish, praebēre.
further, longius; ultra.
fury, fŭror, -oris, *m.*

G

gallant, fortis.
Gallic, Gallĭcus.
game, ludus, -i, *m.*
  hold games, ludos cĕlebrare.
garden, hortus, -i, *m.*
garment, vestīmentum, -i, *n.* ; vestis, -is, *f.*
garrison, praesĭdium, -i, *n.*
gate, porta, -ae, *f.*
gather, collĭgo, -ĕre, -lēgi, -lectum.
Gaul, Gallia, -ae, *f.*
Gaul, a, Gallus, -i, *m.*
gaze at, spectare; intuēri.
general, dux, ducis, *m.* See p. 105, note 3.
  commander-in-chief, impĕrator, -oris, *m.*
  general's tent, praetōrium, -i, *n.*
generally, vulgo.
geniality, cōmĭtas, -atis, *f.*
German, Germānus, -i, *m.*
get out of (*escape*), ēvādo, -ĕre, -vasi, -vasum.
gift, dōnum, -i, *n.* ; mūnus, -eris, *n.*
give, do, dăre, dĕdi, dătum.
  up, trādo; dēdo, -ĕre, -dĭdi, -dĭtum.
  ground, cēdo (-ĕre, cessi, cessum) loco.
give up hope, spem abjĭcio, -ĕre, -jēci, -jectum.
give opportunity, do (dăre, dĕdi, dătum) occāsionem; facio (-ĕre, fēci, factum) pŏtestatem. Voc. 100.
glad, to be, gaudeo, -ēre, gavisus sum. Rule 22, p. 124.
gladly, lībenter.
gloomy, tristis.
glory, glōria, -ae, *f.* ; dĕcus, -ŏris, *n.*

gloriously, summā laude.
go, eo, ire, ii, itum ; se confero, -ferre, -tuli, collatum.
away, discēdo, -ĕre, -cessi, -cessum ; abeo, -ire, -ii, -itum.
back, regrĕdior, -i, -gressus sum ; rĕdeo,-ire, -ii, -itum.
out, ēgrĕdior, -i, -gressus sum.
well, prospĕre ēvĕnio, -ire, -vēni, -ventum.
god, deus, -i, *m.*
going on, to be, pass. of ăgo, -ĕre, ēgi, actum.
gold, aurum, -i, *n.*
golden, aureus.
good for, to be, prōsum, prodesse, profui ; ex usu *or* usui, sum, esse, fui.
goods, bŏna, -orum, *n. pl.*
govern, rĕgĕre ; admĭnistrare.
government, the, ii qui reipublicae praesunt ; ii qui rempublicam admĭnistrant ; măgistratūs, -uum, *m. pl.*
governor, of a province, proconsul, -ulis, *m.*
grant, do, dăre, dĕdi, dătum ; mandare ; trādo, -ĕre, -dĭdi, -dĭtum.
greatly, magnŏpĕre.
greet, sălūtare.
Greece, Graecia, -ae, *f.*
Greek, Graecus, -i, *m. (or adj.).*
language, lingua Graeca.
green, vĭrĭdis.
grief, dŏlor, -oris, *m.*
groan, gĕmĭtus, -ūs, *m.*
ground, hŭmus, -i (see p. 32) ; terra, -ae, *f.*
to hold one's, in loco persto, -are, -stiti *(sometimes*

ground, to hold one's—
translate by rĕsisto, -ĕre, -stiti ; *or* sustĭnēre).
grudge, invĭdia, -ae, *f.* ; dolor, -oris, *m.*
grumble, quĕror, -i, questus sum.
guard, custos, -odis, *m.*
off one's, imprōvĭdus ; incautus.
to, custōdire.
guest, hospes, -itis, *c.*
guide, dux, ducis, *m.*
guilty, nŏcens.
guise of, in the, mōrĕ, *gen.* ; pro, *abl.*
gulf (bay), sĭnus, -ūs, *m.*

H

halt, consisto, -ĕre, -stiti.
hand, mănus, -ūs, *f.*
in hands of, in pŏtestate.
to be at, adesse.
hang (trans.), suspendo, -ĕre, -pendi, -pensum.
(intr.), pendeo, -ēre, -pependi.
happens, it, accĭdit, -ĕre, -cĭdit ; contingit, -ĕre, -tĭgit. Voc. 128.
happy, fēlix ; beatus.
harass, lăcesso, -ĕre, lacessivi, lacessitum.
harbour, portus, -ūs, *m.*
hard, diffĭcĭlis.
hardly, vix ; aegre.
hardship, lăbor, -oris, *m.*
harm, mălum, -i, *n.* ; damnum, -i, *n.*
harvest, messis, -is, *f.*
hasten, prŏpĕrare ; festinare.
hateful to, to be hated by, ŏdio esse. Voc. 85.
hatred, ŏdium, -i, *n.*

havoc, stragēs, -is, *f.*
head, căput, -itis, *n.*
heal, mĕdēri, sānare.   Voc. 61.
healthy (*of persons*), sānus;
    vălĭdus.
    (*of places*), sălūber, -bris,
    -bre.
hear, audire.
heat, călor, -oris, *m.*
heavy, grăvis.
height, altĭtūdo, -dinis, *f.*
helmet, gălea, -ae, *f.*
help, auxĭlium, -i, *n.*
    to, jŭvare; succurro, -ĕre,
    -curri, -cursum;   sub-
    vĕnio, -ire, -vēni, -ven-
    tum.   Voc. 61.
    to be a, auxĭlio, subsĭdio esse.
here, hic.
    (*implying motion*), hūc.
hesitate, dŭbĭtare.
hide, cēlare; condo, -ĕre, -didi,
    -dĭtum.
high, altus.
higher, sŭpĕrior.
highway, via, -ae, *f.*
hill, collis, -is, *m.*
hinder, impĕdire; obsto, -are,
    -stiti.
historian, scriptor (-oris, *m.*)
    rerum.
hitherto, adhuc.
hold, tĕneo, -ēre, tenui, ten-
    tum.
hold out (*of supplies*), sup-
    pĕto, -ĕre, -petivi.
    (=*resist*), rĕsisto, -ĕre, -stiti.
    on one's course, cursum
    tĕneo, -ēre, tenui, tentum.
    one's ground, rĕsisto, -ĕre,
    -stiti; in lŏco persto,
    -are, -stiti.
    (*occupy*), occŭpare.
hold command, impĕrium ob-
    tĭneo, -ēre, -tĭnui,- tentum.

hold cheap, parvi, mĭnĭmi
    aestĭmare.
holy, săcer, -cra, -crum.
home, dŏmus, -ūs (*some 2nd*
    decl. forms), *f.*   See p. 32.
homes, pĕnātes, -ium, *m. pl.*
    (*household gods*) ; *or* fŏci,
    -orum, *m. pl.* (*hearths*).
honour, honor, -oris, *m.*
honour, for the sake of, hŏnōris
    causā.
honourable (*of persons*), prŏ-
    bus.
    (*of things*), hŏnestus.
hope, spēs, -ei, *f.*
    to, spērare.
    give up, spem abjĭcio, -ĕre,
    -jēci, -jectum.
horse, ĕquus, -i, *m.*
horse-soldier, ĕquĕs, -itis, *m.*
hospitality, hospĭtium, -i, *n.*
host, hospĕs, -itis, *m.*
hostage, obsĕs, -idis, *c.*
hour, hōra, -ae, *f.*
house, dŏmus, -ūs (*some 2nd*
    decl. forms), *f.*; *or* aedes,
    -ium, *f. pl.*
household, fămĭlia, -ae, *f.*
how, quam.
    (*in what manner ?*), quŏ-
    mŏdo; quemadmodum.
    great ? quantus.
    long ? quamdiu.
    many ? quot, *indecl. adj.*
    often ? quŏties.
however, tămen.
humour, mōrem gĕro, -ĕre,
    gessi, gestum, *dat.*
hunger, fămes, -is, *f.*
hungry, to be, ēsŭrire.
hurl, jăcio, -ĕre, jēci, jactum ;
    injĭcio, -ĕre, -jēci, -jectum.
hurry, festīnare; prŏpĕrare.
hurt, laedo, -ĕre, laesi, laesum ;
    nŏcēre.   Voc. 61.

husband, vir, viri, *m.* ;
    mărītus, -i, *m.*

I

idle, ignāvus.
if, si.
ignorance, inscientia, -ae, *f.*
ignorant of, inscius; impĕrītus.
ill, aeger, -gra, -grum.
    to be, aegrōtare.
    take, aegre fero, ferre, tuli,
    latum.
imagine, reor, rēri, ratus sum.
immediately, stătim.
immense, ingens.
importance, to be of, interesse;
    rēfert, -ferre, -ttulit. Voc.
    109.
impose tribute, impōno (-ĕre,
    -posui, -positum) trĭbū-
    tum.
impossible, it is, fiĕri non
    pŏtest (quin).
impregnable, inexpugnăbilis.
impression on, to make, com-
    mŏveo,   -ēre,   -mōvi,
    -mōtum.
in, in, *abl.*
incite, addūcĕre.
increase (*trans.*), augeo, -ēre,
    auxi, auctum.
    (*intr.*), cresco, -ĕre, crevi,
    cretum.
incur, subeo, -ire, -ii, -itum.
incursion, to make an, incur-
    sionem făcio, -ĕre, fēci,
    factum.
indeed, quĭdem.
    (*really*), rēvērā.
    (*at least*), certe; saltem.
independence, lībertas, -tatis, *f.*
indignant, to be, irascor, -i,
    iratus sum.
indignation, īra, -ae, *f.* ; dŏlor,
    -oris, *m.*

induce, to, addūcĕre.
inexperienced. See '*ignorant*.'
infantry, pĕdĭtatus, -ūs, *m.* ;
    pĕdĭtes, -um, *m. pl.*
inferior, infĕrior.
infirm, infirmus.
inflict on, affício, -ĕre, -fēci,
    -fectum (*acc. of person,
    abl. of thing*); infero,
    -ferre, -tuli, illatum (*dat.
    of person, acc. of thing*).
influence, auctōrĭtas, -tatis, *f.*
    to have very great, pluri-
    mum vălēre.
inform, certiorem (aliquem)
    făcio, -ĕre, fēci, factum.
infringe upon, dēmĭnuo, -ĕre,
    -minui, -minutum.
inhabit, incŏlo, -ĕre, -colui,
    -cultum.
inhabitants, incŏlae, -arum,
    c. pl.
    (*of a town*), oppĭdāni, -orum,
    m. pl.
    (*of a city*), cīves, -ium, *m. pl.*
injure, laedo, -ĕre, laesi, lae-
    sum ; nŏcēre. Voc. 61.
injury, injūria, -ae, *f.* ; dam-
    num, -i, *n.*
innocent, insons; innŏcens.
inquiry, hold an, quaestiōnem
    hăbēre de, *abl.*
insolence, arrŏgantia, -ae, *f.* ;
    superbia, -ae, *f.*
inspire, to, injĭcio, -ĕre, -jēci,
    -jectum (*acc. of thing,
    dat. of person*).
instead of, lŏco, *gen.*
insult, contŭmēlia, -ae, *f.* ;
    injūria, -ae, *f.*
intend, to, in animo habēre.
intend, I, mihi in animo est.
intention (*with the intention of*),
    eo consĭlio ut.
interior, pars (-rtis, *f.*) interior.

into, in, *acc.*

invade, incursionem făcio (-ĕre, fēci, factum) in, *acc.*; invādo, -ĕre, -vasi, -vasum.

invasion, incursio, -ionis, *f.*

invite, to, invītare.

involved in, to be, occurro, -ĕre, -curri, -cursum.

Ireland, Hĭbernia, -ae, *f.*

Irish, Hĭbernĭcus.

Irishman, Hĭbernus, -i, *m.*

iron, ferrum, -i, *n.* (*adj.* ferreus).

island, insŭla, -ae, *f.*

issue, ēventus, -ūs, *m.*; exĭtus, -ūs, *m.*

J

jealousy, invĭdia, -ae, *f.*

jest, jŏcus, -i, *m.*

join, to, (*trans.*), conjungo, -ĕre, -junxi, -junctum. (*intr.*), se conjungĕre cum, *abl.*

journey, ĭter, itineris, *n.*

joy, gaudium, -i, *n.*; laetĭtia, -ae, *f.*

joyful, laetus.

judge, jūdex, -dicis, *m.*

Jupiter, Juppĭter, Jovis, *m.*

just as, just as much as, aeque ac; haud ălĭter ac. Rule 30, p. 178.

justify, excūsare.

K

keep, conservare. (*observe*), cŏlo, -ĕre, colui, cultum. (*one's word*), fĭdem praesto, -are, -stiti, -stitum.

key, clāvis, -is, *f.*

kill, interfĭcio, -ĕre, -fēci, -fectum. (*cut down*), occĭdo, -ĕre, -cīdi, -cisum. (*murder*), nĕcare. (*massacre*), trŭcīdare.

kind, sort, gĕnus, -eris, *n.*

kind, bĕnignus.

kindly, *adv.* benigne.

kindness, bĕnignitas, -tatis, *f.*; humānĭtas, -tatis, *f.*; bĕnĕvŏlentia, -ae, *f.* *act of kindness*, beneficium, -i, *n.*

king, rex, regis, *m.*

kingdom, regnum, -i, *n.*

kingly, rēgius.

kingly power, regnum, -i, *n.*

knight, ĕques, -itis, *m.*

know, scire. See Syn. (*ascertain*), cognosco, -ĕre, -nōvi, -nĭtum. *not to*, nescire. *it is well known*, constat.

knowledge (*of things*), cognĭtio, -ionis, *f.* (*of persons*), consuetudo, -dinis, *f.*

L

labour, lăbor, -oris, *m.*

lack, to, cărēre. See Syn., ' *want.*'

ladder, scāla, -ae, *f.*

laden, ŏnĕratus.

land (*trans.*), expōno, -ĕre, -posui, -posĭtum. (*intr.*), e nave egrĕdior, -i, -gressus sum.

land, ăger, agri, *m.*; patria, -ae, *f.* See Syn.

landing, egressus, -ūs, *m.*

last, (*most recent*), proximus. (*of a series*), ultimus. *at*, tandem.

last, to the, ad extrēmum.
late at night, multā nocte.
　till late in the night, ad
　　multam noctč ı.
　too, sēro.
lately, nūper.
latter, hic (*opp. to* ille).
launch, dēdūcěre.
law, lex, lēgis, *f.*
　pass a, lēgem jŭbeo, -ēre,
　　jussi, jussum.
　propose a, lēgem fero, ferre,
　　tuli, latum.
　law of nations, jus (juris, *n.*)
　　gentium.
　contrary to, contra jus gen-
　　tium.
lawful, fas, *indecl.*; *or use*
　līcet.
lay down, dēpōno, -ěre, -posui,
　-posĭtum.
lead, dūcěre.
lead back, rědūcěre.
　out, ēdūcěre.
　round, circumdūcěre.
　aside, dēdūcěre.
leader, dux, ducis, *m.*
learn, disco, -ěre, didici.
　(*ascertain*), cognosco, -ěre,
　　-nōvi, -nĭtum ; compěrio
　　-ire, -peri, -pertum.
least, at, certe ; saltem.
leave, rělinquo, -ěre, -līqui,
　-lictum.
leave one's post, loco cēdo,
　-ěre, cessi, cessum.
leave behind, rělinquo, -ěre,
　-līqui, -lictum.
leave, by your, pāce tua.
legion, lěgio, -ionis, *f.*
legionary, lěgiōnārius mīles,
　-itis, *m.*
leisure, ōtium, -i, *n.*
lend, mandare.
length, at, tandem.

lessen, dēmĭnuo, -ěre, -minui,
　-minutum.
let, allow, sĭno, -ěre, sīvi,
　sĭtum.
let down, dēmitto, -ěre, -misi,
　-missum.
let go, dīmitto, -ěre, -misi,
　-missum ; ŏmitto, -ěre,
　-misi, -missum.
letter, ěpistola, -ae, *f.* ; littěrae,
　-arum, *f. pl.*
levy, hold a, dēlectum hăbēre.
liable to, obnoxius.
liberate, līběrare.
liberty, lībertas, -tatis, *f.*
lie, jăcēre.
　(*speak falsely*), mentiri.
lieutenant (*general*), lēgātus,
　-i, *m.*
life, vīta, -ae, *f.*
light, lux, lucis, *f.*
like, sĭmĭlis.
line of battle, ăcies, -iei, *f.*
lines (*of army*), mūnītiones,
　-um, *f. pl.*
listen, audire, (pārēre).
litter, lectīca, -ae, *f.*
little, parvus ; exĭguus.
little, a, paulum.
　(*with comp.*), paulo.
　too, părum, *adv.* (*used as
　　noun with partitive gen.*).
　for a little time, paulisper.
little by little, paulātim.
live (*exist*), vīvo, -ěre, vixi,
　victum.
live in, hăbĭtare in, *abl.* ;
　incŏlo, -ěre -colui, -cul-
　tum.
long, longus.
　(*of time only*), diuturnus.
　(*for a long time*), diu, *adv.*
　(*now for a long time*), jam-
　　prīdem ; jamdūdum. See
　　p. 155, n. 2.

long (*as long as*), dōnec;
  quoad. Rule 25, p. 140.
(=*provided that*),dum; dummŏdo. Rule 27, p. 146.
look after, cūrare.
looks (*expression*), vultus, -ūs,
  m.
lose (*let slip*), āmitto, -ĕre,
  -misi, -missum.
(*wilfully*), perdo, -ĕre, -dĭdi,
  -dĭtum. See Syn.
lose heart, animum dēmitto,
  -ĕre, -misi, -missum.
loss, incommŏdum, -i, *n.*;
  damnum, -i, *n.*
  with great (*of a battle*),
  maxima strāge, *or* multis
  amissis.
lost, to be, actum est de (*abl.*)
  =*it is all over with.*
lot, sors, -rtis, *f.*
loud, *use* magnus.
love, amare; dīlĭgo, -ĕre, -lexi,
  -lectum.
loyal, fĭdēlis.
loyalty, fĭdes, -ei, *f.*; fĭdēlĭtas,
  -atis, *f.*
luxury, luxus, -ūs, *m.*

M

mad, insānus.
  to be, fŭrĕre.
magistrate, măgistratus, -ūs,
  m.
maidens (*servants*), mĭnistrae,
  -arum, *f. pl.*; fămŭlae,
  -arum, *f. pl.*
maimed, saucius.
main road, via, -ae, *f.*
mainly, imprīmis.
majority, major pars (partis,
  f.), *with part. gen.*; plērique, *adj. pl.*
make (*cause that*), effĭcio (-ĕre,
  -fēci, -fectum) ut (final).

make, trial of, expĕrior, -iri,
  -pertus sum; temptare.
man (*human being*), hŏmo,
  -mini *m.*
  (*indivi ual of male sex*),
  vir, ᵥiri, *m.*
  to a, ad unum.
  to man (*vb.*), compleo, -ēre,
  -plēvi, -pletum.
manner, mŏdus, -i, *m.*
  (*custom*), mōs, moris, *m.*
many, multi.
  times (*larger*), multis partibus.
  how, quot, *indecl. adj.*
march, ĭter, itineris, *n.*
  to, iter făcio, -ĕre, fēci,
  factum; contendo, -ĕre,
  -tendi, -tentum.
  a forced, magnum iter,
  itineris, *n.*
  on the, in *or* ex itinere.
  to continue, iter continuare.
marry (*woman as subject*),
  nūbo,-ĕre, nupsi, nuptum.
  (*man as subject*), dūcĕre.
  Voc. 61.
marsh, pălus, -udis, *f.*
marvellous, mīrus.
massacre, caedes, -is, *f.*
master (*of pupils*), măgister,
  -tri, *m.*
  (*of slaves*), dŏmĭnus, -i, *m.*
  of the horse, măgister (-tri,
  m.) equitum.
match for, par.
matters a great deal, it, multum, *or* magni interest.
  Voc. 109.
mean, vŏlo (velle, volui) dīcĕre.
  (*indicate*), signĭfĭcare.
means (*manner, way*), mŏdus,
  -i, *m.*
  by this, ĭta.
  by no, haudquāquam.

meanwhile, intĕrim ; intĕrea.

meet, obviam eo, ire, ivi, itum, dat.

(*obtain*), nanciscor, -i, nactus sum.

meeting, concilium, -i, *n.* ; conventus, -ūs, *m.*

mention above, to, supra com-mĕmŏrare.

mercenaries, mercēnārii mīl-ĭtes, -um, *m. pl.*

merchandise, merces, -ium, *f. pl.*

message, nuntius, -i, *m.*

messenger, nuntius, -i, *m.*

middle, mĕdius.   See note, p. 5.

might, with all one's, summā vi.

mile, mille passūs, -uum, *m. pl.*

miles, two, duo milia (-ium, *n. pl.*) passuum.

mind, ănĭmus, -i, *m.*
    (*intellect*), mens, -ntis, *f.*
    See Syn. *with minds made up*, obstĭnatis ănĭmis.

mindful, mĕmor.

misfortune, călămĭtas, -tatis, *f.* ; mălum,-i, *n.*

moat, fossa, -ae, *f.*

mob, turba, -ae, *f.* ; multĭtūdo, -dinis, *f.*

mock, irrīdeo, -ēre, -risi, -risum.

modern times, in, his tem-pŏribus.

money, pĕcūnia, -ae, *f.*

month, mensis, -is, *m.*

moon, lūna, -ae, *f.*

moreover, praetĕrea.
    (=*now, continuing a narra-tive*), autem.

morning, in the, māne.

mortal (*subject to death*), mor-tālis.
    (*causing death*), mortĭfer.

most, plērique, *adj.*

mother, māter, -tris, *f.*

mound, tŭmŭlus, -i, *m.* ; agger, -geris, *m.*

mountain, mons, montis, *m.*

mouth, ōs, oris, *n.*
    (*entrance*), ostium, -i, *n.* ; adĭtus, -ūs, *m.*

move, mŏveo, -ēre, mōvi, motum.
    (*affect*), commŏveo, -ēre, -mōvi, -motum.

much, just as much as, aeque ac.

too much, nimius, *adj.* ; nĭmium (*used as noun*) ; nĭmis, *adv.*

mule, mūlus, -i, *m.*

multitude (*great number*), mul-tĭtūdo, -dinis, *f.*
    (*common people*), plebs, plebis, *f.*

N

name, nōmen, -inis, *n.* (*by name, named*), nōmĭne).

narrow, angustus ; artus.

nation, gens, -ntis, *f.*   See Syn. ' *people.*'

naval, nāvālis.

near, prŏpe.

near, to be, adsum, -esse, -fui.

nearest, proximus, *followed by dat., or* ab *with abl.*

nearly, paene ; fĕrē.

necessary, nĕcessarius.

necessity, nĕcessĭtas, -tatis, *f.*

neck, collum, -i, *n.* ; cervīces, -um, *f. pl.*

need, ĕgēre ; indĭgēre.   Voc. 134.
    (*be without*), cărēre.

needs money, he, opus est ei pĕcūniā.

neglect, neglĭgo, -ĕre, neglexi,
　　neglectum.
negligence, neglĭgentia, -ae, *f.*
neighbour, neighbouring, vīc-
　　īnus; fīnĭtĭmus.
neither . . . *nor*, nec . . . nec ;
　　neque . . . neque.
never, nunquam.
nevertheless, tămen; nĭhĭlō-
　　mĭnus.
new, nŏvus.　See Syn.
　　(=*fresh*), rĕcens.
news, nuntius, -i, *m.*
　　what ? quid nŏvi ?
　　to bring, affero, -ferre, attuli,
　　　　allatum ;　refero, -ferre,
　　　　rettuli, relatum.
next, proxĭmus.
night, nox, noctis, *f.*
　　by, noctu.
　　until late in the, ad multam
　　　　noctem.
no (*adj.*), nullus.
noble, nōbĭlis.
nobody, no one, nēmo (*acc.*
　　neminem, *no gen. or abl.* ;
　　m.) (*adj.* nullus).
none the less, nĭhĭlōmĭnus.
noon, mĕrĭdies, -ei, *m.*
north, septentriones, -um,
　　m. pl.
not only . . . *but also*, non solum
　　. . . sed etiam.
not yet, nondum.
nothing, nĭhil.
notice, animadverto, -ĕre,
　　-verti, -versum.
now, jam.
　　(*at present time*), nunc.
　　(*continuing narrative*),
　　　　autem.
nowadays, his tempŏribus.
now for a long time, jamprī-
　　dem; jamdūdum.　See p.
　　155, note 2.

number, nŭmĕrus, i, *m., only
　　singular.*
　　a great number, multitudo,
　　　　-dinis, *f.*
nymph, nympha, -ae, *f.*

O

oath, jusjūrandum,　jurisju-
　　randi, *n.*
obey, to, pārēre.
object was, his, id egit ut.
observe (*keep*), cŏlo, -ĕre, colui,
　　cultum.
　　(*notice*), ănĭmadverto, -ĕre,
　　　　-verti, -versum.
obstacle, diffĭcultas, -tatis, *f.*
obstinacy, pertĭnācia, -ae, *f.*
obstinate, pertinax.
obstinately, obstĭnate.
occupy, occŭpare.
off (*promontory, etc.*), contra,
　　acc.
offence, noxa, -ae, *f.*; dēlictum,
　　-i, *n.*
offend, offendo, -ĕre, -fendi,
　　-fensum, *acc.*; displĭcēre,
　　dat.
offer, offero, -ferre, obtuli,
　　oblatum.
office (*of state*), hŏnor, -oris,
　　m.
officer,　praefectus,　-i,　*m.* ;
　　lēgātus, -i, *m.*　See p. 55,
　　note 2.
often, saepe.
　　as often as, quŏties.　See
　　　　Rule 26, p. 144.
old (*that has lasted a long time*),
　　vĕtus.　See Syn.
　　(*belonging to former times*),
　　　　antīquus.
　　old man, senex, senis, *m.*
　　ten years old, etc.　See p. 32.
older, nātu major ; senior.

once (*upon a time*), ălĭquando; ōlim.
at once, stătim.
one . . . another (*of several*); alius . . . alius.
the one . . . the other (*two contrasted*), alter . . . alter.
on one side . . . on the other, ab altera parte . . . ab altera.
with one another, inter se.
one in ten, decimus quisque, *lit., each tenth man.*
only, sōlum ; tantum; mŏdo.
onset, impĕtus, -ūs, *m.*
open, ăpertus.
   to, ăpĕrio, -ire, aperui, apertum.
   to be, pătēre.
   throw open, patĕfacio, -ĕre, -fēci, -factum.
openly, ăperte.
opinion, sententia, -ae, *f.*
   to give an, sententiam fero, ferre, tuli, latum.
opportunity, făcultas, -tatis, *f.*; lŏcus, -i, *m.*; occāsio, -ionis, *f.*
   to give an, do (dăre, dĕdi, dătum)occasionem; făcio, (-ĕre, fēci, factum), potestatem, *gen.* Voc. 100.
   should an opportunity offer, dătā occāsione.
oppose, obsto, -are, obstiti; obsisto, -ĕre, -stiti; rĕsisto, -ĕre, -stiti.
opposite to, contra, *acc.*, e regione, *gen.*
opposite (*bank, etc.*), alter.
oppress, to, vexare; opprĭmo, -ĕre, -pressi, -pressum.
or (*in statements*), aut.
   (*in questions*). See **Exx.** 110, 112.

oracle, ōrācŭlum, -i, *n.*
orator, ōrātor, -oris, *m.*
ordain to, ēdīcĕre.
order, discĭplīna, -ae, *f.*
   to lose, ŏmitto (-ĕre, -misi, -missum) discĭplīnam.
   (*in close*), confertus; conferto agmīne.
order (*command*), jussum, -i, *n.*
   by order of, jussu.
   without the order of, injussu.
   (*vb.*) *command*, jŭbeo, -ēre, jussi, jussum ; impĕrare.
origin, ŏrīgo, -ginis, *f.*
other people, belonging to, ălĭēnus.
others (*all others*), cētĕri; rĕlĭqui.
otherwise than, ălĭter ac. Rule 30, p. 178.
ought, dēbēre.
outpost, stătio, -ionis, *f.*
outside, extra, *acc.*
overcome, sŭpĕrare.
   (*with fear*, etc.) perculsus.
overtake, assĕquor; consĕquor, -i, -secutus sum.
overthrow, sterno; prosterno, -ĕre, -stravi, -stratum.
owe, dēbēre.
   it is owing to you, per te stat (p. 132).
ox, bos, bovis, *c.*

P

pace, passus, -ūs, *m.*
pacify, pācare.
pain, dŏlor, -oris, *m.*
palace, rēgia, -ae, *f.*
panic, păvor, -oris, *m.*
pardon, vĕnia, -ae, *f.*
   to, ignosco, -ĕre, -nōvi, -notum.
parent, părens, -ntis, *c.*

part, pars, -rtis, *f.*
part in, to take, interesse.
particularly, praeter omnes.
partly . . . *partly*, partim . . .
partim.
pass, saltus, -ūs, *m.*; angustiae, -arum, *f.*
spend, ăgo, -ĕre, ēgi, actum.
by, praetĕreo, -ire, -ii, -itum.
past, praetĕritus.
the, praeterĭta, -orum, *n. pl.*
path (byway), trāmes, -itis, *m.*
patiently, aequo ănĭmo.
pay, stīpendium, -i, *n.*
to, solvo, -ĕre, solvi, solutum.
peace, pax, pacis, *f.*
peasant, agrĭcŏla, -ae, *m.*; rusticus, -i, *m.*
penalty, poena, -ae, *f.*
undergo, poenam sŭbeo, -ire, -ii, -itum.
people (population, nation), pŏpŭlus, -i, *m.* See Syn.
(persons), homines, -um, *m. pl.*
(common), plebs, -bis, *f.*; vulgus, -i, *n.*
perceive, sentio, -ire, sensi, sensum.
perform, fungor, -i, functus sum.
perhaps, forte; fortasse; forsĭtan, (forsitan *always takes subj.*).
peril, to bring into, in pĕrīculum addūcĕre.
perish, pĕreo, -ire, -ii, -itum.
(of ship), frangor, -i, fractus sum.
perjury, perjūrium, -i, *n.*
permit, sĭno, -ĕre, sīvi, sĭtum.
Persian, Persa, -ae, *m.*
persuade, persuādeo, -ēre, -suasi, -suasum. Rules 11, 12, pp. 62, 64.

pestilence, pestis, -is, *f.*; pestĭlentia, -ae, *f.*
philosopher, săpiens, -ntis, *m.*; phĭlŏsŏphus, -i, *m.*
philosophy, phĭlŏsŏphia, -ae, *f.*
pierce, transfīgo, -ĕre, -fixi, -fixum.
piece (of money), nummus, -i, *m.*
piety (duty, natural affection), pĭĕtas, -tatis, *f.*
pile up, congĕro, -ĕre, -gessi, -gestum.
pitch a camp, to, castra pōno, -ĕre, posui, positum; castra mūnire.
pity, mĭsĕret, *impers.* See Voc. 128.
place, lŏcus, -i, *m.*; *pl.* loca, *n.*
first, princĭpatus, -ūs, *m.*
(vb.) pono, -ĕre, posui, positum.
before (prefer), antepōno, -ĕre, -posui, -positum.
to take the place of, succēdo, -ĕre, -cessi, -cessum.
plague, pestĭlentia, -ae, *f.*; pestis, -is, *f.*
plain, campus, -i, *m.*; plānĭties, -ei, *f.*
plainly, ăperte; plāne.
plan, consĭlium, -i, *n.*
to form a, consĭlium căpio, -ĕre, cepi, captum; consilium ineo, -ire, -ii, -itum.
play (of artillery), immitto (-ĕre, -misi, -missum) tēla.
play, lūdo, -ĕre, lusi, lusum.
pleasant, jūcundus.
please, plăcēre; jŭvo, -are, jūvi, jūtum. Voc. 61.
pleases, it, jŭvat; lĭbet; plăcet. Voc. 128.

plunder, vastare; dīrĭpio, -ĕre; -rĭpui, -reptum; spŏliare; (*nn.*) praeda, -ae, *f.*
Po, Pădus, -i, *m.*
poet, poēta, -ae, *m.*
point out, ostendo, -ĕre, -tendi, -tentum *or* -tensum; monstrare.
poison, vĕnēnum, -i, *n.*
poor, pauper.
population, pŏpŭlus, -i, *m.*
position, lŏcus, -i, *m.* (*pl.* loca, *n.*).
to take up a, consīdo, -ĕre, -sedi, -sessum.
possession, get, pŏtiri.
possible, use făcĕre, *or* fiĕri possum, posse, potui.
as soon as, quam prīmum.
post, to leave one's, lŏco cēdo, -ĕre, cessi, cessum.
power, pŏtentia, -ae, *f.*; pŏtestas, -tatis, *f.* See Synonyms.
(*energy*), vīs (*acc.* vim, *abl.* vi), *f.*
kingly, regnum, -i, *n.*
with all one's, summā vī.
powerful, pŏtens.
practise, stŭdēre; exercēre.
praise, laus, laudis, *f.*; *vb.* laudare.
pray, ōrare; prĕcari.
prayers, prĕces, -um, *f. pl.*
prefer, mālo, malle, malui.
prepare, părare.
for, se părare ad.
for battle, arma expĕdire.
presence of mind, to show, impăvĭdus esse; se intrĕpĭde gĕro, -ĕre, gessi, gestum.
presence of, in, coram, *abl.*
present, dōnum, -i, *n.*
to be, adsum, -esse, -fui.

preserve, conservare.
press hard, urgeo, -ēre, ursi; prĕmo, -ĕre, pressi, pressum.
on, insto, -are, -stiti, *dat.*
pressed hard, to be, lăbōrare.
pretend, sĭmŭlare.
prevail, sŭpĕrare.
prevent, prŏhĭbēre.
prey, praeda, -ae, *f.*
price, prĕtium, -i, *n.* See p. 48.
at a low, vīli.
pride (*spirit*), ănĭmus, -i, *m.*; sŭperbia, -ae, *f.*
priest, priestess, săcerdos, -otis, *m. or f.*
prison, carcer; vincula, -orum; *n. pl.*, ' *bonds.*'
put in, in carcĕrem (vincŭla) conjĭcio, -ĕre, -jēci, -jectum.
prisoner, captīvus, -i, *m.*
prisoner, take, căpio, -ĕre, cēpi, captum; captīvum făcio, -ĕre, fēci, factum.
private (*not in office*), prīvātus.
produce, ēdo, -ĕre, -didi, -dĭtum.
prolong a war, bellum dūcĕre.
promise to, prōmitto, -ĕre, -misi, -missum; pollĭcēri.
promontory, prōmontōrium, -i, *n.*
proof, indĭcium, -i, *n.*
property, bŏna, -orum, *n. pl.*; res, rei, *f.*
private, res fămĭliāris.
prophet, prophetess, vātes, -is, *c.*
propose (*intend*), in ănĭmo hăbēre.
(*a law*), fero, ferre, tuli, latum.
proscribe, proscrībo, -ĕre, -scripsi, -scriptum.

prospect, (*hope*), spes, -ei, *f.*
prosperity, res (rerum, *f. pl.*)
  prospĕrae.
prosperous, fēlix.
protection, to be, praesĭdio
  esse. Voc. 85.
  to be under, fĭdem sĕqui
  (*alicujus*).
proud, sŭperbus.
prove, demonstrare.
  prove oneself false, se praebēre infĭdēlem.
provide, praebēre.
provided that, dum; dummŏdo
  (p. 146).
province, prōvincia, -ae, *f.*
provision, rem frūmentāriam
  expĕdire.
provisions, commeatus, -ūs,
  m. ; cĭbus, -i, *m.*
provoke, lăcesso, -ĕre, -ivi,
  -itum; incĭtare.
prudent, prūdens.
punish, pūnire; poenā *or* sup-
  plĭcio affĭcio, -ĕre, -fēci,
  -fectum.
punishment, poena, -ae, *f.*;
  supplĭcium, -i, *n.*
purpose, for this, ad hoc.
  for the purpose of, causā, *gen.*
  (*after its case*).
  on, consulto; de industriā.
  on purpose to, eo consilio
  ut.
purpose, to no, frustrā; nēquicquam.
pursue, sĕquor; persĕquor, -i,
  -secutus sum. See Syn.,
  ' *follow.*'
put back, rĕpōno, -ĕre, -posui,
  -posĭtum.
  on trial, reum facio, -ĕre,
  fēci, factum; nōmen de-
  fero, -ferre, -tuli, -latum;
  adj., reus.

put out to sea, ēvĕhor, -i,
  -vectus sum.
  to death, interfĭcio, -ĕre,
  -fēci, -fectum.

Q

quantity, cōpia, -ae, *f.*
quarters, at close, commĭnus.
quickly, cĕlĕrĭter.
quiet, tranquillus; (*nn.*) quĭes,
  -etis, *f.*
quite, admŏdum.

R

rabble, turba, -ae, *f.*
race (*birth*), gĕnus, -eris, *n.*
  tribe, family), gens, -ntis, *f.*
raiment, vestis, -is, *f.*
raise a siege, relinquo (-ĕre,
  -līqui, -lictum) obsĭdiō-
  nem; obsĭdĭone dēsisto,
  -ĕre, -stiti.
  (*of relieving army*), obsidione lĭbĕrare.
rampart, vallum, -i, *n.*
range, within, intrā conjectum
  tēli.
rank, ordo, -dinis, *m.*
  first, prīma ăcies, -ei, *f.*
rash, tĕmĕrārius; inconsultus.
rashly, tĕmĕre; inconsulte.
rashness, tĕmĕritas, -tatis, *f.*
ravage, pŏpŭlari; vastare.
reach, pervĕnio (-ire, -vēni,
  -ventum) ad, *acc.*
read, lĕgo, -ĕre, lēgi, lectum.
  through, perlĕgo, -ĕre, -lēgi,
  -lectum.
reading, lectio, -ionis, *f.*
readily, lĭbenter.
ready, get, părare; compărare.
  to, părātus, *with inf.*
really, rēvērā.
rear, in the, a tergo.

rearguard, nŏvissimum agmen, -minis, *n.*

reason that, *for the*, propterea quod.

rebel, rĕbellis, -is, *c.*

recall, rĕvŏcare.

call to mind, rĕpĕto, -ĕre, -ivi, -itum, *acc.* ; 1ĕminiscor, -i, *gen.*

receive, accĭpio, -ĕre, -cēpi, -ceptum.

recent, rĕcens.

recently, nūper.

recognise, agnosco, -ĕre, -nōvi, -nĭtum.

recollect, rĕmĭniscor, -i, *gen.*

I recollect, vĕnit mihi in mentem.

recollection, mĕmŏria, -ae, *f.*

recommend, suādeo, -ēre, suasi, suasum.

recover (*trans.*), rĕcĭpio, -ĕre, -cēpi, -ceptum ; (*intr.*), se rĕficio, -ĕre, -fēci, -fectum.

recruit, tīro, -onis, *m.*

red, rŭber, -bra, -brum.

reduce, redĭgo, -ĕre, -ēgi, -actum.

refer (*to senate*), rĕfero, -ferre, rettuli, relatum.

refrain, tempĕrare ; prohĭbēri.

refuge, *to seek*, *to fly for*, confūgio (-ĕre, -fūgi) ad, *acc.*

refuse, nōlo, nolle, nolui ; rĕcūsare. Voc. 170.

regard as, dūcĕre ; hăbēre pro.

regiment, cŏhors, -rtis, *f.*

regret, deplōrare.

(*be sorry for*), paenitet.

reinforcements, supplēmentum, -i, *n.* ; nŏvae cōpiae, -arum, *f. pl.*

reject, rējĭcio, -ĕre, -jēci, -jectum ; respuo, -ĕre, -spui, -sputum.

rejoice, gaudeo, -ēre, gavisus sum. Rule 22, p. 124.

relate, narrare.

relief, auxĭlium, -i, *n.*

relieve, *to*, succēdo, -ēre, -cessi, -cessum, *dat.* ; sublevare.

from a siege, lībĕrare obsĭdione.

relying on, frētus, *abl.*

remain, măneo, -ēre, mansi, mansum.

faithful to Caesar, fĭdem Caesaris sĕquor, -i, secutus sum.

remarkable, insignis ; praeclārus.

remedy, rĕmĕdium, -i, *n.*

remember, memini, -isse ; memor sum, esse, fui.

remembrance, mĕmŏria, -ae, *f.*

remind, admŏnēre.

remove, transfero, -ferre, -tuli, -latum.

renew, redintegrare.

battle, redintegrare *or* restĭtuŏ (-ĕre, -stitui, -stitutum) proelium.

repair, reficio, -ĕre, -fēci, -fectum.

repay, reddo, -ĕre, reddidi, redditum.

repeatedly, ĭdentĭdem.

repel, *repulse*, rĕpello, -ĕre, -puli, -pulsum.

repent of, paenĭtet. Voc. 128.

replace, rĕpōno, -ĕre, -posui, -positum.

reply, respondeo, -ēre, -spondi, -sponsum.

report, nuntiare ; rĕfero, -ferre, -ttuli, -latum.

resentment, dŏlor, -oris, *m.* ; invĭdia, -ae, *f.*

reserves, subsĭdia, -orum, *n. pl.*

resign se abdĭcare.

resist, resisto, -ĕre, -stiti.
resolutely, constanter; obstĭnāte.
resolution, constantia, -ae, *f.*
resolve, constĭtuo, -ĕre, -stitui, -stitutum.
resolved minds, with, obstĭnatis animis.
responsible for, auctor, -oris, *m., with gen.*
  to be responsible for, rătionem reddo, -ĕre, reddidi, redditum (*to render an account*).
rest, the, cētĕri; rĕlĭqui; rĕlĭqua pars, -rtis, *f.*
rest (*vb.*), quiesco, -ĕre, quievi, quietum; se rĕfĭcio, -ĕre, -fēci, -fectum.
restrain, tempĕrare. Voc. 61.
result, eventus, -ūs, *m.*; exĭtus, -ūs, *m.*
  to, ēvĕnio, -ire, -vēni, -ventum; ēvādo, -ĕre, -vasi, -vasum.
results, it, evĕnit, -ire, -vēnit.
retreat, se recĭpio, -ĕre, -cēpi, -ceptum; pĕdem rĕfero, -ferre, -ttuli, -latum.
  sound a retreat, receptui cano, -ĕre, cecini. Voc. 85.
return (*intr.*), redeo, -ire, -ii, -itum; regredior, -i, -gressus sum.
  trans. (=give back), reddo, -ĕre, reddidi, redditum.
revenge, poena, -ae, *f.*; ulciscendi lĭbīdo, -dinis, *f.*
  to, vindĭcare.
  (*take vengeance on*), ulciscor, -i, ultus sum; poenam sūmo (-ĕre, sumpsi, sumptum) de, *abl.*
review, rĕcensēre.

revolt, dēfectio, -ionis, *f.*
  from, dēfĭcio (-ĕre, -fēci, -fectum) ab, *abl.*
revolution, res (rerum, *f. pl.*) novae.
reward (*vb.*), praemio affĭcio, -ĕre, -fēci, -fectum.
  (*nn.*) praemium, -i, *n.*
Rhine, Rhēnus, -i, *m.*
Rhone, Rhŏdănus, -i, *m.*
rich, dīves.
riches, dīvĭtiae, -arum, *f. pl.*
ride, ĕquo vĕhor, -i, vectus sum.
ride at anchor, sto (stare, steti) in ancŏris.
right, it is, oportet. Voc. 128.
rightly, jūre.
riot, tŭmultus, -ūs, *m.*
ripe (*ready, early*), mātūrus.
ripen, maturescĕre.
rise, surgo, -ĕre, surrexi, surrectum; orior; coorior, -iri, -ortus sum.
rising ground, lŏcus (-i, *m. pl.* -a, *neut.*) ēditus.
risk, pĕrīclĭtari.
  run risk, pĕrīcŭlum subeo, -ire, -ii, -itum.
risk all, rem in summum discrīmen addūcĕre.
risk one's life, periculum capitis subeo, -ire, -ii, -itum.
river, flŭvius, -i, *m.*; flūmen, -inis, *n.*
  up, adverso flūmĭne; in adversum flumen.
  down, sĕcundo flumine.
road, via, -ae, *f.*
  (*route*), ĭter, itineris, *n.*
  make a, viam (ĭter) mūnire.
rob, spŏliare.
robber, latro, -onis, *m.*
robes of state (*of senators*), tŭnĭca (-ae, *f.*) lātĭclāvia.

rock, saxum, -i, *n.*; rupes, -is, *f.*
rod, virga, -ae, *f.*
Rome, Rōma, -ae, *f.*
Roman, Rōmānus.
rout, fundo, -ĕre, fudi, fusum; fŭgare.
  utterly, prōflīgare.
rule, rĕgĕre; regnare.
run, curro, -ĕre, cucurri, cursum.
run out, prōcurro, -ĕre, -curri, -cursum.
  short, dēfĭcio, -ĕre, -fēci, -fectum.
  the risk, in pĕrīculum addūci.
  away, aufŭgio, -ĕre, -fūgi, -fugitum.
rush into, irruo, -ĕre, -rui.
  out, eruo, -ĕre, -rui, -rutum; effundor, -i, -fusus sum.
  forward, prōruo, -ĕre, -rui, -rutum.

S

sacred, săcer, -cra, -crum.
sacrilegious, sacrĭlĕgus.
sad (*feeling sad*), *gloomy*, tristis.
  (*showing sadness*), maestus.
safe, *in safety*, tūtus; incŏlŭmis.
safety, sălus, -utis, *f.*
said he, inquit.
sail, nāvĭgare.
  past, *or along*, praetervĕhor, -i, -vectus sum.
  along coast, ōram lĕgo, -ĕre, lēgi, lectum.
  to set sail, solvo (-ĕre, solvi, solutum) navem.
sailor, nauta, -ae, *m.*

sake of, *for the*, causā, *gen.* (*following its case*); pro, *abl.*
sally, *sortie*, ēruptio, -ionis, *f.*
salvation of, *to be*, sălūti esse. Voc. 85.
same as, *the*, īdem ac.
same time, *at the*, sĭmul.
satisfy, sătisfăcio, -ĕre, -fēci, -factum.
  (*indulge*), indulgeo, -ĕre, indulsi, indultum.
savage, saevus.
save, servare.
say, dicĕre.
  men say, *it is said*, fĕrunt.
scale, ascendo, -ĕre, -scendi, -scensum.
scarcely, vix; aegrē.
scatter (*trans.*), dispergo, -ĕre, -persi, -persum.
  (*intr.*), *use passive*.
schoolmaster, măgister, -tri, *m.*
scorn, contemptus, -ūs, *m.*; contemptio, -ionis, *f.*
  vb. See ' *despise.*'
scout, explōrator, -oris, *m.*; specŭlator, -oris, *m.*
scruples (*religious*), rēlĭgio, -ionis, *f.*
sea, măre, -is, *n.*
sea, *to put out to*, evĕhor, -i, -vectus sum.
search for, quaero, -ĕre, quaesivi, quaesitum; pĕto, -ĕre, petivi, petitum.
seat of war, sēdes (-is, *f.*) belli.
secretly, clam.
see to, cūrare. See Voc. 149.
see to it that, *take care that*, cūra ut.
seek, quaero, -ĕre, quaesivi, quaesitum; pĕto, -ĕre, petivi, petitum.

291

seek refuge, confŭgio (-ĕre, -fūgi) ad, *acc.*

seem, videor, -ēri, visus sum.

seize, căpio, -ĕre, cēpi, captum. See Syn. ' *take*.'

(*snatch*), răpio, -ĕre, rapui, raptum.

(*arrest*), comprĕhendo, -ĕre, -prehendi, -prehensum.

seldom, *rarely*, rāro.

sell, vendo, -ĕre, -dĭdi, -dĭtum.

senate, sĕnatus, -ūs, *m.*; patres, -um, *m. pl.*

house, cūria, -ae, *f.*

senator, sĕnātor, -oris, *m.*

send, mitto, -ĕre, misi, missum.

away, dīmitto, -ĕre, -misi, -missum.

back, reddo, -ĕre, -ddĭdi, -ddĭtum ; rĕmitto, -ĕre, -misi, -missum.

for, arcesso, -ĕre, -ivi, -itum.

forwards, praemitto, -ĕre, -misi, -missum.

to the aid, subsĭdio mitto, -ĕre, misi, missum ; submitto, -ĕre, -misi, -missum.

sentence, to undergo, poenam subeo, -ire, -ii, -itum.

sentinels, vĭgĭliae, -arum, *f. pl.*; custōdes, -um, *m. pl.*

separate, sējungo, -ĕre, -junxi, -junctum.

serious, grăvis.

serve, to, prōsum, prodesse, profui ; servire.

(*as soldier*), stīpendia mĕrēre (*sometimes* mĕrēre *alone*).

sesterce, sestertius, -i, *m.*

set free, to, libĕrare.

out, prŏfĭciscor, -i, -fectus sum.

set sail, solvo (-ĕre, solvi, solutum) navem ; ancŏram tollo, -ĕre, sustuli, sublatum.

settlement, cŏlōnia, -ae, *f.*

several, complures.

severe, grăvis.

severely, grăvĭter.

share (*divide*), partiri.

(*take part in*), partĭceps (-cipis, *c.*) esse.

shed, effundo, -ĕre, -fudi, -fusum.

shield, scūtum, -i, *n.*

ship, nāvis, -is, *f.*

(*of war*), nāvis longa.

ship (*merchant, or transport*), nāvis (-is, *f.*) ŏnĕrāria.

shipwreck, naufrăgium, -i, *n.*

shipwrecked, ejectus in lītore *or* lītus.

to be, naufrăgium făcio, -ĕre, fēci, factum.

shirk, vītare ; detrectare.

shoot, to (*missiles*), mitto, -ĕre, misi, missum.

shore, lītus, -oris, *n.* ; ōra, -ae, *f.*

short, brĕvis.

to run short, dēfĭcio, -ĕre, -fēci, -fectum.

shout, clāmor, -oris, *m.*

to, clāmare.

show, ostendo, -ĕre, -tendi, -tentum *or* tensum ; demonstrare. See Syn.

courage, virtutem praesto, -are, -stiti, -stitum.

show oneself brave, se fortem praebēre.

shower, imber, -bris, *f.*

(*of missiles*), vis (*acc.* vim, *abl.* vi) *f.* ; multĭtudo, -dinis, *f.* ; crēbra tēla, *n. pl.*

shut up, claudo, -ĕre, clausi,
    clausum.
Sicily, Sĭcīlia, -ae, *f.*
sick, aeger, -gra, -grum.
    to be, aegrōtare.
side, lătus, -eris, *n.*
    (*of a river*), rīpa, -ae, *f.*
    to be on our, sto (-are, stĕti,
    stătum) a nobis.
    on the one . . . on the other, ab
    altera parte . . . ab altera.
    on this side of, citra, *acc.*
sides, on all, undĭque; passim.
    on both, utrimque.
siege, obsĭdio, -ionis, *f.*
    to raise a, relinquo (-ĕre,
    -līqui, -lictum) obsĭdio-
    nem; obsĭdĭone dēsisto,
    -ĕre, -stiti.
    to relieve from, libĕrare
    obsĭdione.
sight, conspectus, -ūs, *m.*
sight of, to catch, conspĭcio,
    -ĕre, -spexi, -spectum;
    conspĭcari.
sign, signum, -i, *n.*
signal for, signum, *gen.*
    to serve as, signo esse. Voc.
    85.
signally, so, tantā strāge.
signs of office, insignia, -ium,
    n. pl.
silence, sĭlentium, -i, *n.*
silent, sĭlens; tăcĭtus.
    to be (*make no noise at all*),
    sĭlēre.
    to be (*not to speak*), tăcēre.
silently, silentio.
silver, argentum, -i, *n.*
since, quŏniam; cum. Rule
    22, p. 124.
    (*from the time when*), ex
    quo tempore.
sink (*trans.*), submergo, -ĕre,
    -mersi, -mersum.

sister, sŏror, -oris, *f.*
sit, sĕdeo, -ēre, sēdi, sessum.
size, magnĭtūdo, -dinis, *f.*
skill, sollertia, -ae, *f.*
    (*gained by experience*), pĕr-
    ītĭa, -ae, *f.*; ūsus, -ūs, *m.*
skin (*of men*), cŭtis, -is, *f.*
    (*of beasts*), pellis, -is, *f.*
slaughter, trŭcīdare.
    (*nn.*) caedes, -is, *f.*
slave, servus, -i, *m.*
slavery, servĭtus, -tutis, *f.*
slay, to, occīdo, -ĕre, -cīdi,
    -cisum; trŭcīdare. See
    Syn., ' *kill.*'
sleep, dormire.
slight, aspernari.
slip, lābor, -i, lapsus sum.
    let, dīmitto, -ĕre, -misi,
    missum; omitto, -ĕre,
    -misi, -missum.
slope, clīvus, -i, *m.*
slow, lentus.
small, parvus; exĭguus.
    so, tantŭlus.
smile, rīsus, -ūs, *m.*
    to, subrīdeo, -ēre, -risi,
    -risum.
snow, nix, nĭvis, *f.*
so (*with adv. and adj.*), tam.
    Voc. 6.
    (*in such a way*), ĭta.
    (*to such an extent*), adeo.
    great, tantus.
    many, tot.
    much (*adv.*), tantŏpere;
    tantum.
    often, tŏties.
soil (*ground*), sŏlum, -i, *n.*
soldier, mīles, -itis, *m.*
    of line, mīles (-itis, *m.*),
    lĕgionarius.
some, nonnulli, *pl.*
some days after, ăliquot post
    diebus.

293

some . . . others, alii . . . alii.
sometimes, nonnunquam; interdum.
son, fīlius, -i, *m.*
  of, nātus. Ex. 87.
song, cantus, -ūs, *m.*
soon, mox; brĕvi (tempore).
  as soon as, simulac. Rule 25, p. 140.
  as soon as possible, quam primum.
sorrow, dŏlor, -oris, *m.*
sorry, use paenĭtet. Voc. 128.
sound, sŏnus, -i, *m.*; sonĭtus, -ūs, *m.*
sound a retreat, to, rĕceptui căno, -ĕre, cecini, cantum.
south, mērīdĭes, -diei, *f.*
sow, to, sĕro, -ĕre, sēvi, sătum.
Spain, Hispānia, -ae, *f.*
Spaniard, Hispānus, -i, *m.*
Spanish, Hispānicus.
spare, parco, -ĕre, peperci, parsum.
Spartan, Lacedaemŏnius, -i, *m.*
speak, lŏquor, -i, locutus sum.
speaker, ōrātor, -oris, *m.*
spear, hasta, -ae, *f.*
speech, ōrātio, -ionis, *f.*
  to make a, orationem habēre.
speed, cĕlĕrĭtas, -tatis, *f.*
spend, ăgo, -ĕre, ēgi, actum.
splendid, insignis.
spoil, spŏlia, -orum, *n. pl.*
sports, ludi, -orum, *m. pl.*
spring, vēr, vēris, *n.*
spy, spĕcŭlator, -oris, *m.*
squadron, āla, -ae, *f.*; turma, -ae, *f.*
staff (*officers*), lēgāti, -orum, *m. pl.*
stand, sto, -are, steti, stătum.
  firm, rĕsisto, -ĕre, -stiti; in loco persto, -are, -stiti.

stand, by, adsto, -are, -stiti.
  for the consulship, consŭlatum pĕto, -ĕre, -ivi, -itum.
standards, to advance, signa fero, ferre, tuli, latum.
start, prŏfīciscor, -i, -fectus sum.
starvation, fămes, -is, *f.*
starve, făme pereo, -ire, -ii, -itum.
state, cīvĭtas, -tatis, *f.*
  adj., publĭcus.
state of affairs, in this, quae cum ita sint, essent.
statue, stătua, -ae, *f.*
stay, măneo, -ēre, mansi, mansum; morari.
steal, abrĭpio, -ĕre, -ripui, -reptum.
stealthily, furtim.
steep, praeruptus.
still (*till now*), adhuc.
  (*even*), etiam.
sting (*provoke*), incĭtare; lăcesso, -ĕre, -ivi, -itum.
stone, lăpis, -idis, *m.*
storm, tempestas, -tatis, *f.*
  to, expugnare.
story, fābŭla, -ae, *f.*
  to tell a, narrare.
straight (*adv.*), directo.
  (*make straight for*), recto ĭtĭnĕre pĕto, -ĕre, -ivi, -itum.
strange, mīrus; mīrābilis.
stranger, hospes, -itis, *c.*; advĕna, -ae, *c.*
straw, not care a, flocci non făcio, -ĕre, fēci, factum.
stream, rīvus, -i, *m.*
street, via, -ae, *f.*
strength, rōbur, -oris, *n.*; vires, -ium, *f. pl.*

stretch out, to, extendo, -ĕre, -tendi, -tentum; porrĭgo, -ĕre, -rexi, -rectum.

strict, sĕvērus.

(careful), dīlĭgens.

strike, to, percŭtio, -ĕre, -cussi, -cussum; fĕrio, -ire.

a camp, castra mŏveo, -ēre, mōvi, motum.

terror, injĭcio (-ĕre, -jēci, -jectum) terrorem, *dat.*

stroke, mulceo, -ēre, mulsi.

strong, firmus; vălĭdus.

strongly, vălĭde.

stubbornly, ācriter.

stumble, prōlābor, -i, -lapsus sum.

stupefied, obstŭpĕfactus.

subdue, sŭbĭgo, -ĕre, -ēgi, -actum; in pŏtestatem rĕdĭgo, -ĕre, -ēgi, -actum.

subject, imperio subjectus.

to (liable to), obnoxius.

succeed, get on well, prōfĭcio, -ĕre, -fēci, -fectum.

turn out well, prospere ēvĕnio, -ire, -vēni, -ventum.

success, successus, -ūs, *m.*

success, without, frustra; nēquicquam.

win a, rem prospĕre gĕro, -ĕre, gessi, gestum.

such, tālis.

such . . . as, tālis . . . quālis.

suddenly, sŭbĭto.

suffer, pătior, -i, passus sum.

suffering, dŏlor, -oris, *m.*

sufferings, măla, -orum, *n. pl.*

sufficient, sătis.

to be (of supplies), suppĕto, -ĕre, -ivi, -itum.

suitable, ĭdōneus.

suits, it, convĕnit, -ire, -vēnit.

sum, summa, -ae, *f.*

summer, aestas, -tatis, *f.*

summon, arcesso, -ĕre, -ivi, -itum.

back, rĕvŏcare.

sumptuous, lautus.

sun, sōl, solis, *m.*

sunset, solis occāsus, -ūs, *m.*

superior, to be, praesto, -are, -stiti, -stătum.

superstition, superstĭtio, -ionis, *f.*; nĭmia *or* prāva rĕlĭgio, -ionis, *f.* ; ĭnanis tĭmor (-oris, *m.*) deorum.

supper, cēna, -ae, *f.*

supply, praebēre.

support (military), subsĭdia, -orum, *n. pl.*

to, sustĭnēre; tŏlĕrare. See Syn., ' *bear*.'

(aid), adjŭvare.

supreme power, summa (-ae, *f.*) impĕrii.

sure, to be, pro certo habēre.

surmount, sŭpĕrare.

surpass, sŭpĕrare; praesto, -are, -stiti, -stĭtum.

surprise, opprĭmo, -ĕre, -pressi, -pressum.

surrender (trans.), trādo, -ĕre, -dĭdi, -dĭtum; dēdo, -ĕre, -dĭdi, -dĭtum.

(intr.), se dēdo, -ĕre, -dĭdi, -dĭtum.

surround, circumvĕnio, -ire, -vēni, -ventum; cingĕre.

survive, supersum, -esse, -fui.

surviving, superstes.

sustain (encourage), confirmare.

swear, jūrare.

swim, nătare.

sword, glădius, -i, *m.*

Syracusan, Syrācūsanus.

Syracuse, Syracusae, -arum, *f. pl.*

T

take, *capture,* căpio, -ĕre, cēpi, captum.
away, aufero, -ferre, abstuli, ablatum.
from, prīvare.
by storm, expugnare.
captive, căpio, -ĕre, cēpi, captum.
ill, aegre fero, ferre, tuli, latum.
part in, intersum, -esse, -fui.
to flight, terga verto, -ĕre, verti, versum.
the place of, succēdo, -ĕre, -cessi, -cessum.
up arms, arma sūmo, -ĕre, sumpsi, sumptum.
up one's position, consīdo, -ĕre, -sedi, -sessum.
take on board, in nāvem excĭpio, -ĕre, -cēpi, -ceptum.
taking place, to be, ăgor, -i, actum.
talent *(money),* tălentum, -i, *n.*
talents, ingĕnium, -i, *n.*
talk, lŏquor, -i, locutus sum.
tax, vectīgal, -alis, *n.*
teach, dŏceo, -ēre, -ui, -tum.
tear, lăcrĭma, -ae, *f.*
tell *(inform),* certiorem facio, -ĕre, fēci, factum.
(order), imperare; jubeo, -ēre, jussi, jussum. Ex. 75.
(tell a story), narrare.
temper, mens, -ntis, *f.*; ănĭmus, -i, *m.*
temple, templum, -i, *n.* ; aedes, -is, *f. (sing. only).*
tempt, temptare.
ten, *one in (each tenth man),* decimus quisque.

tent, tăbernācŭlum, -i, *n.*
tenth, *one,* decima pars, partis, *f.*
tenths, *three,* tres decimae partes.
terms, condĭtiones, -um, *f. pl.*
terms, *on equal,* aequo Marte; aequa contentione.
terrible, terrĭbĭlis.
terrify, terrēre.
territories, fīnes, -ium, *m. pl.* *(in sing.* finis=*boundary).*
terror, *to inspire with,* injicio (-ĕre, -jēci, -jectum) terrorem, *dat.*
thank, grātias ăgo, -ĕre, ēgi, actum, *dat.*
theft, furtum, -i, *n.*
then, tum; tunc.
(=next), deinde.
therefore, ĭtăque.
thereupon, deinde; quo facto.
thick, densus.
thicket, virgultum, -i, *n.*
thief, fūr, furis, *m.*
think, pŭtare; existĭmare; arbitrari.
I almost, haud scio an.
thirds, *two,* duae partes, -ium, *f.*
thirst, sĭtis, -is, *f.*
threats, mĭnae, -arum, *f. pl.*
threaten, mĭnari. Voc. 61.
(by proximity), immĭnēre; insto, -are, -stiti.
threatening, mĭnax.
throw, jăcio, -ĕre, jēci, jactum.
away, abjĭcio, -ĕre, -jēci, -jectum.
throw a bridge over a river, pontem in flumine făcio, -ĕre, fēci, factum.
thus, ĭta; sic; hoc mŏdo.
Tiber, Tĭbĕris, -is, *m.*
time, tempus, -oris, *n.*
at the same, sĭmul.

time, for a little, paulisper.
for a long, diu.
in, ad tempus; tempŏri.
in a short, brĕvi (tempŏre).
till that, ad id tempŏris.
time, to waste, tempus tĕro,
-ĕre, trīvi, tritum.
for some, aliquamdiu.
now for a long, jamprīdem;
jamdūdum. (P. 155, n. 2.)
in our, nostrā aetāte; his
tempŏrĭbus.
tinge, tinguo, -ĕre, tinxi, tinctum.
tired, defessus.
tired of, to be, pĭget; taedet.
Voc. 128.
to-day, hŏdie.
toga, tŏga, -ae, *f.*
together, ūnā.
to-morrow, crās.
too late, sēro.
little, părum, *adv., used as
noun.*
much, nĭmius, *adj.*; nĭmium,
adv., used as noun.
top. See note, p. 5.
torment, torture, crŭciare.
torture, crŭciātus, -ūs, *m.*
touch, tango, -ĕre, tetigi, tactum.
towards, erga, *acc.*
evening, sub vespĕrum.
town, oppĭdum, -i, *n.*
town, people of, oppĭdāni,
-orum, *m. pl.*
traitor, prōdĭtor, -oris, *m.*;
perfĭdus, -i, *m.*
transfer, transfero, -ferre, -tuli,
-latum.
traveller, viator, -oris, *m.*
treachery, prōdĭtio, -ionis, *f.*
treason, (accuse of), mājestatis
accūsare.
treasure, thēsaurus, -i, *m.*

treat, affĭcio, -ĕre,-fēci,-fectum.
well, bĕnĕfĭcio affĭcio, -ĕre,
-fēci, -fectum.
for, ăgo (-ĕre, ēgi, actum)
de *abl.*
treaty, foedus, -eris, *n.*
tree, arbor, -oris, *f.*
trench, fossa, -ae, *f.*
trial of, to make, expĕrior, -iri,
expertus sum; temptare.
to be on, reus esse.
to put on, reum aliquem
făcio, -ĕre, fēci, factum;
nomen alicujus defero,
-ferre, -tuli, -latum.
tribe, trĭbus, -ūs, *f.*
tribune (of people), trĭbūnus
(-i, *m.*) plēbis.
(of soldiers), trĭbūnus (-i, *m.*)
mīlĭtum.
tribute, trĭbūtum, -i, *n.*; stīpendium, -i, *n.*; vectī-
gal, -alis, *n.*
trick, dŏlus, -i, *m.*; ars, artis, *f.*
triumph (procession), trium-
phus, -i, *m.*
in triumph, victor, -oris, *m.*
troop (of horse), turma, -ae, *f.*
troops, cōpiae, -arum, *f. pl.*
Troy, Trōja, -ae, *f.*
true, vērus.
trust, credo, -ĕre, credĭdi, credĭ-
tum; committo, -ĕre,
-misi, -missum. Voc. 61.
truth, to tell the, vēra dico, -ĕre,
dixi, dictum.
try, cōnari.
turn, in turn, invicem; singuli.
back, revertor, -i, -versus
sum.
round (intr.), convertor, -i,
-versus sum; se con-
verto, -ĕre, -verti.
two divisions, in, bĭpartīto
tyrant, tyrannus, -i, *m.*

U

unaccustomed, insuētus.
unanimously, consensu (omnium).
  approved, *to be*, omnium consensu comprŏbari.
uncertain, dŭbius.
unconquerable, indŏmĭtus; invictus.
under, sub. p. 245.
  arms, in armis.
undergo sentence, poenam subeo, -ire, -ii, -itum.
understand, intellegĕre.
undertake, suscĭpio, -ĕre, -cēpi, -ceptum.
unexpected, sŭbĭtus; inŏpīnātus.
unfortunate, infēlix; fūnestus.
union, consensus, -ūs, *m.*
universe, mundus, -i, *m.*
unjust, injustus.
unlike, dissĭmĭlis.
unmolested, incŏlŭmis.
unmoved, immōtus.
unshaken, immōtus.
until, dum; dōnec; quoad. Rule 25, p. 140.
  (*prep.*), usque ad.
untouched, intĕger, -gra, -grum.
unwilling, invītus.
  to be, nōlo, nolle, nolui.
unworthy, indignus.
upright, prŏbus.
upset, ēverto, -ĕre, -verti, -versum.
urge, hortari; admŏnēre.
  on, urgeo, -ēre, ursi.
use, ūtor, -i, usus sum.
useful, ūtĭlis.
useless, ĭnūtĭlis.
utmost (*extreme*), summus.
  to do one's, id ăgo (-ĕre, ēgi, actum) ut (*final*).

V

vain, in, frustra; nēquicquam.
value, aestĭmare.
vanguard, primum agmen, -inis, *n.*
various, vărius; dīversus.
vengeance on, to take, ulciscor, -i, ultus sum; poenas sūmo (-ĕre, sumpsi, sumptum) de, *abl.*
veteran, vĕtĕranus, -i, *m.* (*or adj.*).
vexed, to be, aegre fero, ferre, tuli, latum.
victorious, to come off, ēvādo (-ĕre, -vasi, -vasum) victor.
victory, to win a, victoriam rĕportare.
vigorous, ălăcer, -cris, -cre.
vigour, alacritas, -tatis, *f.*
village, vīcus, -i, *m.*; pagus, -i, *m.*
vine, vītis, -is, *f.*
vineyard, vīnētum, -i, *n.*
violate, viŏlare.
violence, vis (*acc.* vim, *abl.* vi), *f.*
virtue, virtus, -utis, *f.*
visit, to, viso, -ĕre, visi.
voice, vox, vocis, *f.*
  with a loud, magna voce.
vow, to, jūrare; se jurejurando obstringo, -ĕre, -strinxi, -strictum.

W

waggon, plaustrum, -i, *n.*
wage war, bellum gĕro, -ĕre, gessi, gestum; bellum infero, -ferre, -tuli, illatum.
wait, măneo, -ēre, mansi, mansum.

wait, for, exspectare.
wake, excĭtare.
wall, mūrus, -i, *m.* ; moenia, -ium, *n. pl.*
wander, văgari ; errare.
war, bellum, -i. *n.*
    prepare for, bellum părare.
    declare, indīcĕre.
want, inŏpia, -ae, *f.*
    (*vb.*), carēre; egēre. See Syn.
warn, admŏnēre.
warning, exemplum, -i, *n.*
warrior, jŭvĕnis, -is, *m.*
waste time, to, tempus tĕro, -ĕre, trīvi, tritum.
watch, spectare ; intuēri.
    about the third, de tertia vĭgĭlia.
way (*manner*), mŏdus, -i, *m.*
way (*route*), via, -ae, *f.*
weak, infirmus ; invălĭdus.
weakness (*want of energy*), infirmĭtas, -tatis, *f.* ; imbecillĭtas, -tatis, *f.* (animi, consilii).
    (*of forces, etc.*), *use* exiguus (*small*).
wealth, dīvĭtiae, -arum, *f. pl.*
weapon, tēlum, -i, *n.*
wear, passive of induo, -ĕre, -dui, -dutum *or* vestire.
weary, fessus; *or use* taedet. Voc. 128.
weave, to, texo, -ĕre, -ui, textum.
weep, lacrĭmare.
weigh anchor, ancŏram tollo, -ĕre, sustuli, sublatum.
well, bene.
west, solis occāsus, -ūs, *m.* ; oc cĭdens, -entis, *m.*
western, (terra) quae ad occasum solis spectat.
what news ? quid nŏvi.
    sort of ? quālis.

when ? quando.
whence ? (*where from ?*) unde.
whenever, quandocunque.
where ? ŭbi ; quā.
whereupon, quo facto.
whether . . . or (*double cond.*) seu . . . seu ; sive . . . sive, (*double question*), utrum . . . an.
which of two ? ŭter.
whilst, dōnec; quoad. Rule 25, p. 140.
white, albus; candĭdus.
whither, where to ? quo.
who ? quis; quisnam; *adj.*, qui.
whoever, whatever, quisquis ; quicumque.
whole, tōtus ; omnis; ūniversus. See Syn.
wholly, omnīno.
why ? cur; quārē ; quămobrem.
wide, lātus.
wife, uxor, -oris, *f.*
willingly, lĭbenter.
win (*obtain*), nanciscor, -i, nactus sum ; ădĭpiscor, -i, adeptus sum.
win a victory, victoriam rĕportare.
wind, ventus, -i, *m.*
wing, āla, -ae, *f.*
winter, hĭems, -emis, *f.*
    quarters, hīberna, -orum, *n. pl.*
wisdom, săpientia, -ae, *f.*
wise, săpiens ; prūdens.
    in no, haudquāquam.
wiser than to, sapientior quam qui. Rule 18, p. 110.
wish to (*be willing*), vŏlo, velle, volui.
wish not to (*be unwilling*), nōlo, nolle, nolui.